Literacy

Anthology

Compiled by Bill Laar

Series consultant: Margaret Stillie
Illustrations © STP 2000; by: Dick Barton, Louise Barton, Harry Bell, Harriet Buckley, Abigail Conway, Tamsin Cook, Beverly Curl, Mike Dodd, Jackie East, Felicity House, Rosalind Hudson, Michelle Ives, Karen Kett, Jean de Lemos, Darin Mount, Pat Murray, Tony O'Donnell, Tim Oliver, Rhiannon Powell, Zara Slattery, Margaret Theakston, Noriko Toyama, Lisa Williams, Sarah Wimperis.

The acknowledgements on page 303 constitute an extension of this copyright page.

First published by

Stanley Thornes Publishers Ltd
Ellenborough House
Wellington Street
Cheltenham
GL50 1YW

00 01 02 03\ 10 9 8 7 6 5 4 3 2

A catalogue record for this book is available from the British Library.

ISBN 0-7487-4830-X

Design by Oxprint Design / STP.
Page make up by Aetos Ltd, Bathampton, Bath.
Printed and bound in Spain by Graficas Estella S.A.

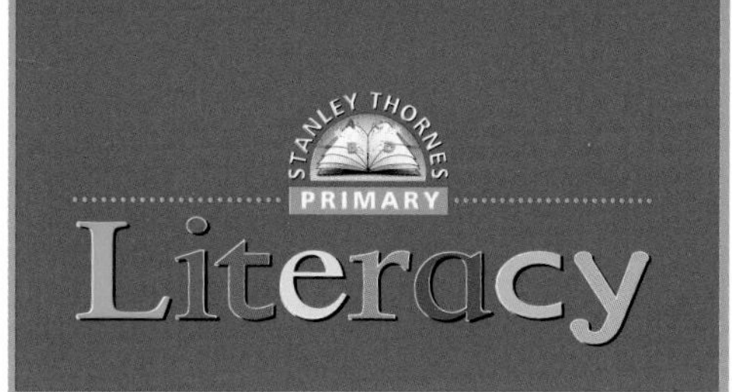
STANLEY THORNES
PRIMARY
Literacy

Contents

Literacy

Anthology Extracts

Saint George and the Dragon

by Geraldine McCaughrean

The still, deep pool lay in a hollow below the high wooden fence of the hilltop town. Every day the women came down to draw its water. Their sheep drank at its banks, and a few straggling roses bloomed, in coils of bramble, along the water's edge.

Then, one morning, the women walking down to the water dropped their empty buckets, ran back, and closed the city gates, sobbing with fright. Climbing to the top of the palisade, they peeped over.

A dragon, born in the deepest crevices of the bottomless pool, had dragged itself out on to the bank and lay coiled around it.

A wreath of sinew and claw. Its red mouth gaped as it panted in the hot sun. Its ragged teeth bulged through rolled green lips. And awake or asleep, its lidless eyes stared and its claws stretched and withdrew, stretched and withdrew in the waterside mud. Its foul breath hung in a green haze. Its father was Evil, its mother Darkness, and its name was Wickedness.

That night it left the pool, lifting its heavy haunches and heaving its scaled belly off the ground. Lizard-like, it cut a track through the mud, dragging its thorny tail. The people

herded their livestock into the city and shut the gates on the dragon.

But what good is a wooden fence against breath fuming with fire?

One corner of the town was set ablaze, and its crumbling ash blew away in the morning wind.

The dragon ate two dogs, before thrashing back to the pool to coil itself around the water.

Next day, the people opened the gates just wide enough to push two sheep out on to the plain. The animals stood bleating, then trotted down towards the water in the hollow. Suddenly, the shape of the dragon lurched up over them! Fleece and flesh, it tore them to pieces.

Two sheep were fed to the dragon every day, though sometimes, after its meal, it would still slither towards the city and scratch its back against the timber fence.

From the high window of the palace, Princess Sabra watched with a pale face, and asked: "What will happen when there are no more sheep?"

Before the last sheep was gone, the people began to draw lots in the most terrible of lotteries. The name of every man, woman and child was entered, and one name drawn out each day: one person turned out of the city, side by side with a sheep as food for the dragon.

Soon, the sound of wailing hung like a cloud over the city. Men eyed one another across the street and thought: "I hope his name will be drawn before mine."

One day, the wailing came from the palace itself. The Princess Sabra's name had been drawn in the lottery.

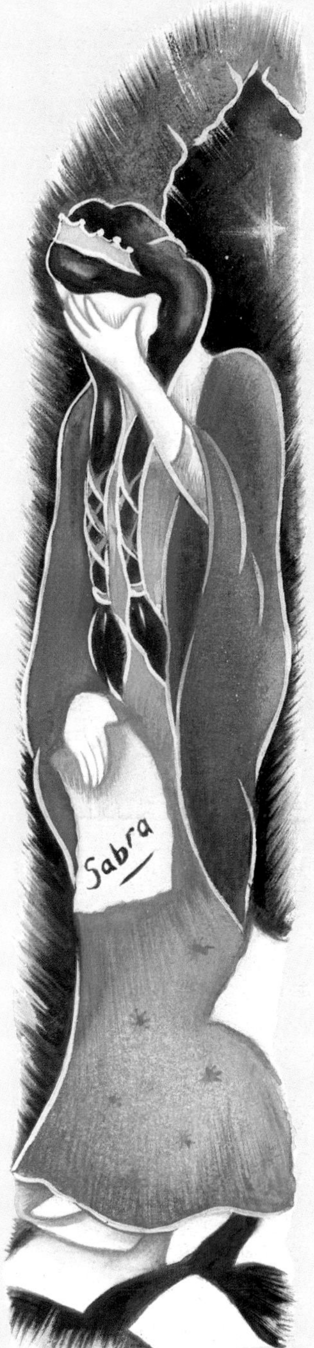

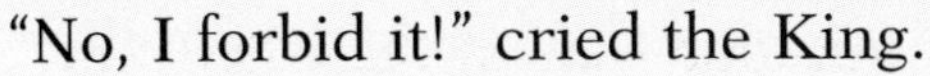

"No, I forbid it!" cried the King.

"It is law," said the town governors. "You made it so."

"But she is so good and pure, and I love her so very much!"

"We loved our daughters," said the old women, "but still they were fed to the dragon when their turn came."

"But she's so small and fragile – a poor morsel for a hungry dragon!"

"Then go in her place!" shouted the people. "What good have you been to us since the dragon came?"

And when he saw rebellion in their faces the King gave up his daughter. "Don't let me see her again, or I may change my mind."

Not far away, a horseman was riding up a steep hill when his horse stopped and began to paw the ground, blowing sharply through its nostrils. The rider himself was aware of a charred, acrid smell in the air. From the top of the hill, he looked down on devastation.

In the hollow below, there lay a fouled and festering pool. Beyond it, a fortified town had its gates closed in siege.

Turning its head idly in his direction, a dragon, its flightless wings half spread, paused in its slinking, lizard-like scuttle, and let out a roar.

The flash of sunlight on a bridge, and the white of the horse itself, had caught the dragon's eye. At the same moment, a speck of white and gold flickered to its left: a golden-haired maiden dressed in a lightly blowing smock was being tied to the stake where the beast looked daily for its dinner.

The girl cast one imploring look towards the town. But the windows of her father's palace were empty. Her head fell forward in despair.

The dragon threw out a contemptuous roar at the rider and turned to devour its white morsel of meat...

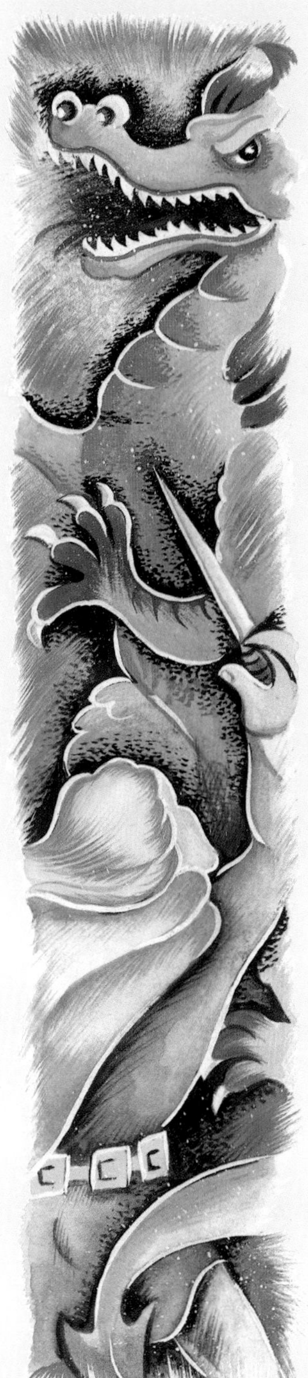

"Hear this, beast, I am George of Lydda, and a pure man!" The rider's voice barely reached the dragon across the wilderness. "Turn and fight me – for surely your father was Evil, your mother Darkness, and you are Wickedness itself!" George levelled his long lance.

The dragon's jaws – gaping over the Princess – clashed shut. It snaked on its haunches, and its wings beat the air.

A column of fuming fire belched from its nostrils. But the soldier, galloping towards it across the plain, raised a shield over his own and his horse's head, and the fire was turned aside. The brightness of the sun on shield and helmet seemed to madden the rampaging beast.

George's noble white horse carried him into the very shadow of the dragon. Its green paw reached out to snatch him from his saddle. The lance slapped the dragon's shoulder, but the scales were tough like leather, rough like stone.

Horse and dragon cannoned together. The mare's foamy sweat spattered the dragon's green flank. A moment later, the massive tail lashed round, but the horse stood back on its haunches and sprang across its thorns.

George's lance struck the beast's snout and shattered like an icicle.

For a moment, he stared into the lidless eyes, then he threw up his shield again, to keep off the cauldron-breath.

The dragon struck him a blow with its horny wing that pitched him to the ground. George threw off his helmet, and snatched the broad sword from his saddle.

As vast jaws opened to devour the soldier where he stood, he ran in under the towering green chest and plunged in the sword where a heart should lie.

But the creature had no heart!

A spurt of black blood spattered George's shield. But the dragon only threw back its head and gave a gargled roar. Its claws tore the young man's cloak into seven ragged strips.

Once more George drove in the sword – drove it into the gaping red jaw. It was torn from his grasp as the beast thrashed its head from side to side.

For a moment, the lumbering body threatened to capsize and crush George. And as he put both hands on the dragon's flank to push it away, smoke rose from the palms of his gloves. With the groaning slowness of a falling tree, the creature crashed down on to its side.

George left it where it lay, and ran to the side of the Princess, lifted up her face, and said:

"The danger is almost past. I see that you are a pure and lovely maiden. Give me your sash, please, for the dragon is not dead."

With the sash, he circled the lolling green head.

In the depths of the beast's cavernous body, its furious fire was extinguished. In the depths of its eyes, too, the wildness and wickedness went out. The vanquished dragon laid down its head on George's lap: its breathing calm, its breath harmless to the sweet and unscorched air.

Together, Sabra and George led a peaceful dragon through the streets of the town and it lay down at the gates of the palace.

"Stranger," said the delighted King, "where you are from I do not know. But end your journey here, with my palace for your home and my daughter for your wife!"

"I cannot," said George, (though he looked at the Princess with longing in his eyes). "I have other dragons to vanquish."

His horse was brought to him, her white mane scorched and her white tail charred. And slipping his arm from between Sabra's two white hands, George mounted and rode away.

Though Sabra watched for him from the window of the highest palace tower, he never returned.

Afterword

The details of the life of George the Saint are few and uncertain. Even the execution exacted by Emperor Diocletian on 23 April AD 303 may have been of another man, another among the numberless Christian martyrs. But that he lived and died is proven: it is his death which is commemorated on Saint George's Day.

The exploits of George the Dragon-slayer are altogether more vivid – adventures of a sort that were being told with relish 2,000 years ago. English Crusaders carried home the stories, adding a story of their own – of a vision that rallied them at the battle of Antioch in 1309. They acted out his fight in their miracle plays, vaunted him in their church windows, took him so to heart that Edward III lighted on him in 1348 as a fit patron for England.

And yet the Dragon-slayer was an amalgamation of shadows, a pooling of myths. He is the Greek Perseus who saved Andromeda from the sea monster; Christ who slays the satanic beast in Revelation; Renewal which conquers Death; Good which conquers Evil. The Slayer probably never existed: he is a figment of universal imagination. But he stepped out of folklore to the aid of an obscure young man ingloriously tortured to death long ago in Asia Minor. As a result, the young man was immortalized: Saint George, Patron Saint of England.

The Wreck of the Zanzibar

by Michael Morpurgo

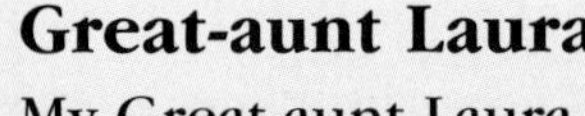

Great-aunt Laura

My Great-aunt Laura died a few months ago. She was a hundred years old. She had her cocoa last thing at night, as she usually did, put the cat out, went to sleep and never woke up. There's no better way to die.

I took the boat across to Scilly for the funeral – almost everyone in the family did. I met again cousins and aunts and uncles I hardly recognised, and who hardly recognised me. The little church on Bryher was packed, standing room only. Everyone on Bryher was there, and they came from all over the Scilly Isles, from St Mary's, St Martin's, St Agnes and Tresco.

We sang the hymns lustily because we knew Great-aunt Laura would enjoy a rousing send-off. Afterwards we had a family gathering in her tiny cottage overlooking Stinking Porth Bay. There was tea and crusty brown bread and honey. I took one mouthful and I was a child again. Wanting to be on my own, I went up the narrow stairs to the room that had been mine when I came every summer for my holidays. The same oil lamp was by the bed, the same peeling wallpaper, the same faded curtains with the red sailing boats dipping through the waves.

I sat down on the bed and closed my eyes. I was eight years old again and ahead of me were two weeks of sand and sea, and boats and shrimping, and oystercatchers and gannets, and Great-aunt Laura's stories every night before she drew the curtains against the moon and left me alone in my bed.

Someone called from downstairs and I was back to now.

Everyone was crowded into her sitting-room. There was a cardboard box open in the middle of the floor.

"Ah, there you are, Michael," said Uncle Will.

He was a little irritated, I thought.

"We'll begin then."

And a hush fell around the room. He dipped into the box and held up a parcel.

"It looks as if she's left us one each," said Uncle Will. Every parcel was wrapped in old newspaper and tied with string, and there was a large brown label attached to each one. Uncle Will read out the names. I had to wait some minutes for mine. There was nothing I particularly wanted, except Zanzibar of course, but then everyone wanted Zanzibar. Uncle Will was waving a parcel at me.

"Michael," he said, "here's yours."

I took it upstairs and unwrapped it sitting on the bed. It felt like a book of some sort, and so it was, but not a printed book. It was handmade, handwritten in pencil, the pages sewn together. The title on the cover read *The Diary of Laura Perryman* and there was a watercolour painting on the cover of a four-masted ship keeling over in a storm and heading for the rocks. With the book there was an envelope.

I opened it and read.

> Dear Michael,
>
> When you were little I told you lots and lots of stories about Bryher, about the Isles of Scilly. You know about the ghosts on Samson, about the bell that rings under the sea off St Martin's, about King Arthur still waiting in his cave under the Eastern Isles.
>
> You remember? Well, here is my story, the story of me and my

twin brother Billy whom you never knew. How I wish you had. It is a true story and I did not want it to die with me.

When I was young I kept a diary, not an everyday diary. I didn't write in it very often, just whenever I felt like it. Most of it isn't worth the reading and I've already thrown it away – I've lived an ordinary sort of life. But for a few months a long, long time ago, my life was not ordinary at all. This is the diary of those few months.

Do you remember you always used to ask where Zanzibar came from? (You called him "Marzipan" when you were small.) I never told you, did I? I never told anyone. Well, now you'll find out at last.

Goodbye, dear Michael, and God bless you.

Your great-aunt Laura.

P.S. I hope you like my little sketches. I'm a better artist than I am a writer, I think. When I come back in my next life – and I shall – I shall be a great artist. I've promised myself.

* * *

The Diary of Laura Perryman (1907)

January 20th

"Laura Perryman, you are fourteen years old today."

I said that to the mirror this morning when I wished myself "Happy Birthday". Sometimes, like this morning, I don't much want to be Laura Perryman, who's lived on Bryher all her life and milks cows. I want to be Lady Eugenia Fitzherbert with long red hair and green eyes, who wears a big wide hat with a white ostrich feather and who travels the world in steamships with four funnels. But then, I also want to be Billy Perryman so I can row out in the gig and build boats and run fast. Billy's fourteen too – being my twin brother, he would be. But I'm not Lady

Eugenia Fitzherbert, whoever she is, and I'm not Billy; I'm me. I'm Laura Perryman and I'm fourteen years old today.

Everyone is pleased with me, even Father, because I was the one who spotted the ship before they did on St Mary's. It was just that I was in the right place at the right time, that's all. I'd been milking the cows with Billy, as usual, and I was coming back with the buckets over Watch Hill when I saw sails on the horizon out beyond White Island. It looked like a schooner, three-masted. We left the buckets and ran all the way home.

The gig was launched in five minutes. I watched the whole thing from the top of Samson Hill with everyone else. We saw the St Mary's gig clear the harbour wall, the wind and the tide in her favour. The race was on. For some time it looked as if the St Mary's gig would reach the schooner first, as she so often does, but we found clear water and a fair wind out beyond Samson and we were flying along. I could see the Chief holding on to the mast, and Billy and Father pulling side by side in the middle of the boat. How I wanted to be one of them, to be out there rowing with them. I can handle an oar as well as Billy. He knows it, everyone knows it. But the Chief won't hear of it – and he's the coxswain – and neither will Father. They think that's an end of it. But it isn't. One day, one day... Anyway, today we won the race, so I should be pleased about that, I suppose.

The St Mary's boat lost an oar. She was left dead in the water and had to turn back. We watched our gig draw alongside the schooner and we all cheered till we were hoarse. Through the telescope I could see the Chief climbing up the ladder to pilot the schooner into St Mary's. I could see them helping him on board, then shaking hands with him. He took off his cap and waved and we all cheered again. It would mean money for everyone, and there's precious little of that around. When the gig came back into Great Porth we were all there to meet her. We helped haul her up the beach. She's always lighter when we've won. Father hugged me and Billy winked at me. It's an American ship, he says, the *General Lee*, bound for New York.

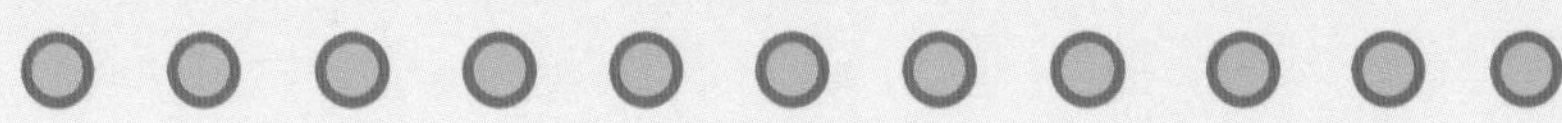

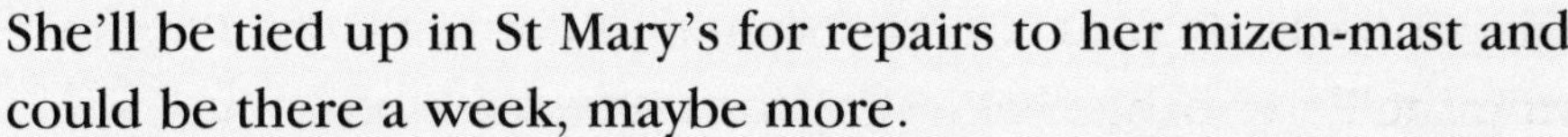

She'll be tied up in St Mary's for repairs to her mizen-mast and could be there a week, maybe more.

This evening, Billy and I had our birthday cake from Granny May as usual. The Chief and crew were all there as well, so the cake didn't last long. They sang "Happy Birthday" to us and then the Chief said we were all a little less poor because Laura Perryman had spotted the *General Lee*. And I felt good. They were all smiling at me. Now's the time, I thought, I'll ask them again.

"Can I row with Billy in the gig?"

They all laughed and said what they always said, that girls don't row in gigs. They never had.

I went to the hen-house and cried. It's the only place I can cry in peace. And then Granny May came in with the last piece of cake and said there are plenty of things that women can do, that men can't. It doesn't seem that way to me. I want to row in that gig, and I will. One day I will.

Billy came into my room just now. He's had another argument with Father – this time the milk buckets weren't clean enough. There's always something, and Father will shout at him so. Billy says he wants to go to America and that one day he will. He's always saying things like that. I wish he wouldn't. It frightens me. I wish Father would be kinder to him.

February 12th The Night of the Storm

A terrible storm last night and the pine tree at the bottom of the garden came down, missing the hen-house by a whisker. The wind was so loud we never even heard it fall. I'm sure the hens did. We've lost more slates off the roof above Billy's room. But we were lucky. The end of Granny May's roof has gone completely. It just lifted off in the night. It's sitting lopsided across her escallonia hedge. Father's been up there all day trying to do what he can to keep the rain out. Everyone would be there helping, but there isn't a building on the island that hasn't been battered. Granny May just sat down in her kitchen all day and shook her head. She wouldn't come away. She kept saying she'll never be able to pay for a new roof and where will she go and what will she do? We stayed with her, Mother and me, giving her cups of tea and telling her it will be all right.

"Something'll turn up," Mother said. She's always saying that. When Father gets all inside himself and miserable and silent, when the cows aren't milking well, when he can't afford the timber to build his boats, she always says, "Don't worry, something'll turn up".

She never says it to me because she knows I won't believe her. I won't believe her because I know she doesn't believe it herself. She just says it to make him feel better. She just hopes it'll come true. Still, it must have made Granny May feel better. She was her old self again this evening, talking away happily to herself. Everyone on the island calls her "a mad old stick". But she's not really mad. She's just old and a bit forgetful. She does talk to herself, but then she's lived alone most of her life, so it's not surprising really. I love her because she's my granny, because she loves me, and because she shows it. Mother has persuaded her to come and stay for a bit until she can move back into her house again.

Billy's in trouble again. He went off to St Mary's without telling anyone. He was gone all day. When he got back this evening he never said a word to me or Granny May. Father buttoned his lip for as long as he could. It's always been the same with Father and Billy. They set each other off. They always have. It's Billy's fault really, most of the time anyway. He starts it. He does things without thinking. He says things without thinking. And Father's like a squall. He seems calm and quiet one moment and then... I could feel it coming. He banged the table and shouted. Billy had no right going off like that, he said, when there was so much to be put right at Granny May's. Billy told him he'd do what he pleased, when he pleased and he wasn't anyone's slave. Then he got up from the table and ran out, slamming the door behind him. Mother went after him. Poor Mother, always the peacemaker.

Father and Granny May had a good long talk about "young folk today", and how they don't know how lucky they are these days and how they don't know what hard work is all about. They're still at it downstairs. I went in to see Billy just a few minutes ago. He's been crying, I can tell. He says he doesn't want to talk. He's thinking, he says. That makes a change, I suppose.

February 14th

Granny May's roof has been patched up. She moved back home yesterday. We are on our own again.

Father said at breakfast he thought Molly would calve down today and that Billy and me should keep an eye on her. Billy went off to St Mary's and I went up to check Molly this afternoon on my own. She was lying down by the hedge, her calf curled up beside her. He looked as if he was sleeping at first, but he wasn't. There were flies on his face and his eyes weren't blinking. He was dead, and I couldn't make Molly get up. I pushed her and pushed her, but she wouldn't move. I didn't tell Father because I knew how angry he'd be. We should have been there, Billy or me – one of us should have been there. I fetched Mother instead. She couldn't get Molly on her feet either, so in the end we had to call Father from the boatshed. He tried everything, but Molly just laid her head down on the grass and died.

Father sat beside her, stroked her neck and said nothing. But I knew what he was thinking. We only had four cows and we'd just lost the best of them. Then he looked up and said, "Where's that boy?"

Mother tried to comfort him, but he wouldn't even answer her.

"Just you wait till he gets back, just you wait." That was all he said.

Billy came back at sundown. I saw him come sailing up Tresco Channel. I ran down to Green Bay to tell him about Molly, to warn him about Father. Then I saw that he was not alone.

"This is Joseph Hannibal," said Billy. "He's American, off the *General Lee* in St Mary's."

Joseph Hannibal is a bear of a man with a bushy black beard and twitchy eyebrows that meet in the middle so he always looks angry. I never had a chance to tell Billy about Molly. He'd brought Joseph Hannibal back to see the island, he said, and they went off together up towards Hell Bay.

I didn't see them again until supper. Father sat in a stony silence and Mother smiled all the time, thinly, like she does when she is worried. But after a time she was doing what I was doing, what Billy was doing, what even Father was doing. We were all listening to Joseph Hannibal.

He's been all over the world, the South Sea Islands, Australia, Japan, China, the frozen North. He's sailed on tea clippers, on steamships, and he's been whaling too.

"Yessir," he went on, puffing at his pipe, "I've seen whales longer than this entire house and that's the honest truth."

You had to listen to him – I mean, you wanted to listen. You wanted him to go on all night. Then Mother said we should go up to bed – that we had the cows to milk early in the morning. Billy said he wasn't tired, that he'd be up later. He stayed where he was. Father looked at him hard, but Billy didn't seem to notice. He had eyes only for Joseph Hannibal.

He still doesn't know about Molly, and he's still down there now talking to Joseph Hannibal.

There's something about Joseph Hannibal, something I don't like, but I'm not sure what it is. One thing I am sure of though. As soon as he's gone Father's going to have something to say, and when he does I wouldn't want to be in Billy's shoes.

I'm trying to stay awake by writing this, so I can warn him about Molly, but my eyes are pricking and I can hardly keep them open.

July 21st

My house is not my home any more. It's a place I live in. My island is a prison and I am quite alone. Mother and Father are strangers to each other. Billy has been gone for over four months now. There's been no letter, no word. We scarcely ever speak of him. It's as if he never lived.

I went to his room this morning and found Mother sitting on his bed staring at the wall, rocking back and forth. She had his blue jersey on her lap. I went and sat beside her. She tried to smile but couldn't. She hasn't smiled since Billy left.

I do the morning milking on my own now. That's when I most miss Billy. I talk to the cows and they listen. Maybe they understand too – I hope so. They're not milking at all well – I think perhaps they're missing Billy, like everyone else. They aren't eating properly either. Their coats are staring, and they're not licking themselves. They're just not how they should be.

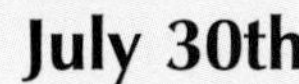

July 30th

In church today I was listening to the vicar. It was as if he was speaking just to me. He said we mustn't hope for anything at all in this life, only in the next life. I think I understand what he means. You only get disappointed if you hope.

Every night – like tonight, when I've finished this – I lie in the darkness and hope and pray that Billy will come back. I pray out loud, just in case God can't hear me hoping. And every morning, as soon as I wake up, I go to the window and hope to see him running up the path. But each day he isn't there makes even hoping more hopeless.

September 8th

Today I found a turtle. I think it's called a leatherback turtle. I found one once before, but it was dead. This one has been washed up alive.

Father had sent me down to collect driftwood on Rushy Bay. He said there'd be plenty about after a storm like that. He was right.

I'd been there for half an hour or so heaping up the wood, before I noticed the turtle in the tideline of piled seaweed. I thought at first he was just a washed-up tree stump covered in seaweed.

He was upside down on the sand. I pulled the seaweed off him. His eyes were open, unblinking. He was more dead than alive, I thought. His flippers were quite still, and held out to the clouds above as if he was worshipping them. He was massive, as long as this bed, and wider. He had a face like a two hundred year old man, wizened and wrinkled and wise with a gently-smiling mouth.

I looked around, and there were more gulls gathering. They were silent, watching, waiting; and I knew well enough what they were waiting for. I pulled away more of the seaweed and saw that the gulls had been at him already. There was blood under his neck where the skin had been pecked. I had got there just in time. I bombarded the gulls with pebbles and they flew off protesting noisily, leaving me alone with my turtle.

I knew it would be impossible to roll him over, but I tried anyway. I could rock him back and forth on his shell, but I could not turn him over, no matter how hard I tried. After a while I gave up and sat down beside him on the sand. His eyes kept closing slowly as if he was dropping off to sleep, or maybe he was dying – I couldn't be sure. I stroked him under his chin where I thought he would like it, keeping my hand well away from his mouth.

A great curling stormwave broke and came tumbling towards us. When it went hissing back over the sand, it left behind a broken spar. It was as if the sea was telling me what to do. I dragged the spar up the beach. Then I saw the turtle's head go back and his eyes closed. I've often seen seabirds like that. Once their heads go back there's nothing you can do. But I couldn't just let him die. I couldn't. I shouted at him. I shook him. I told him he wasn't to die, that I'd turn him over somehow, that it wouldn't be long.

I dug a deep hole in the sand beside him. I would lever him up and topple him in. I drove the spar into the sand underneath his shell. I drove it in again and again, until it was as deep as I could get it. I hauled back on it and felt him shift. I threw all my weight on it and at last he tumbled over into the hole, and the right way up, too. But when I scrambled over to him, his head lay limp in the sand, his eyes closed to the world. There wasn't a flicker of life about him. He was dead. I was quite sure of it now. It's silly, I know – I had only known him for a few minutes – but I felt I had lost a friend.

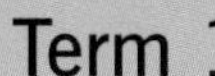

I made a pillow of soft sea lettuce for his head and knelt beside him. I cried till there were no more tears to cry. And then I saw the gulls were back. They knew too. I screamed at them, but they just glared at me and moved in closer.

"No!" I cried. "No!"

I would never let them have him, never. I piled a mountain of seaweed on top of him and my driftwood on top of that. The next tide would take him away. I left him and went home.

I went back to Rushy Bay this evening, at high tide, just before nightfall, to see if my turtle was gone. He was still there. The high tide had not been high enough. The gulls were gone though, all of them. I really don't know what made me want to see his face once more. I pulled the wood and seaweed away until I could see the top of his head. As I looked it moved and lifted. He was blinking up at me. He was alive again! I could have kissed him, really I could. But I didn't quite dare.

He's still there now, all covered up against the gulls, I hope. In the morning...

I had to stop writing because Father just came in. He hardly ever comes in my room, so I knew at once something was wrong.

"You all right?" he said, standing in the doorway. "What've you been up to?"

"Nothing," I said. "Why?"

"Old man Jenkins. He said he saw you down on Rushy Bay."

"I was just collecting the wood," I told him, as calmly as I could, "like you said I should." I find lying so difficult. I'm just not good at it.

"He thought you were crying, crying your eyes out, he says."

"I was not," I said, but I dared not look at him. I pretended to go on writing in my diary.

"You are telling me the truth, Laura?" He knew I wasn't, he knew it.

"Course," I said. I just wished he would go.

"What do you find to write in that diary of yours?" he asked.

"Things," I said. "Just things."

And he went out and shut the door behind him. He knows something, but he doesn't know what. I'm going to have to be very careful. If Father finds out about the turtle, I'm in trouble. He's only got to go down to Rushy Bay and look. That turtle would just be food to him, and to anyone else who finds him. We're all hungry, everyone is getting hungrier every day. I should tell him. I know I should. But I can't do it. I just can't let them eat him.

In the morning, early, I'll have to get him back into the sea. I don't know how I'm going to do it, but somehow I will. I must. Now it's not only the gulls I have to save him from.

The Dancing Bear

by Michael Morpurgo

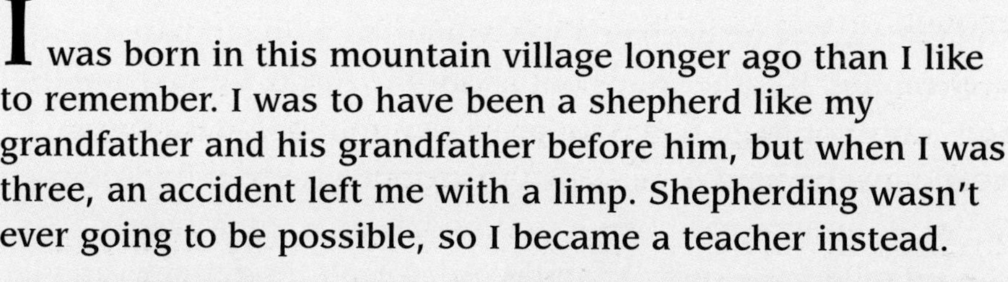

I was born in this mountain village longer ago than I like to remember. I was to have been a shepherd like my grandfather and his grandfather before him, but when I was three, an accident left me with a limp. Shepherding wasn't ever going to be possible, so I became a teacher instead.

For nearly forty years now, I have been the schoolmaster here. I live alone in a house by the school, content with my own company and my music. To play my hunting horn high in the mountains, and to hear its echo soaring with the eagles, is as close as I have been to complete happiness.

Yet I suppose you could say that I became a sort of shepherd after all: I shepherd children instead of sheep, that's all. I teach them, and I'm a kind of uncle to them even after they've left school. They think I'm a bit eccentric – I play my horn and I talk to myself more than I should. Like all children, they can be a bit cruel from time to time. They call me "Three Legs" or "Long John Silver" when they think I'm not listening, but you have to put up with that.

We are people whose lives are ruled by sheep, by the seasons, and above all by the mountains. We make cheese here, sheep's cheese. You won't find a better cheese anywhere, that's a promise. Almost all the families have a flock of sheep which they graze in the fields around the village, but when the snows clear, they take them up on to the mountain pastures for the sweet summer grass. The cows go too, and the horses and the pigs.

Snow cuts us off for at least three months of every winter, sometimes more, and then we are left to ourselves. But it's a peaceful place at any time of year. The winding road from the valley ends in the village square. Beyond us are the mountains, and beyond the mountains, the sky. We are a world of our own and we like it that way. We are used to it. The life is hard but predictable. People are born, people die. We have our blizzards and our droughts, no one ever has enough money and the roof always needs repairing.

Nothing ever really disturbed our life until some ten years ago, when a small bear came down out of the mountains. Nothing was ever to be the same again.

Roxanne was about seven years old at the time. An orphan child, she lived with her grandfather, who was a dour and unloving man. She was a solitary girl, but never lonely, I think. At school, she appeared to be a dreamer, a thinker. After school, with her grandfather busy in his fields, she would often wander off by herself, watching rabbits, maybe, or following butterflies. She was forever going missing. Then her grandfather would come shouting around the village for her. When he found her, he would shake her or even hit her. I protested more than once, but was told to mind my own business. A friendless, bitter old man, Roxanne's grandfather was interested in nothing unless there was some money in it. Roxanne was a nuisance to him. She knew it – and everyone knew it. But he was the only mother and father she had.

It was a Sunday morning in April. We were in the café before lunch. The old man was going on about Roxanne again, and how she ate him out of house and home. He'd had a bit too much to drink, I think, but then he was often that way.

"Gone off again, she has," he grumbled. "God knows what she gets up to. Nothing but trouble, that girl."

Just then we heard shouting in the village square and, glad of any diversion, we all went out to look. Roxanne was staggering towards us, clutching a bear cub in her arms, with its arms wrapped around her neck. She'd been scratched on her face and on her arms, but it didn't seem to bother her. She was laughing and breathless with joy.

"Bruno!" she said. "He's called Bruno. I was down by the stream. I was just throwing sticks and I felt something stroking my neck. I turned round and there he was. He patted my shoulder. He's my very own bear. Grandpa. He's all alone. He's hungry. I can keep him, can't I? Please?"

If we hadn't been there – and half the village was there by now – I think the old man might have grabbed the bear cub by the scruff of the neck and taken him right back where he came from.

"Look at him," he said. "He's half starved. He's going to die anyway. And besides, bears are for killing, not keeping. You know how many sheep we lose every year to bears? Dozens, I'm telling you, dozens."

Some people were beginning to agree with him. I looked at Roxanne and saw she was looking up at me. Her eyes were filled with tears.

"Maybe" – I was still thinking hard as I spoke – "if you kept him, you know, just for a while. It wouldn't cost much: some waste milk and an old shed somewhere. And just suppose" – I was talking directly to the old man now – "just suppose you made 'bear' labels for your honey jars – you could call it 'Bruno's Honey'. Everyone would hear about it.

They'd come from miles around, have a little look at the bear and then buy your honey. You'd make a fortune, I'm sure of it."

I'd said the right thing. Roxanne's grandfather had his beehives all over the mountainside, and everyone knew that he couldn't sell even half the honey he collected. He nodded slowly as the sense of it dawned on him. "All right," he said. "We'll try it. Just for a while, mind."

Roxanne looked at me and beamed her thanks. She went off with Bruno, followed by an excited cavalcade of village children who took turns to carry him.

That afternoon, they made him a bed of bracken at the back of one of the old man's barns, and fed him a supper of warm ewe's milk from a bottle. They dipped his paw in honey and made him suck it. After that he helped himself. Later when I passed the barn on my evening walk, I heard Roxanne singing him to sleep. She sang quite beautifully.

In no time at all, Bruno became one of the village children; nobody was afraid of him, as he was always gentle and biddable. He'd go splashing with them in the streams; he'd romp with them in the hay barns; he'd curl himself up in a ball and roll with them helter-skelter down the hillsides. He was more than a playmate, though. He was our mascot, the pride of the village.

To begin with, he never strayed far from Roxanne. He would follow her everywhere, almost as if he were guarding her. Then one day – and by this time, Roxanne was maybe ten or eleven – he broke out of his barn and followed her to school.

I was sitting at my desk sharpening pencils and the class was settled at its work, when Bruno's great panting face appeared at the window, tongue lolling out and drooling. Roxanne managed to shut him in the woodshed where he stayed till lunch, happily sharpening his claws on the logs.

Not much school-work was done *that* day.

Hurricane Summer

by Robert Swindells

We played games of course, same as before, except now our favourite game was soldiers. We'd pick sides and toss a coin. If you lost the toss you had to be the Germans, which meant you couldn't win.

The village was our battleground. The British would chase the Germans along the High Street and in and out of gardens, yards and alleyways. The Germans cheated a lot – hiding inside the church or ganging up five against one – but the British always fought fair. Our battles usually ended on the Green, where the Germans would be caught in the open and mown down with tommy guns. They always died dramatically – throwing up their arms and rolling over three or four times in the grass before finally coming to rest. There were benches here and there round the rim of the Green and sometimes, on warm days, the climax of the battle would be watched by a few old villagers sitting out enjoying the sunshine.

On the particular day I want to tell you about, Sam Drury was there, twitching and blinking as usual.

Sam was the village barber, and we weren't supposed to stare at him. It was hard not to, because of the twitching and blinking. Sam had fought in the trenches in World War I and had shell-shock. Us kids weren't sure what that meant, but our parents said he'd come home from Flanders twenty years ago twitching and blinking and hadn't stopped since. It didn't keep him from being a good barber, but it was hard not to crack up laughing when he was cutting your hair and you could see him in the mirror.

Anyway, this particular day he was on one of the benches, and I was a German. When I got shot, I fell with a cry and rolled over and over, coming to rest spreadeagled on my back with my eyes shut. I was lying there, listening to the British making tommy gun noises, when a voice whispered, "You never get up, you know, once you're down."

I opened my eyes and saw Sam Drury looking down at me. I hadn't realised I was so close to his bench.

"P-pardon?"

He blinked rapidly. "I said, you never get up once you're down. Not when it's real."

"I... I know that, Mr Drury." I could feel my cheeks going red. "We're playing, that's all. It's just a game."

"A game. Yes." He gazed across the Green. The Germans were all dead. The British were standing at a distance, staring at Sam.

"We thought it was a game in 1914," he murmured. "Couldn't wait to enlist." He smiled crookedly. "It was the girls, you see. And the songs. *'Goodbye, Dolly Grey'. 'Tipperary'*. They made us feel like heroes. Should've been us, lad, marching through the village. Bags of swank." He shook his head. "Different down Salisbury Plain though, and when we finally reached the Front we thought we'd arrived in Hell. Wounded on stretchers in the mud, blind and screaming. Dead mules, bloated and covered in flies. The filthy, inescapable stink. Gulping rum at dawn so you'd be drunk enough to go over the top instead of lying in the bottom of the trench blubbing for your ma, which is what you'd do if you was sober. Don't show none of that, do they, in their recruiting posters? Ain't no songs about it neither."

He sniffled, wiping his cheek with the back of his hand. "It's goodbye Dolly Grey though – they got that bit right." He slumped forward, dangling his hands between his knees. "She don't want you no more, see? Not when you can't hold your head still nor stop blinking."

He was crying. There's nothing more embarrassing to a kid than a grown up crying. I didn't know where to put myself. What to say. The other Germans had stopped being dead and were standing with the British, staring across at us. I got up quietly. Sam Drury seemed to have forgotten I was there and I tiptoed away. But whenever I played soldiers after that, I kept thinking about the stuff he'd mentioned. Spoiled it a bit, I can tell you, but not as much as something that happened a few weeks later.

The Computer Nut

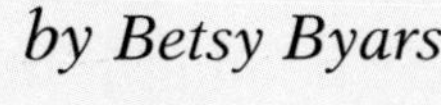

by Betsy Byars

"Your planet is known as the laughing planet. Did you know that? Yours is the only planet in the whole universe where there's laughing."

So says BB9, whose main ambition in life is to make people laugh. Which is why he chooses to contact Kate to help him with his mission. From her self-portrait drawn on her father's computer, it looks as if she has a sense of fun and would definitely enjoy a good laugh.

But who is BB9? Is he really a creature from outer space, or is this all a big hoax? The Computer Nut has a job on her hands to find out just exactly what's going on.

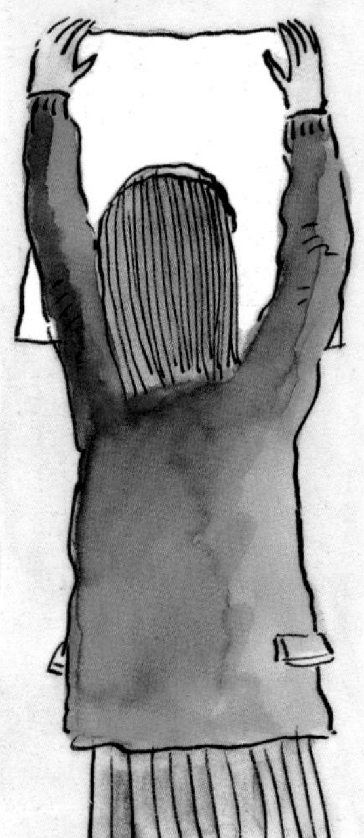

Self-Portrait of a Computer Nut

Kate was drawing a picture of herself on her father's computer. She had been working for an hour. She was half finished when Miss Markham came and stood in the doorway behind her.

"I'm ready to close the office now, Kate," she said.

Kate flicked her hair behind her ears. She did not answer. She continued to turn the thumbwheels, drawing lines between the dots. Her eyes watched the screen intently.

"Kate, did you hear me? The last patient has left. Your father has gone to the hospital. I'm ready to close the office now."

"Go ahead, I'll lock the doors when I leave."

"You know that's against your father's orders."

"Well, I've *got* to finish this. It's homework and it's due tomorrow."

"Katie –"

"Miss Markham, this is the first art assignment I've ever been interested in. Last week you know what we did? We made Indian signs out of yarn, and before that we pasted macaroni on cardboard. Now, *finally*, we are doing something I'm interested in, and I've got to finish."

Miss Markham crossed the room and stood behind Kate. She watched the screen as Kate connected the dots for her mouth. "That does *not* look like homework."

"It is! Our assignment is to do a self-portrait."

"On a computer?"

"No. We're supposed to use our imaginations. Willie Lomax is doing a collage out of candy wrappers. His freckles are M&Ms. He's calling it Sweet Freak."

"What are you calling yours?"

"Self-Portrait of a Computer Nut."

"Good title."

"I like it." Kate smiled without glancing around.

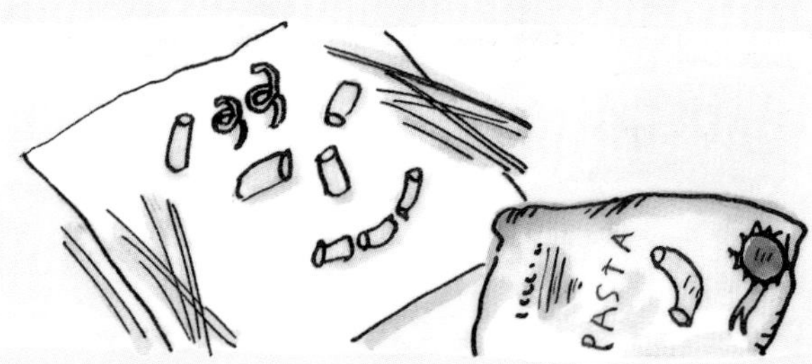

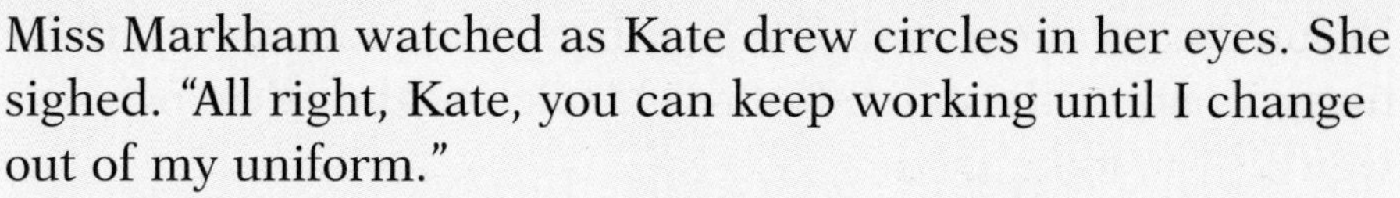

Miss Markham watched as Kate drew circles in her eyes. She sighed. "All right, Kate, you can keep working until I change out of my uniform."

"Thanks."

"But then you have *got* to leave whether you're through or not."

"I'll be through."

As Miss Markham started for the door, she added, "If you're not, you'll have to call it 'Unfinished Portrait of a Computer Nut'. Ten minutes, Kate."

"Right."

With her eyes watching the screen, Kate drew the straight lines for her hair. She paused to look at what she'd done. "Not bad." She typed "Self-Portrait of a Computer Nut" beneath the picture. Then she pushed the button marked "Hard Copy" and waited while the machine printed the picture.

When the sheet of paper slid out of the side, Kate picked it up. "That does look like me," she said to herself.

She turned to shut off the computer and saw Miss Markham in the doorway. "Perfect timing," Kate said. She held up her picture. "What do you think?"

"Not bad. Your hair's never that neat, though."

"I know, and I also have more freckles, and braces on my teeth."

She eyed the sheet of paper critically. "Well, it's better than Willie's candy portrait. You know what happened last summer? I meant to tell you this. Willie went to the same computer camp as I did, and when we were checking in, his suitcase fell open, and there was a real thin layer of clothes – one T-shirt and a pair of socks – and the whole rest of the suitcase was junk food. He had enough Snickers to –"

"Kate, I have not got time to talk about Willie Lomax."

"I don't want to talk about him either!" Kate said quickly. She turned back to the computer to hide her expression. "I just wanted you to know that next time he's in for a checkup do not believe him when he says he has stuck to his diet."

Kate slipped out the disk containing the drawing program. To change the subject, she said, "Where are you going, Miss Markham? Do you have a date?"

"Not unless I leave right this minute!"

"I'm coming! I'm coming!"

Kate was reaching for the off button when suddenly words began appearing on the screen. She stopped, her hand frozen in mid air.

"That's crazy!"

She glanced at the door to see if Miss Markham had noticed, but Miss Markham was in the outer office, turning off the lights. Kate sank into the chair, her portrait forgotten in her lap.

The words on the screen were:

I HAVE JUST SEEN THE PORTRAIT OF THE COMPUTER NUT AND I WOULD LIKE TO MAKE CONTACT. WILL YOU RECEIVE A MESSAGE, COMPUTER NUT?

Kate read the words a second time. A flutter of excitement moved up her spine. "Miss Markham, could you please come

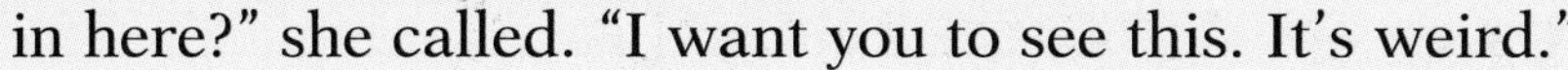

in here?" she called. "I want you to see this. It's weird."

"I am ready to leave, Kate. I am standing by the door with my coat on. My hand is on the doorknob."

"Has this computer been acting funny lately?"

"I am opening the door, Kate."

"Wait! It's happening again!"

REPEAT. I HAVE A MESSAGE FOR THE COMPUTER NUT.
WILL YOU RECEIVE INPUT, YES OR NO?

"I am stepping outside, Kate."

"Miss Markham, somebody is sending me a message. I cannot believe this. On the computer! Somebody saw my portrait and they're sending me a message."

"I am closing the door, Kate."

"Wait! Let me get my message! I – Oh, all right! I'm coming!"

Hurriedly Kate put her hands on the keyboard and typed one word:

TOMORROW

Then she got to her feet and turned off the computer. The screen dimmed and, holding her self-portrait in one hand, she ran for the door.

The Firework Maker's Daughter

by Philip Pullman

Chapter One

A thousand miles ago, in a country east of the jungle and south of the mountains, there lived a Firework-Maker called Lalchand and his daughter Lila.

Lalchand's wife had died when Lila was young. The child was a cross little thing, always crying and refusing her food, but Lalchand built a cradle for her in the corner of the workshop, where she could see the sparks play and listen to the fizz and crackle of the gunpowder. Once she was out of her cradle, she toddled around the workshop laughing as the fire flared and the sparks danced. Many a time she burnt her little fingers, but Lalchand splashed water on them and kissed her better, and soon she was playing again.

When she was old enough to learn, her father began to teach her the art of making fireworks. She began with little Crackle-Dragons, six on a string. Then she learned how to make Leaping Monkeys, Golden Sneezes, and Java Lights. Soon she was making all the simple fireworks, and thinking about more complicated ones.

One day she said, "Father, if I put some flowers of salt in a Java Light instead of cloud-powder, what would happen?"

"Try it and see," he said.

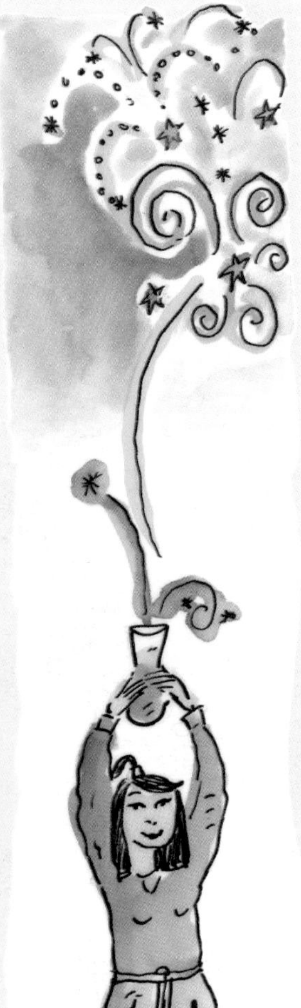

So she did. Instead of burning with a steady green glimmer, it sprayed out wicked little sparks, each of which turned a somersault before going out.

"Not bad, Lila," said Lalchand. "What are you going to call it?"

"Mmm... Tumbling Demons," she said.

"Excellent! Make a dozen and we'll put them into the New Year Festival display."

The Tumbling Demons were a great success, and so were the Shimmering Coins that Lila invented next. As time went on she learned more and more of her father's art, until one day she said, "Am I a proper Firework-Maker now?"

"No, no," he said. "By no means. Ha! You don't know the start of it. What are the ingredients of fly-away powder?"

"I don't know."

"And where do you find thunder-grains?"

"I've never heard of thunder-grains."

"How much scorpion oil do you put in a Krakatoa Fountain?"

"A teaspoonful?"

"*What*? You'd blow the whole city up. You've got a lot to learn yet. Do you really want to be a Firework-Maker, Lila?"

"Of course I do! It's the only thing I want!"

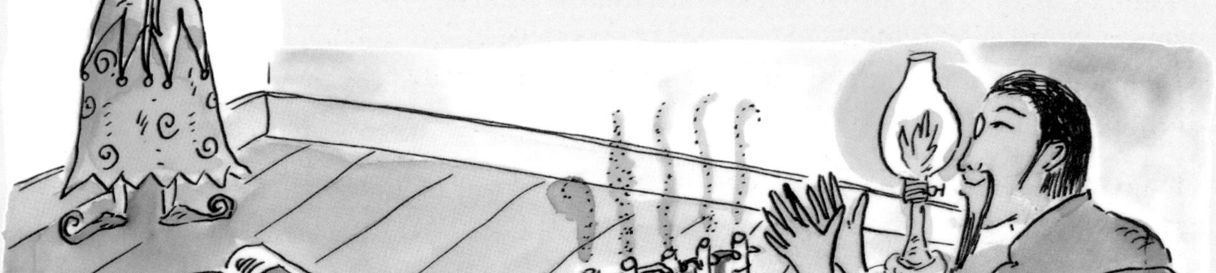

“I was afraid so,” he said. “It’s my own fault. What was I thinking of? I should have sent you to my sister Jembavati to bring you up as a dancer. This is no place for a girl, now I come to think of it, and just look at you! Your hair’s a mess, your fingers are burned and stained with chemicals, your eyebrows are scorched... How am I going to find a husband for you when you look like that?”

Lila was horrified.

“A *husband*?”

“Well, of course! You don’t imagine you can stay here for ever, do you?”

They looked at each other as if they were strangers. Each of them had had quite the wrong idea about things, and they were both alarmed to find it out.

So Lila said no more about being a Firework-Maker, and Lalchand said no more about husbands. But they both thought about them, all the same.

Now the King of that country owned a White Elephant. It was the custom that whenever the King wanted to punish one of his courtiers, he would send him the White Elephant as a present, and the expense of looking after the animal would ruin the poor man; because the White Elephant had to sleep between silk sheets (enormous ones), and eat mango-flavoured Turkish Delight (tons of it), and have his tusks covered in gold leaf every morning. When the courtier had no money left at all, the White Elephant would be returned to the King, ready for his next victim.

Wherever the White Elephant went, his personal servant had to go too. The servant’s name was Chulak, and he was the same age as Lila. In fact, they were friends.

Every afternoon Chulak would take the White Elephant out for his exercise, because the Elephant would go with no-one else,

and there was a reason for this: Chulak was the only person, besides Lila, who knew that the Elephant could talk.

One day Lila went to visit Chulak and the White Elephant. She arrived at the Elephant House in time to hear the Elephant Master losing his temper.

"You horrible little boy!" he roared. "You've done it again, haven't you?"

"Done what?" said Chulak innocently.

"Look!" said the Elephant Master, pointing with a quivering finger at the White Elephant's snowy flanks.

Written all over his side in charcoal and paint were dozens of slogans:

EAT AT THE GOLDEN LANTERN

BANGKOK WANDERERS FOR THE CUP

STAR OF INDIA TANDOORI HOUSE

And right at the very top of the White Elephant's back, in great big letters:

CHANG LOVES LOTUS BLOSSOM <u>TRUE</u> XXX

"Every day this Elephant comes home with graffiti all over him!" shouted the Elephant Master. "Why don't you stop people doing it?"

"I can't understand how it happens, Master," said Chulak. "Mind you, the traffic's awful. I've got to watch those rickshaw-drivers like a hawk. I can't look out for graffiti artists as well – they just slap it up and run."

"But *Chang loves Lotus Blossom True* must have taken a good ten minutes on a stepladder!"

"Yes, it's a mystery to me, Master. Shall I clean it off?"

"All of it! There's a job coming up in a day or two, and I want this animal *clean*."

And the Elephant Master stormed off, leaving Chulak and Lila with the Elephant.

"Hello, Hamlet," said Lila.

"Hello, Lila," sighed the Elephant. "Look what this obnoxious brat has reduced me to! A walking billboard!"

"Stop fussing," said Chulak. "Look, we've got eighteen rupees already – and ten annas from the Tandoori House – and Chang gave me a whole rupee for letting him write that on the top. We're nearly there, Hamlet!"

"The *shame*!" said Hamlet, shaking his great head.

"You mean you charge people money to write on him?" said Lila.

"Course!" said Chulak. "It's dead lucky to write your name on a White Elephant. When we've got enough, we're going to run away. Trouble is, he's in love with a lady elephant at the Zoo. You ought to see him blush when we go past – like a ton of strawberry ice cream!"

"She's called Frangipani," said Hamlet mournfully. "But she won't even look at me. And now there's another job coming up – another poor man to bankrupt. Oh, I hate Turkish Delight! I detest silk sheets! And I loathe gold leaf on my tusks! I wish I was a normal dull grey elephant!"

"No, you don't," said Chulak. "We've got plans, Hamlet, remember? I'm teaching him to sing, Lila. We'll change his name to Luciano Elephanti, and the world'll be our oyster."

"But why are you looking so sad, Lila?" said Hamlet, as Chulak began to scrub him down.

"My father won't tell me the final secret of Firework-Making," said Lila. "I've learned all there is to know about fly-away

powder and thunder-grains, and scorpion oil and spark repellent, and glimmer-juice and salts-of-shadow, but there's something else I need to know, and he won't tell me."

"Tricky," said Chulak. "Shall I ask him for you?"

"If he won't tell me, he certainly won't tell you," said Lila.

"He won't know he's doing it," said Chulak. "You leave it to me."

So that evening, after he'd settled Hamlet down for the night, Chulak called at the Firework-Maker's workshop. It lay down a little winding alley full of crackling smells and pungent noises, between the fried-prawn stall and the batik-painter's. He found Lalchand in the courtyard under the warm stars, mixing up some red glow-paste.

"Hello, Chulak," said Lalchand. "I hear the White Elephant's going to be presented to Lord Parakit tomorrow. How long d'you think his money'll last?"

"A week, I reckon," said Chulak. "Though you never know – we might run away before then. I've nearly got enough to get us to India. I thought I might take up firework-making when we got there. Nice trade."

"Nice trade, my foot!" said Lalchand. "Firework-making is a sacred art! You need talent and dedication and the favour of the gods before you can become a Firework-Maker. The only thing *you're* dedicated to is idleness, you scamp."

"How did you become a Firework-Maker, then?"

"I was apprenticed to my father. And then I had to be tested to see whether I had the Three Gifts."

"Oh, the Three Gifts, eh," said Chulak, who had no idea what the Three Gifts were. Probably Lila did, he thought. "And did you have them?"

"Of course I did!"

"And that's it? Sounds easy. I bet I could pass that test. I've got more than three gifts."

"Pah!" said Lalchand. "That's not all. Then came the most difficult and dangerous part of the whole apprenticeship. Every Firework-Maker –" and he lowered his voice and looked around to make sure no-one was listening – "every Firework-Maker has to travel to the Grotto of Razvani, the Fire-Fiend, in the heart of Mount Merapi, and bring back some of the Royal Sulphur. That's the ingredient that makes the finest fireworks. Without that, no-one can ever be a true Firework-Maker."

"Ah," said Chulak. "Royal Sulphur. Mount Merapi. That's the volcano, isn't it?"

"Yes, you pestilential boy, and already I've told you far more than I should. This is a secret, you understand?"

"Of course," said Chulak, looking solemn. "I can keep a secret."

And Lalchand had the uneasy feeling that he'd been tricked, though he couldn't imagine why.

From The Penguin Dictionary of Surnames

Cameron N "crooked nose, hook-nose" Scots Gaelic. Or, rarely, L – places in Fifes, Stirlings, of same meaning used topographically. 31st commonest surname in Scotland in 1958.

Camm L "Caen" (see **Cain**) or "crooked (river)" Welsh; place (Cam) in Glos. Or N "crooked, cross-eyed, deformed" Scots Gaelic and Welsh, as in *game leg* and Davy Gam at Agincourt.

Cammamile N "camomile" OF from Latin from Greek (= earth-apple). Its blossoms smell like apples, and it is used in pharmacy; but the reason for the N is obscure.

Camp(s) O "warrior" OE (see **Kemp**), or a similar N "battle" OE *camp*; and "(son) of **C-**".

Campbell N "crooked mouth" Scots Gaelic. Seventh commonest surname in Scotland in 1958 (as in 1858), and 31st in Ireland in 1890. Family name of the dukes of Argyll and of six other Scots peers.

Campin L "open country, fertile land" OF; places (Campagne) in Oise, Pas-de-Calais, or the region Champagne (of the same meaning) normanized.

Campion Norman form of OF **Champion**; found in Northants-Lincs

Campton L "place on the crooked (stream)" British+OE; place in Beds.

Candler Norman form of OF **Chandler**.

Cann O "can, pot, bucket, jar" OE, for a maker/seller. Or L

"deep valley (a topographical use of *can*)" OE; place in Dorset. The surname is common in Devon.

Cannan F (for **O/McC-**) "descendant/son of White-Head" or "of Wolfcub" Irish; anglicized spellings of two different Irish septs, often rendered Cannon.

Cannard N "sluggard, wastrel" OF; the inn-sign at C-'s Grave near Shepton Mallet, Somerset, displays a hanged man. A surname of the Bristol area.

Cannel(l) O "cinnamon(-seller)" OF, (*Atte* and *de* forms are lacking to make it L "channel, river-bed, gutter, ditch" OF.) For Manx **Cannell** see **McConnal**. Guppy counted **-ell** only in Norfolk.

Cannington L "farm by the Quantock (= ?rim of a circle) Hills" Keltic + **OE**; place in Somerset.

F: *first name* **L**: *local name*

N: *nickname* **O**: *occupational name*

Clockwork, or All Wound Up

by Philip Pullman

Part One

Once upon a time (when time ran by clockwork), a strange event took place in a little German town. Actually, it was a series of events, all fitting together like the parts of a clock, and although each person saw a different part, no-one saw the whole of it; but here it is, as well as I can tell it.

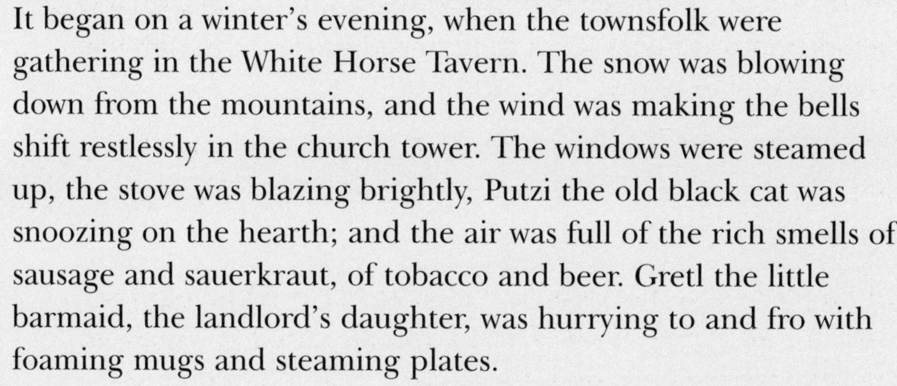

It began on a winter's evening, when the townsfolk were gathering in the White Horse Tavern. The snow was blowing down from the mountains, and the wind was making the bells shift restlessly in the church tower. The windows were steamed up, the stove was blazing brightly, Putzi the old black cat was snoozing on the hearth; and the air was full of the rich smells of sausage and sauerkraut, of tobacco and beer. Gretl the little barmaid, the landlord's daughter, was hurrying to and fro with foaming mugs and steaming plates.

The door opened, and fat white flakes of snow swirled in, to faint away into water as they met the heat of the parlour. The incomers, Herr Ringelmann the clockmaker and his apprentice Karl, stamped their boots and shook the snow off their greatcoats.

"It's Herr Ringelmann!" said the Burgomaster. "Well, old friend, come and drink some beer with me! And a mug for young what's his name, your apprentice."

Karl the apprentice nodded his thanks and went to sit by himself in a corner. His expression was dark and gloomy.

"What's the matter with young thingamajig?" said the Burgomaster. "He looks as if he's swallowed a thundercloud."

"Oh, I shouldn't worry," said the clockmaker, sitting down at the table with his friends. "He's anxious about tomorrow. His apprenticeship is coming to an end, you see."

"Ah, of course!" said the Burgomaster. It was the custom that when a clockmaker's apprentice finished his period of service, he made a new figure for the great clock of Glockenheim. "So we're to have a new piece of clockwork in the tower! Well, I look forward to seeing it tomorrow."

"I remember when my apprenticeship came to an end," said Herr Ringelmann. "I couldn't sleep for thinking about what would happen when my figure came out of the clock. Supposing I hadn't counted the cogs properly? Supposing the spring was too stiff? Supposing – oh, a thousand things go through your mind. It's a heavy responsibility."

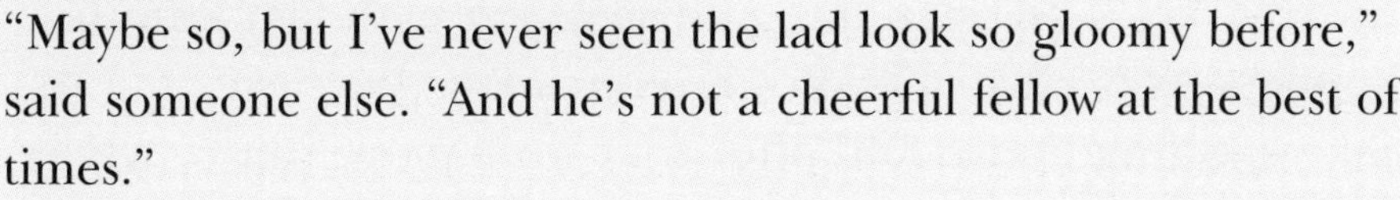

"Maybe so, but I've never seen the lad look so gloomy before," said someone else. "And he's not a cheerful fellow at the best of times."

And it seemed to the other drinkers that Herr Ringelmann himself was a little down-hearted, but he raised his mug with the rest of them and changed the conversation to another topic.

A Lot of Mince Pies

by Robert Swindells

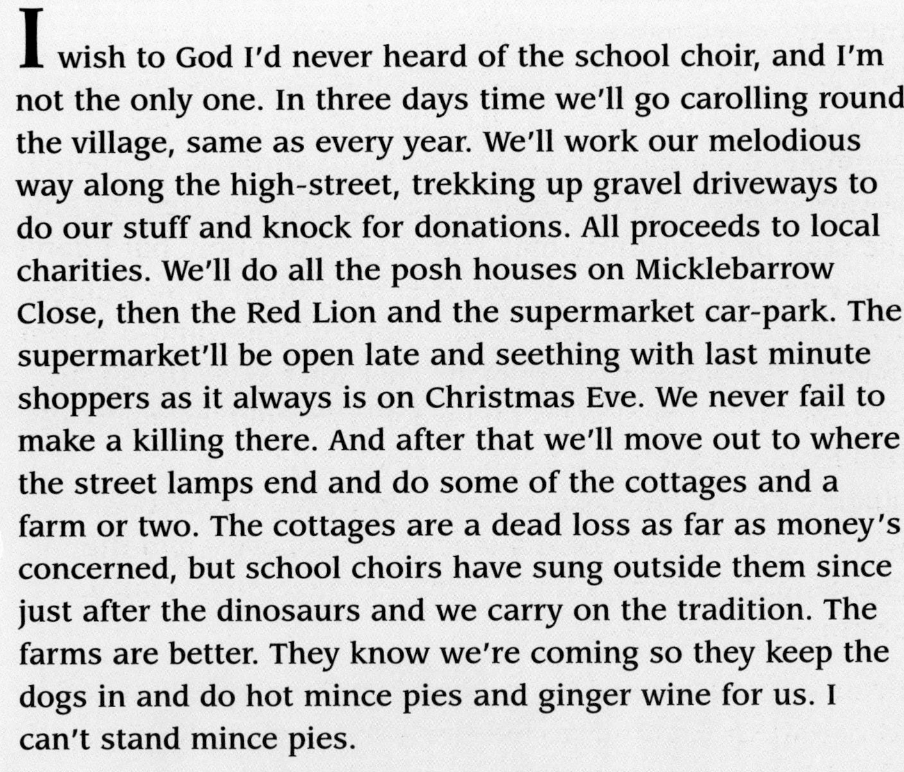

I wish to God I'd never heard of the school choir, and I'm not the only one. In three days time we'll go carolling round the village, same as every year. We'll work our melodious way along the high-street, trekking up gravel driveways to do our stuff and knock for donations. All proceeds to local charities. We'll do all the posh houses on Micklebarrow Close, then the Red Lion and the supermarket car-park. The supermarket'll be open late and seething with last minute shoppers as it always is on Christmas Eve. We never fail to make a killing there. And after that we'll move out to where the street lamps end and do some of the cottages and a farm or two. The cottages are a dead loss as far as money's concerned, but school choirs have sung outside them since just after the dinosaurs and we carry on the tradition. The farms are better. They know we're coming so they keep the dogs in and do hot mince pies and ginger wine for us. I can't stand mince pies.

Anyway, from the minute we troop out of the schoolyard behind old Exley at seven o'clock, the kids'll be waiting for one thing. They'll be waiting for the last house – the Meltons' place, with its tangled garden, crumbling brick, and funny little windows. It's three-quarters of a mile from the village, and the choir usually gets there about nine o'clock. The Meltons'll be waiting, and as soon as we strike up the first number they'll open the door and stand there in carpet-slippers, smiling and swaying a little to the music. They're the most ancient couple you're ever likely to see – my mum says they were old when she was in the choir – but the thing about them is, you can actually see that they're enjoying the carols, and afterwards they make a generous donation and give presents to all the kids. There's always eighteen in the choir and I suppose the Meltons buy the stuff on their Christmas shopping expedition, but I don't know where they go – nobody ever sees them in the village. The presents aren't tatty either – none of your quid-a-dozen made in Taiwan plastic rubbish. They tend to be things like cartridge pens, penknives and wallets and purses made of real leather. Last year I got a calculator. As soon as the singing's over they beckon some kid inside – someone whose face they've taken a fancy to I suppose – and the chosen one reappears a few minutes later with a double armful of little packets.

By now you'll be thinking this sounds like the perfect end to Christmas Eve and wondering why I'm moaning. Hang about, and I'll tell you what happened last year.

The Two-thousand-pound Goldfish

by Betsy Byars

Warren sat in the second row of the theatre, staring up at the screen. A piece of cold popcorn was in his hand, halfway to his mouth, forgotten.

– We've tried everything. Everything! Nothing can stop the monster.

– Wait! There's one thing we haven't tried.

– What?

– The S-F-342 Photo-Atomic cloud.

– But that's never been tested, Professor. There's no guarantee it will work.

– It's our one hope. Tell Doctor Barronni to ready the machine.

– But Professor –

"Warren Otis." The theatre manager was coming down the aisle. "Is there a Warren Otis in the theatre? Warren Otis!"

When his name was called for the third time, Warren straightened. "Oh, that's me. I'm Warren Otis. What do you want?"

"Your grandmother called. You're supposed to go home."

"Is something wrong?"

"She just said you're supposed to go home."

Warren got up out of his seat. Walking backwards so he could watch the pink haze of the S-F-342 Photo-Atomic cloud encircle the monster, he moved slowly, reluctantly, up the aisle.

The monster inhaled some of the S-F-342 and began clawing at the sky. He threw back his head and roared. Drool came out of his mouth.

A poor effect, Warren decided, walking slower. You could see it was a man in a reptile suit now, standing in a pond made up to look like the Pacific Ocean. Economy drool, too – probably corn syrup.

– It's taking effect, Professor. The monster is shrinking.

– Wait! The wind is changing!

– Yes, Professor, the cloud is shifting. It's heading for Los Angeles!

Warren stopped. In the crook of his arm was his half-eaten box of popcorn. It had been there for six hours. Warren ate between features.

"Excuse me," a voice said.

"Sure." Warren shifted to let two girls pass. Eyes on the screen, he felt his way into an aisle seat in the last row.

– We've got to stop it!

– Professor! Look at the monster! It's still shrinking! The cloud works!

– Yes, this means –

– This means that if the cloud hits Los Angeles, it will reduce the entire population to the size of Barbie dolls within ten minutes!

– Yes, Professor, unless …

This was the third time Warren had heard that prediction this afternoon, but it was still awesome. His eyes gleamed.

He envisioned millions of Barbies and Kens running helplessly around Los Angeles, trying to climb up into house-sized beds, making human ladders up to doorknobs, squeaking like mice as they scurried through the streets.

"Excuse me."

"Sure." A fat boy crawled over Warren's knees. He shifted impatiently to keep the screen in sight.

– There may be time enough if –

Warren's lips were moving with the actor's now, forming the words. "If," he and the actor said together, "we can send the cloud back out to –"

"Warren Otis!" It was the manager again. "Is Warren Otis still in the theatre?"

Warren sighed aloud. He got up, head down, and ducked quickly into the lobby. He went around the refreshment centre and out into the street, where he stood for a moment under the marquee.

He never came out of a theatre without sensing all over again the cold drabness of the real world. The same dull line of traffic was in the street, the same dull sky overhead. Even the shadows seemed empty, nothing lurking inside.

Warren zipped up his jacket and pulled his aviator sunglasses down from on top of his head. Frowning slightly, he started down the sidewalk. He felt as dissatisfied as if he had been interrupted in the middle of a dream. He began to eat his cold popcorn.

Catherine Called Birdy

by Karen Cushman

6th day of February, *Feast of Saint Dorothy, a virgin martyr who sent back a basket of fruit from the Garden of Paradise, and celebration of the founding of our village church, Saint Dorothy's, one hundred and seven years ago.*

This might become my favourite feast day if we could celebrate it each year as we did today. First we heard a special Mass, which meant it was twice as long and my mind wandered twice as much and my knees got twice as tired.

After, we all gathered in the hall to eat, feasting on pig's stomach stuffed with nuts and apples, herring with parsnips, and a disgusting peacock, stuffed and roasted with his tail feathers stuck back on.

There was abundant wine as well as ale and cider and perry and we grew quite rowdy as we played Hoodman's Blind. The shallow-brained Lady Margaret, whenever it was her turn to be blindfolded, whiffled here and there around the hall and then wandered into the pantry… Corpus bones! What an odd way to play!

Suddenly there was a commotion as two of my father's men pulled out their swords and started slashing at each other, each accusing the other of sneaking peaks over the blindfold. Everyone moved aside as Richard and Gilbert, cursing and grunting, swung their terrible heavy swords at each other. Up on the tables, where they overturned cups and goblets and stepping in and out of the plates of meat. Onto the benches, which splintered as they swung and missed each other. Over to the walls, where their sharpened weapons cut new rends in the already tattered hangings.

All afternoon they swung until finally they were near too tired to lift their heavy weapons again. Gilbert heaved one last swipe at Richard, which knocked him off his feet. Bellowing about who did what unfairly to whom, their friends joined in, shouting and cursing and grunting along. Then we all joined in, even the cooks and servers swinging their ladles and pothooks. I with no weapon hurled food at whoever was near, pretending I was a crusader battling the heathens with leftover pig's stomach and almond cream.

One group of fighters stumbled into the fire, scattering the burning brands and smouldering ashes into the rushes, which burst into flame. Suddenly the hall floor was ablaze, as the dry rushes caught fire. Even William Steward's shoes were smouldering. William and Gilbert grabbed flagons of wine to pour over the blazing rushes while Richard stamped on the stray sparks… The hot fire seemed to cool our tempers so everyone sat down to drink again amidst the ruins of the table and argue over which side got the better of the other. If I become a saint, I would like my day to be celebrated in just such a fashion.

8th day of February, *Feast of Saint Cuthman, a hermit and beggar who took his crippled mother everywhere with him in a wheelbarrow.*

I spent yesterday doctoring ale head, grumbling guts, and various cuts, gashes, scratches, and burns – including my own. Then just before dinner we found Roger Moreton lying unconscious in the black soggy rushes near the buttery. He sustained a grievous injury in the fight and lay untended all night while we slept. Now he lies in the solar in my parents' bed, still asleep, with cobwebs packed about his wound, his fever raging.

9th day of February, *Feast of Saint Apollonia, who relieves those suffering from toothache.*

Roger's wound has grown black and smells bad. My mother and Morwenna and I do all we can, but his head is no better and his fever no less and his eyes still closed.

10th day of February, *Feast of Saint Scholastica, the first nun.*

Roger died this morning. He never woke up. He was seventeen.

11th day of February, *Feast of Saint Gobnet, virgin and beekeeper.*

Today is Roger's funeral ale, and our hall rings with noise and music and fighting and eating and drinking just as it did the day our brawling killed him. This will go on all night until the funeral Mass tomorrow after which there will be more

feasting. I am in my chamber, for my head aches and my heart grieves, and I have no appetite for food, merriment or company.

11th day of March, *Feast of Saint Oengus the Culdee, an Irish bishop who genuflected frequently and recited the psalms while standing in cold water.*

At Mass today I wondered instead of listening to the sermon, but they were wonderings about holy things, so I trust God was not offended. First I wondered why, after Lazarus was raised from the dead, people did not ask him about heaven and hell and being dead. Were they not curious? Indeed, this may have been our only chance to find out without dying.

Then I wondered why Jesus used his miraculous powers to cure lepers instead of creating an herb or flower that would cure them so we could continue to use it even now when Jesus is in Heaven. When we are on the road, I hate to hear the bell of a leper hiding in the trees until we pass. I know priests say lepers are paying for their great sins, but I know plenty of great sinners who still have their fingers and noses.

And I wondered about how long it took Noah to gather up two of everything for the Ark. The rain was pouring down and his family were driving bears and dogs and horses aboard and old Noah was in the garden catching flies and gnats, digging for worms and dung beetles and maggots. Why did he bother? Did he worry that he got all of them? Were there some disgusting slimy creeping things that Noah never found and so we do not have any more?

Napoleon Bonaparte

by L. du Garde Peach

Napoleon Bonaparte was one of the two greatest soldiers the world has ever known. The other was Alexander the Great, who died more than 2,000 years before Napoleon was born. As well as being a great general, Napoleon made many of the laws under which France is governed today.

Napoleon had more energy, more intelligence and a better brain than any other man in Europe. He was also able to work for twenty hours a day, with only four hours sleep.

All this, combined with his ability to decide instantly and correctly what to do either in a battle or a council chamber, enabled him, a poor boy from Corsica, to become Emperor of France and master of Europe at the age of thirty-five.

Napoleon's mother Letizia.

In 1768 the island of Corsica became part of France, and a year later Charles and Letizia Buonaparte had a son, their second, whom they christened Napoleoné. These names are Italian, because Corsica previously belonged to Italy. Napoleon later changed the spelling to the French form which we know today, and by which he will always be known in history.

We know very little about Napoleon's childhood. Corsica was a small island, and the Corsican people were mostly untaught peasants in revolt against their new French masters. Napoleon's father and, later, Napoleon himself were involved in a rebellion which failed. For a time they were obliged to leave the island.

Charles Buonaparte was related to a family which had belonged to the nobility of Tuscany, in Italy. A friend of the family, Count de Marboeuf, was able to help him to get a grant to send the young Napoleon to a military school at Brienne, in France.

He did not have a very happy time at school. He has been described as gloomy and not good at games. In addition, he spoke French with a strong Corsican accent, and was despised by the boys from rich French families because he was poor.

Napoleon was not a brilliant scholar. He was good at mathematics, and he liked history and geography. But he had a wonderful memory, and all his life he was always able to remember everything he read or heard. When it came to designing fortifications, or planning military exercises, he was far better than any of the other boys.

Because Napoleon was so good at mathematics he was sent to the artillery school in Paris, where his mathematics master reported that he was one of the most intelligent pupils he had ever had. In everything else, he failed to distinguish himself.

He was posted to the La Fère regiment of artillery as a sub-lieutenant, and this was the beginning of his wonderful career as the greatest military commander of his time.

Curriculum Vitae

Name: Bridgid O'Dunply. (Stage name) Daisy Petite.

Age: 24

Position applied for: Lead singer in "The Cool Jellybabies Band".

Education: Glenmagog Primary and Comprehensive schools.

Distinctions in Music, Dance and Physical Education in State Examinations.

Passes in English, Mathematics and Religious Education.

In addition, I was given and satisfactorily carried out positions of responsibility as library helper, playtime monitor, and for a period as Acting Prefect.

School reports, without exception, describe my behaviour as reliable, supportive, hard-working and cheerful.

Further Education: While employed at the Medical Hall I attended evening classes in Word Processing, Financial Accounting and Management, and Office Management at the Glenmagog Institute of Further Education and I satisfactorily completed all these courses. During this time I also secured my driving licence.

Health: I had a prolonged absence from school (six months) in Year 9 due to the fact that I contracted a strain of rheumatic fever. You will see from the attached medical report that I am now completely recovered from this.

Employment: Counter assistant at O'Flaherty's Medical Hall (chemist) in Glenmagog for three years.

Clerical officer and assistant to the Chief Office Manager, Glenmagog Hospital for two years. My responsibilities included general office management, a wide range of secretarial and general reception duties.

Show Business Experience: Member of the Hospital Operatic and Dramatic Society, appearing in the chorus of a number of their musicals, concerts and other shows. As a result of encouragement from the Director and Conductor of the Society I paid for one year-long, part-time professional training in singing, general music and dance at the Galbally Academy of Music and Dramatic Art, and passed in all subjects with distinctions.

Leading roles: The Hospital Operatic and Dramatic Society productions of "Show Boat", "Oklahoma", "Saturday Night Fever", "Grease" and "The Rocky Horror Show". Guest singing artiste in several shows and concerts for The Galbally Music Society, one of the best known amateur theatrical groups in the Midlands. I also took the part of Maria in "West Side Story".

Semi-professional lead vocalist for local bands and groups, including "The Galbally Hoppers", "The Gingerbreads" and "Wow; Wow". With the latter group I made the record "Rocking with Wow; Wow", which got to third place in the national charts.

I have now had four years' experience as a semi-professional and appeared as guest artiste for performances by the major Country and Western bands "The Wailing Hill-Billies" and "The Lonesome Boys". I have continued with courses of professional voice training.

I believe I have now reached a stage in my career when I am capable of fitting the role of lead singer with a professional band. I am a keen fan of the "Jellybabies", I know and love their music and I feel I could present it very successfully.

I hope my curriculum vitae will be of assistance to you in considering my application.

Charles Dickens (1812–1870)

by Bill Laar

Biography

Charles Dickens had a very hard childhood. His father was constantly in trouble and difficulty because he could not manage his business affairs and was often in serious debt. As a result he was sent to prison for a period.

Young Charles, who visited him regularly there, was agonised by the experience – and horrified by prison conditions.

Charles was forced by the family's financial difficulties to go to work in a factory at the age of ten. He hated the life and was devastated by the fact that he was cut off from the chance to be educated. He did receive some schooling later and, as a young newspaper reporter, worked frantically to be a success.

He began to write articles and stories for magazines and at the age of twenty-four he published his novel *Pickwick Papers*. This was a sensational success. After that novels poured from his pen. One of the first of these was *Oliver Twist* which gave people an idea of the shocking conditions which many people, young children included, endured in London in the nineteenth century.

Another of his novels, *Nicholas Nickelby* exposed the cruelty of many boarding schools of the time.

Dickens, in fact, used all his great books to let people know about evils, unfairness and wrong-doing in society. He revealed the injustice of the law at that time, the uncaring way in which working people and poor people were treated and the dreadful conditions in prisons. Many of his books were written in serial form with episodes appearing every month or so. People all over the country, and indeed in America, looked forward to these episodes with feverish excitement. In poor parts of cities some people would save up together to buy each episode and would sit around in a house while a literate person in that street read it to them.

Dickens began to give public readings of extracts from his books, especially those that were frightening, exciting or sensational. People flocked to these readings, but they put a great strain on Dickens' health and led in the end to his death.

Some of his best known novels are: *Great Expectations*; *David Copperfield* which was a kind of autobiographical novel; *Bleak House*; *The Old Curiosity Shop* (people ran crying into the streets of New York when they learned that the heroine of the novel, Little Nell, had been allowed "to die" by Dickens) and *A Tale of Two Cities* a story based on the French Revolution.

Many of his novels have been filmed and made into brilliant TV serials. However, his work may be less frequently read today than it was in his own time because of its length and occasional complexity.

Many people regard him as one of the greatest of all novelists.

Caregivers

from Usborne's Great Lives

Florence Nightingale

The Lady with the Lamp

In 1854, Turkish, French and British soldiers joined forces to fight the Russian army. The war was fought in an area near the Black Sea known as the Crimea. As the number of wounded men increased, nurses were desperately needed.

Florence Nightingale (1820–1910) came from a wealthy English family. She was much admired in London for her nursing work. Sidney Herbert, the Secretary of State for War, asked Florence to gather a team of nurses and set sail for the Crimea.

When she arrived in Turkey, Florence was appalled by the conditions in Scutari Barrack Hospital. She worked 20-hour shifts, converting the filthy, rat-infested wards into a cleaner, brighter, more efficient hospital. Florence's work at the hospital reduced the patient death rate from 42 per cent to just over 2 per cent.

Her patients adored her. They called her "the lady of the lamp" because of her habit of roaming the wards at night with a lantern checking on their comfort and welfare.

By the time Florence returned to England, she was a national heroine. She went on to write about the importance of diet and sanitation for good health. She also began raising money, which she used to found a nursing college, the Nightingale Training School for Nurses, in London.

In 1907, Florence Nightingale became the first woman to be awarded the Order of Merit, which is given to British citizens in recognition of a great contribution to society.

Mary Seacole

A dedicated nurse

A Jamaican woman named Mary Seacole (1805–81) became a nurse in 1850, during an outbreak of a disease called cholera. A few years later, she sailed to England to offer her services as a Crimean War nurse, but was turned down because she was black.

Undeterred, Mary paid for her own passage to the Crimea, and spent the next three years working with Florence Nightingale, providing medical care for the war casualties.

When she returned to England, Mary was praised for her bravery by the same people who had previously rejected her help.

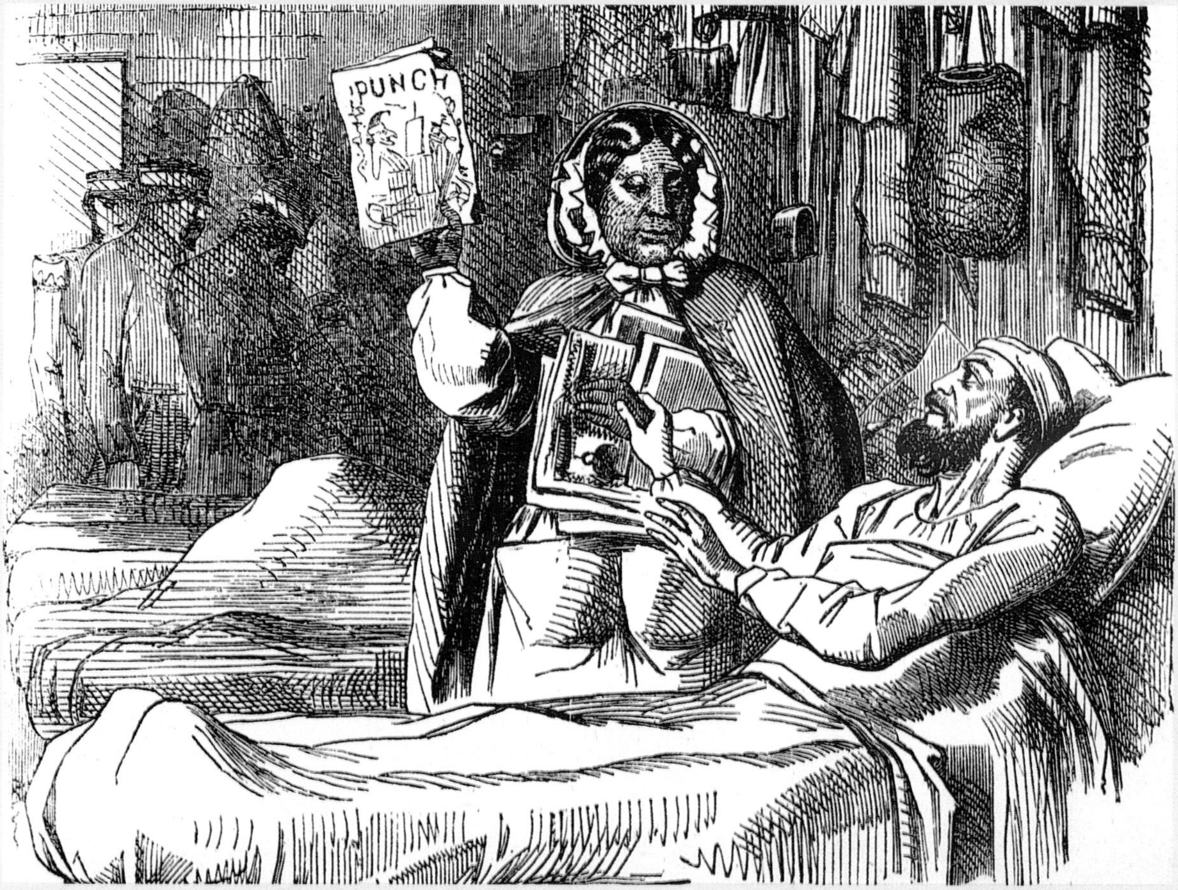

A cartoon from the magazine Punch in 1857, showing Mary Seacole

The Arrival of the Dinosaurs

by D. Norman, A. Milner and A. Miller

Introduction

What is a Dinosaur?

Dinosaurs were very special reptiles. Some were the size of chickens; others may have been as long as jumbo jets. These creatures were the most successful animals that have ever lived on Earth. They dominated the world for nearly 150 million years and were found on every continent during the Mesozoic Era, which is divided into the Triassic, Jurassic and Cretaceous periods. Like reptiles today, dinosaurs had scaly skin and laid their eggs in shells. The earliest dinosaurs ate meat, while later plant-eating dinosaurs enjoyed the lush plant life around them. Dinosaurs are called "lizard-hipped" or "bird-hipped", depending on how their hip bones were arranged. They stood on either four legs or two, and walked with straight legs tucked beneath their bodies. Dinosaurs are the only reptiles that have ever been able to do this.

Before the Dinosaurs

The Earth began 4,600 million years ago. Its long history is divided into different periods, during which an amazing variety of life forms developed or died out. In the beginning, single-celled algae and bacteria formed, or evolved, in the warm seas that covered most of the planet. In the Palaeozoic Era, more complex plants and animals appeared in the sea: worms, jellyfish and hard-shelled molluscs swarmed in shallow waters and were eaten by bony fish.

When plants and animals first appeared on land, they were eaten by amphibians that had evolved from fish with lungs and strong fins. Some amphibians then evolved into reptiles that did not lay their eggs in water. Early reptiles developed into turtles and tortoises, lizards, crocodiles, birds, and the first dinosaurs. They dominated the world for millions of years.

millions of years ago	4,600	2,500	570	439	408	362	290	245
	Precambrian Era		**Palaeozoic Era**					
	Archaean	Proterozoic	Cambrian	Ordovician	Silurian	Devonian	Carboniferous	Permian
Origin of the Earth	First algae and single-celled bacteria appeared in the seas.	First animals with soft bodies and many cells. They looked like worms and jellyfish.	First sponges, segmented worms and hard-shelled animals.	First animals with back-bones; jaw-less fish, then sharks and bony fish.	First land plants. Sea scorpions up to 2m (7ft) dominated the seas.	The Age of Fishes and the first land animals with backbones.	The Age of Amphibians. Primitive reptiles hunted insects and small amphibians.	Many species of reptiles that ate plants and meat. Trilobites disappear.

From *Dinosaurs* by Dr A. Milner

Death Comes to Paradise

Massive death toll likely

Yes, unbelievable though it may seem, The Bugle is here, in the form of roving correspondent, Joe Malloy, the man with the mission to bring you the stories from the danger spots of the world.

I stand here, the only international reporter, in scenes of indescribable horror and chaos. How I got here is another story, but one journey through Hell and two helicopters later I am reporting one of the most terrible disasters of recent years.

There is nothing left of this village but crumbling walls, a church tower leaning over at a crazy angle like some drunken giant, and in the snow-covered debris a few survivors searching in despair for any others. But they search in vain. Everything has been swept away by the savage floods of ice-filled water which still roar past me as I stand here on the devastated mountain side.

Right across this region, a score of other villages have almost certainly been destroyed as well, as if Death has come to walk in Paradise, a place of beauty, well known to many British tourists.

I wondered how I could possibly convey to you the horror of it all. And then I saw them, scattered in the snow, a few pathetic toys: a sad-faced clown, flaxen-haired dolls and a little model car that will never run again. And I knew as I looked at them that these, more than anything, would help the readers of The Bugle to realise that disaster had come to Paradise.

But like a candle in the dark there is one piece of hope. And yes, I can tell you with pride – it comes from the British Army! A small detachment of paratroopers, engaged in top secret training on the other side of the Alps, are battling their way through with expert help and supplies. Everyone else may fail but with the paras on the way, hope is alive again.

Floods Devastate Alps Tourist Region

Hundreds die as villages swept away

Yesterday and last night, for the second time in less than three years, the region of Northern Alpine Italy, bordering on Austria was devastated by fierce floods, with severe damage to life and property. Experts believe that the unexpected floods are the result of premature and simultaneous melting of the Alpine snows as a result of global warming.

While information from the region is as yet vague and uncertain it seems likely, judging by radio messages from the area, that the death toll exceeds a hundred people. In addition, it seems certain that many are injured and in need of urgent medical attention. Emergency services, however, are struggling to get through to the villages, isolated as they are in this high mountainous region, often almost inaccessible from the outside world for parts of the winter. There are reports, as yet unconfirmed, that a detachment of British troops, engaged in winter training in the mountains nearby, has made its way through to the area and is providing what support it can.

The Italian Government last night issued a statement through the Ministry of Information indicating that sections of the national air force and army, including the crack Alpine Legion, are on stand-by to provide all necessary support. The Government statement went on to say that the services would move into action today whatever the weather conditions, with food, medical supplies and tents for the survivors. In the meantime weather experts are monitoring conditions, anxious to predict any further flood movement in the high mountains. We understand that the Italian Air Force will employ their state-of-the-art helicopters to evacuate villagers to places of safety at the foot of the Alps.

The beautiful region will be familiar to some in the United Kingdom. It has never been a favourite with skiers, largely due to the unpredictable weather conditions that probably led to the present catastrophe, but is visited regularly by those who look for peace and quiet amid scenes of grandeur. Sadly that peace has been rudely shattered, at least for a time.

"Driver's Action Prevents Carnage"

Only quick thinking and resolute action on the part of lorry driver Steve Harper averted what could have been a horrendous accident, and possible loss of life, in the town last Friday afternoon. As it was, seven people, suffering injuries ranging from cuts and bruises to fractures, concussion and shock, were ferried by ambulance to the Accident and Emergency department of nearby Willowbrook hospital. Most were allowed home after treatment; however, two patients are still detained, although both are now out of any danger.

The incident occurred on Windmill Hill which is well known to local people as an accident Black Spot. According to eye-witnesses, whose views are supported by police evidence, the lorry's brakes had failed and it was out of control from the moment it began its descent of the treacherous hill.

The driver, who sustained broken ribs and severe lacerations, attempted to halt the lorry by using the hand brake. However, he realised almost immediately that the only way to avoid a disaster was to run the vehicle off the road. Otherwise the lorry would have plunged into the Shopping Centre, almost certainly leaving a trail of destruction in its

wake. As it was, the lorry demolished the bus shelter injuring, as reported, a number of the people waiting there, who were unable to get out of the way in time.

There was widespread praise for the driver, Mr Harper, without whose action the consequences could have been so much worse.

As *The Herald* was going to press there were forceful calls from local inhabitants for urgent action by the Council. There is a general view that unless major safety measures are implemented, the hill will be the scene – and the cause – of something much more serious than occurred last Friday.

The Herald pursues the matter further in our Leading Article this week and makes a series of practical suggestions designed to make Windmill Hill a safe place for all who live or drive there.

William Shakespeare

(1564 –1616)

by Bill Laar

Shakespeare was born in the Warwickshire town of Stratford-upon-Avon. We do not know a great deal about his early life, but it is thought he occasionally got into trouble with the law, and possibly had to leave the town to avoid being charged with poaching deer.

He went to London and became an actor, appearing at the famous Globe Theatre in plays by various dramatists.

Soon he began to write plays himself, often producing them very quickly and seldom taking trouble to correct or alter what he had written. The plays were written to be acted, not to be sold in bookshops and kept in libraries. They were written by hand to provide sufficient copies for the actors, who often had to share scripts. Later, as the plays were copied out for other performances in other places, lines and words were often written down wrongly. As a result, scholars are still arguing about the exact meaning of some of the things Shakespeare wrote.

In Tudor times there was great enthusiasm for the theatre, and people rich and poor, old and young flocked to the Globe and other theatres. To satisfy the wide social range of people who came to see his plays (many people were illiterate, superstitious and ignorant) Shakespeare put in ghosts, battles, murders and rude and vulgar jokes.

He wrote many plays, together with beautiful poetry. His plays include comedies (*A Midsummer Night's Dream; The Merchant of Venice; As You Like It; Twelfth Night*), tragedies (*Romeo and Juliet; Hamlet; King Lear; Othello; Macbeth*); Greek and Roman plays (*Troilus and Cressida; Antony and Cleopatra; Julius Caesar; Coriolanus*) and history plays (*Richard II; Richard III; Henry IV, Parts I and II*; and *Henry V*).

Towards the end of his life, Shakespeare made enough money to be able to retire to Stratford and live the life of a gentleman.

Many people think he may be the greatest writer who ever lived. His plays are performed every day all over the world in very many different languages.

Some of the beautiful language is, at first, a little strange to us today, but one soon understands it and the plays themselves are wonderful and thrilling.

Julius Caesar

by William Shakespeare

Act three Scene 2

1st Pleb — Stay, ho! and let us hear Mark Antony.

3rd Pleb — Let him go up into the public chair.
We'll hear him. Noble Antony, go up.

Antony — For Brutus' sake, I am beholding to you.

4th Pleb — What does he say of Brutus?

3rd Pleb — He says, for Brutus' sake He finds himself beholding to us all.

4th Pleb — 'Twere best he speak no harm of Brutus here!

1st Pleb — This Caesar was a tyrant.

3rd Pleb — Nay, that's certain. We are blest that Rome is rid of him. ...

Antony — Friends, Romans, countrymen, lend me your ears.
I come to bury Caesar, not to praise him.
The evil that men do lives after them,
The good is oft interred with their bones;
So let it be with Caesar. The noble Brutus
Hath told you Caesar was ambitious.
If it were so, it was a grievous fault,
And grievously hath Caesar answer'd it.
Here, under the leave of Brutus and the rest,
– For Brutus is an honourable man;
So are they all, all honourable men –
Come I to speak in Caesar's funeral.
He was my friend, faithful and just to me;
But Brutus says he was ambitious,
And Brutus is an honourable man.
He hath brought many captives home to Rome,
Whose ransom did the general coffers fill:

Did this in Caesar seem ambitious?
When that the poor have cried, Caesar hath wept;
Ambition should be made of sterner stuff:
Yet Brutus says he was ambitious,
And Brutus is an honourable man.
You all did see that on the Lupercal
I thrice presented him a kingly crown,
Which he did thrice refuse. Was this ambition?
Yet Brutus says he was ambitious,
And sure he is an honourable man.
I speak not to disprove what Brutus spoke,
But here I am to speak what I do know.
You all did love him once, not without cause;
What cause withholds you then to mourn for him?
O judgement, thou art fled to brutish beasts,
And men have lost their reason. Bear with me.
My heart is in the coffin there with Caesar,
And I must pause till it come back to me.

1st Pleb Methinks there is much reason in his sayings.

2nd Pleb If thou consider rightly of the matter,
Caesar has had great wrong.

3rd Pleb Has he, masters?
I fear there will a worse come in his place.

4th Pleb Mark'd ye his words? He would not take the crown;
Therefore 'tis certain he was not ambitious.

1st Pleb If it be found so, some will dear abide it.

2nd Pleb Poor soul! His eyes are red as fire with weeping.

3rd Pleb There's not a nobler man in Rome than Antony.

4th Pleb Now mark him; he begins again to speak.

Antony But yesterday the word of Caesar might
Have stood against the world; now lies he there,
And none so poor to do him reverence.
O masters! if I were dispos'd to stir
Your hearts and minds to mutiny and rage,
I should do Brutus wrong, and Cassius wrong,
Who, you all know, are honourable men.

I will not do them wrong; I rather choose
To wrong the dead, to wrong myself and you,
Than I will wrong such honourable men.
But here's a parchment with the seal of Caesar;
I found it in his closet; 'tis his will.
Let but the commons hear this testament,
Which, pardon me, I do not mean to read,
And they would go and kiss dead Caesar's wounds,
And dip their napkins in his sacred blood,
Yea, and beg a hair of him for memory,
And, dying, mention it within their wills,
Bequeathing it as a rich legacy
Unto their issue.

4th Pleb — We'll hear the will. Read it, Mark Antony.

All — The will, the will! We will hear Caesar's will!

Antony — Have patience, gentle friends; I must not read it.
It is not meet you know how Caesar lov'd you.
You are not wood, you are not stones, but men;
And being men, hearing the will of Caesar,
It will inflame you, it will make you mad.
'Tis good you know not that you are his heirs;
For if you should, O, what would come of it?

4th Pleb — Read the will! We'll hear it, Antony!
You shall read us the will, Caesar's will!

Antony — Will you be patient? Will you stay awile?
I have o'ershot myself to tell you of it.
I fear I wrong the honourable men
Whose daggers have stabb'd Caesar; I do fear it.

4th Pleb — They were traitors. Honourable men!

All — The will! – The testament!

2nd Pleb — They were villains, murderers! The will! Read the will!

Antony — You will compel me then to read the will?
Then make a ring about the corpse of Caesar,
And let me show you him that made the will.
Shall I descend? and will you give me leave?

All Come down.

2nd Pleb Descend.

[Antony comes down]

Antony If you have tears, prepare to shed them now.
You all do know this mantle. I remember
The first time ever Caesar put it on;
'Twas on a summer's evening in his tent,
That day he overcame the Nervii.
Look, in this place ran Cassius' dagger through:
See what a rent the envious Casca made:
Through this the well-beloved Brutus stabb'd;
And as he pluck'd his cursed steel away,
Mark how the blood of Caesar follow'd it,
As rushing out of doors, to be resolv'd
If Brutus so unkindly knock'd or no;
For Brutus, as you know, was Caesar's angel.
Judge, O you gods, how dearly Caesar lov'd him.
This was the most unkindest cut of all;
For when the noble Caesar saw him stab,
Ingratitude, more strong than traitors' arms,
Quite vanquish'd him: then burst his mighty heart;
And in his mantle muffling up his face,
Even at the base of Pompey's statue
(Which all the while ran blood) great Caesar fell.
O, what a fall was there, my countrymen!
Then I, and you, and all of us fell down,
Whilst bloody treason flourish'd over us.
O, now you weep, and I perceive you feel
The dint of pity. These are gracious drops.
Kind souls, what weep you when you but behold
Our Caesar's vesture wounded? Look you here!
Here is himself, marr'd, as you see, with traitors.

1st Pleb O piteous spectacle!

2nd Pleb O noble Caesar!

3rd Pleb O woeful day!

4th Pleb O traitors! villains!

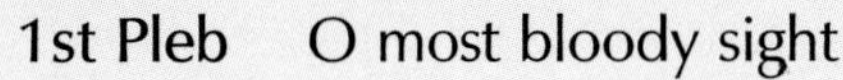

1st Pleb O most bloody sight!

2nd Pleb We will be revenged.

All Revenge! About! Seek! Burn! Fire! Kill! Slay!
Let not a traitor live.

Antony Stay, countrymen.

1st Pleb Peace there! Hear the noble Antony.

2nd Pleb We'll hear him, we'll follow him, we'll die with him.

Antony Good friends, sweet friends, let me not stir you up
To such a sudden flood of mutiny.
They that have done this deed are honourable.
What private griefs they have, alas, I know not,
That made them do it. They are wise and honourable,
And will, no doubt, with reasons answer you.
I come not, friends to steal away your hearts.
I am no orator, as Brutus is,
But, as you know me all, a plain blunt man,
That love my friend; and that they know full well
That gave me public leave to speak of him.
For I have neither wit, nor words, nor worth,
Action, nor utterance, nor the power of speech
To stir men's blood; I only speak right on.
I tell you that which you yourselves do know,
Show you sweet Caesar's wounds, poor poor dumb mouths,
And bid them speak for me. But were I Brutus,
And Brutus Antony, there were an Antony
Would ruffle up your spirits, and put a tongue
In every wound of Caesar that should move
The stones of Rome to rise and mutiny.

All We'll mutiny.

1st Pleb We'll burn the house of Brutus.

3rd Pleb Away then! Come, seek the conspirators.

Antony Yet hear me, countrymen. Yet hear me speak.

All Peace, ho! Hear Antony, most noble Antony.

Antony Why, friends, you go to do you know not what.
Wherein hath Caesar thus deserv'd your loves?
Alas! you know not: I must tell you then.
You have forgot the will I told you of.

All Most true. The will! Let's stay and hear the will.

Antony Here is the will, and under Caesar's seal
To every Roman citizen he gives,
To every several man, seventy-five drachmas.

2nd Pleb Most noble Caesar! We'll revenge his death.

3rd Pleb O royal Caesar!

Antony Hear me with patience.

All Peace, ho!

Antony Moreover, he hath left you all his walks,
His private arbours, and new-planted orchards,
On this side Tiber; he hath left them you,
And to your heirs for ever: common pleasures,
To walk abroad and recreate yourselves.
Here was a Caesar! when comes such another?

1st Pleb Never, never! Come away, away!
We'll burn his body in the holy place,
And with the brands fire the traitors' houses.
Take up the body.

2nd Pleb Go fetch fire

3rd Pleb Pluck down benches.

4th Pleb Pluck down forms, windows, any thing.

[Exeunt Plebeians with the body]

Antony Now let it work. Mischief, thou art afoot,
Take thou what course thou wilt!

From Reynard the Fox

by John Masefield 1878–1967

The fox knew well, that before they tore him,
They should try their speed on the downs before him,
There were three more miles to the Wan Dyke Hill,
But his heart was high, that he beat them still.
The wind of the downland charmed his bones
So off he went for the Sarsen Stones.

The moan of the three great firs in the wind,
And the Ai of the foxhounds died behind,
Wind-dapples followed the hill-wind's breath
On the Kill Down gorge where the Danes found death;
Larks scattered up; the peewits feeding
Rose in a flock from the Kill Down Steeding.
The hare leaped up from her form and swerved
Swift left for the Starveall, harebell-turved.
On the wind-bare thorn some longtails prinking
Cried sweet, as though wind-blown glass were chinking.
Behind came thudding and loud halloo,
Or a cry from hounds as they came to view.

The pure clean air came sweet to his lungs,
Till he thought foul scorn of those crying tongues.
In a three mile more he would reach the haven
In the Wan Dyke croaked on by the raven.
In a three mile more he would make his berth
On the hard cool floor of a Wan Dyke earth,
Too deep for spade, too curved for terrier,
With the pride of the race to make rest the merrier.
In a three mile more he would reach his dream,
So his game heart gulped and he put on steam.

Like a rocket shot to a ship ashore
The lean red bolt of his body tore,
Like a ripple of wind running swift on grass,
Like a shadow on wheat when a cloud blows past,
Like a turn at the buoy in a cutter sailing
When the bright green gleam lips white at the railing,
Like the April snake whipping back to sheath,
Like the gannet's hurtle on fish beneath,
Like a kestrel chasing, like a sickly reaping,
Like all things swooping, like all things sweeping,
Like a hound for stay, like a stag for swift,
With his shadow beside like spinning drift.

Past the gibbet-stock all stuck with nails,
Where they hanged in chains what had hung at jails,
Past Ashmundshowe where Ashmund sleeps,
And none but the tumbling peewit weeps,
Past Curlew Calling, the gaunt grey corner
Where the curlew comes as a summer mourner,
Past Blowbury Beacon shaking his fleece,
Where all winds hurry and none brings peace;
Then down, on the mile-long green decline
Where the turf's like spring and the air's like wine,
Where the sweeping spurs of the downland spill
Into Wan Brook Valley and Wan Dyke Hill.

On he went with a galloping rally
Past Maesbury Clump for Wan Brook Valley.
The blood in his veins went romping high,
"Get on, on, on to the earth or die,"
The air of the downs went purely past
Till he felt the glory of going fast,
Till the terror of death, though there indeed,
Was lulled for a while by his pride of speed;
He was romping away from hounds and hunt,
He had Wan Dyke Hill and his earth in front,
In a one mile more when his point was made,
He would rest in safety from dog or spade;
Nose between paws he would hear the shout
Of the "gone to earth" to the hounds without,
The whine of the hounds, and their cat feet gadding,
Scratching the earth, and their breath pad-padding;
He would hear the horn call hounds away,
And rest in peace till another day.
In one mile more he would lie at rest
So for one mile more he would go his best.
He reached the dip at the long droop's end
And he took what speed he had still to spend.

So down past Maesbury beech clump grey,
That would not be green till the end of May,
Past Arthur's Table, the white chalk boulder,
Where pasque flowers purple the down's grey shoulder,
Past Quichelm's Keeping, past Harry's Thorn,
To Thirty Acre all thin with corn.
As he raced the corn towards Wan Dyke Brook,
The pack had view of the way he took,
Robin hallooed from the downland's crest,
He capped them on till they did their best.
The quarter mile to the Wan Brook's brink
Was raced as quick as a man can think.
And here, as he ran to the huntsman's yelling,
The fox first felt that the pace was telling;
His body and lungs seemed all grown old,
His legs less certain, his heart less bold,
The hound-noise nearer, the hill slope steeper,
The thud in the blood of his body deeper,
His pride in his speed, his joy in the race,
Were withered away, for what use was pace?
He had run his best, and the hounds ran better.
Then the going worsened, the earth was wetter.
Then his brush drooped down till it sometimes dragged,
And his fur felt sick and his chest was tagged
With taggles of mud, and his pads seemed lead,
It was well for him he'd an earth ahead.
Down he went to the brook and over,
Out of the corn and into the clover,
Over the slope that the Wan Brook drains,
Past Battle Tump where they earthed the Danes,
Then up the hill that the Wan Dyke rings
Where the Sarsen Stones stand grand like kings.

Seven Sarsens of granite grim,
As he ran them by they looked at him;
As he leaped the lip of their earthen paling
The hounds were gaining and he was failing.

He passed the Sarsens, he left the spur,
He pressed up hill to the blasted fir,
He slipped as he leaped the hedge; he slithered;
"He's mine," thought Robin. "He's done; he's dithered."
At the second attempt he cleared the fence,
He turned half right where the gorse was dense,
He was leading hounds by a furlong clear.
He was past his best, but his earth was near.
He ran up gorse to the spring of the ramp,
The steep green wall of the dead men's camp,
He sidled up it and scampered down
To the deep green ditch of the dead men's town.

Within, as he reached that soft green turf,
The wind, blowing lonely, moaned like surf,
Desolate ramparts rose up steep,
On either side, for the ghosts to keep.
He raced the trench, past the rabbit warren,
Close-grown with moss which the wind made barren,
He passed the spring where the rushes spread,
And there in the stones was his earth ahead.
One last short burst upon failing feet –
There life lay waiting, so sweet, so sweet,
Rest in a darkness, balm for aches.

The earth was stopped. It was barred with stakes.

With the hounds at head so close behind
He had to run as he changed his mind.
This earth, as he saw, was stopped, but still
There was one earth more on the Wan Dyke Hill
A rabbit burrow a furlong on,
He could kennel there till the hounds were gone.
Though his death seemed near he did not blench,
He upped his brush and ran the trench.

He ran the trench while the wind moaned treble,
Earth trickled down, there were falls of pebble.
Down in the valley of that dark gash
The wind-withered grasses looked like ash.
Trickles of stones and earth fell down
In that dark valley of dead men's town.
A hawk rose from a fluff of feathers,
From a distant fold came a bleat of wethers.
He heard no noise from the hounds behind
But the hill-wind moaning like something blind

He turned the bend in the hill and there
Was his rabbit-hole with its mouth worn bare;
But there with a gun tucked under his arm
Was young Sid Kissop of Purlpits Farm,
With a white hob ferret to drive the rabbit
Into a net which was set to nab it.
And young Jack Cole peered over the wall,
And loosed a pup with a "Z'bite en, Saul!"
The terrier pup attacked with a will,
So the fox swerved right and away down hill.

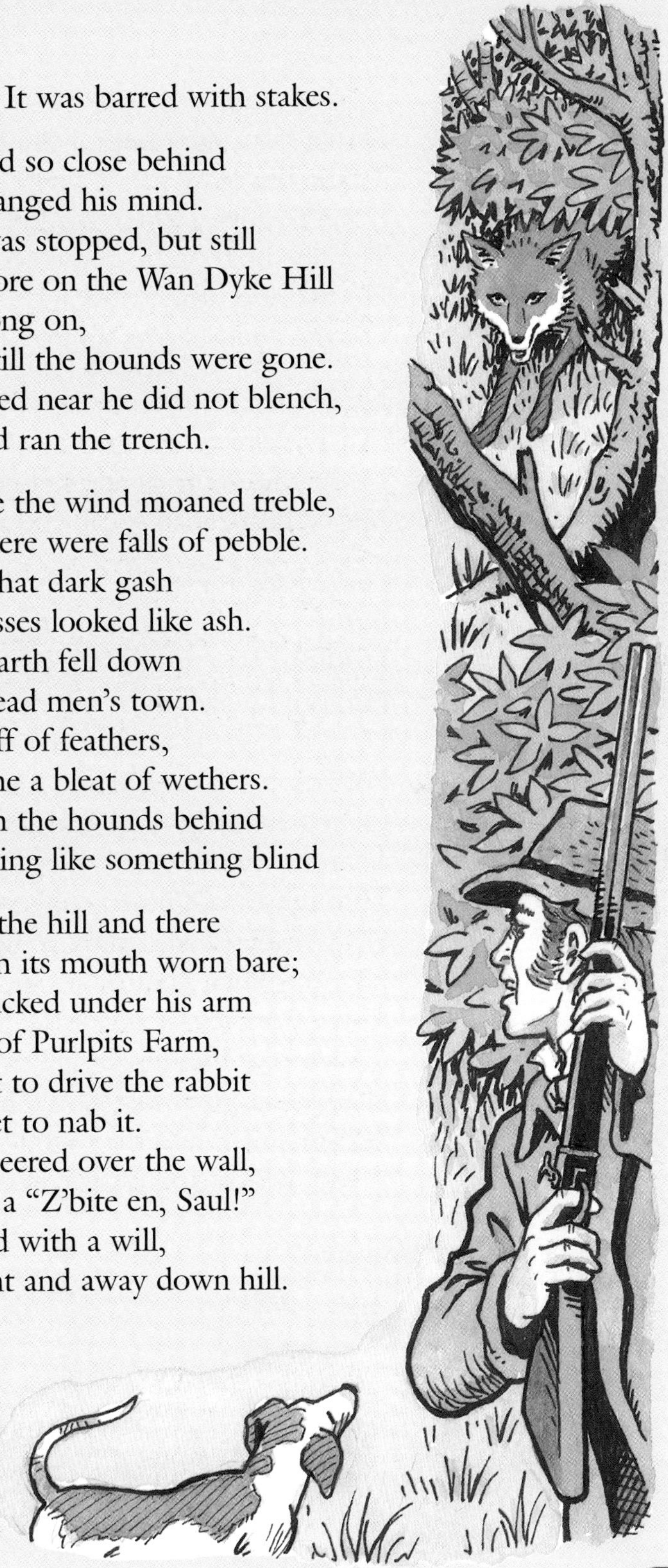

Down from the ramp of the Dyke he ran
To the brackeny patch where the gorse began,
Into the gorse, where the hill's heave hid
The line he took from the eyes of Sid;
He swerved downwind and ran like a hare
For the wind-blown spinney below him there.

He slipped from the gorse to the spinney dark
(There were curled grey growths on the oak tree bark);
He saw no more of the terrier pup,
But he heard men speak and the hounds come up.

He crossed the spinney with ears intent
For the cry of hounds on the way he went;
His heart was thumping, the hounds were near now,
He could make no spring at a cry and cheer now,
He was past his perfect, his strength was failing,
His brush sag-sagged and his legs were ailing.
He felt as he skirted Dead Men's Town,
That in one mile more they would have him down.
Through the withered oak's wind-crouching tops
He saw men's scarlet above the copse,
He heard men's oaths, yet he felt hounds slacken
In the frondless stalks of the brittle bracken.
He felt that the unseen link which bound
His spine to the nose of the leading hound
Was snapped, that the hounds no longer knew
Which way to follow nor what to do;

That the threat of the hounds' teeth left his neck,
They had ceased to run, they had come to check,
They were quartering wide on the Wan Hill's bent.

The terrier's chase had killed his scent.

He heard bits chink as the horses shifted,
He heard hounds cast, then he heard hounds lifted,
But there came no cry from a new attack;
His heart grew steady, his breath came back.

He left the spinney and ran its edge
By the deep dry ditch of the blackthorn hedge;
Then out of the ditch and down the meadow,
Trotting at ease in the blackthorn shadow
Over the track called Godsdown Road,
To the great grass heave of the gods' abode.
He was moving now upon land he knew:
Up Clench Royal and Morton Tew,
The Pol Brook, Cheddesdon and East Stoke Church,
High Clench St. Lawrence and Tinker's Birch,
Land he had roved on night by night,
For hot blood-suckage or furry bite,
The threat of the hounds behind was gone;
He breathed deep pleasure and trotted on.

Great Expectations

by Charles Dickens

Chapter 1

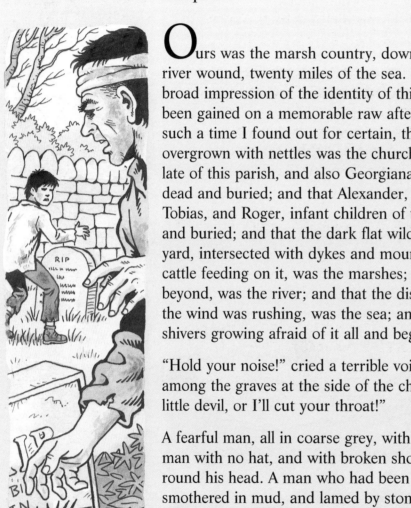

Ours was the marsh country, down by the river, within, as the river wound, twenty miles of the sea. My first most vivid and broad impression of the identity of things, seems to me to have been gained on a memorable raw afternoon towards evening. At such a time I found out for certain, that this bleak place overgrown with nettles was the churchyard; and that Philip Pirrip, late of this parish, and also Georgiana wife of the above, were dead and buried; and that Alexander, Bartholomew, Abraham, Tobias, and Roger, infant children of the aforesaid, were also dead and buried; and that the dark flat wilderness beyond the churchyard, intersected with dykes and mounds and gates, with scattered cattle feeding on it, was the marshes; and that the low leaden line beyond, was the river; and that the distant savage lair from which the wind was rushing, was the sea; and that the small bundle of shivers growing afraid of it all and beginning to cry, was Pip.

"Hold your noise!" cried a terrible voice, as a man started up from among the graves at the side of the church porch. "Keep still, you little devil, or I'll cut your throat!"

A fearful man, all in coarse grey, with a great iron on his leg. A man with no hat, and with broken shoes, and with an old rag tied round his head. A man who had been soaked in water, and smothered in mud, and lamed by stones, and cut by flints, and stung by nettles, and torn by briars; who limped, and shivered, and glared and growled; and whose teeth chattered in his head as he seized me by the chin.

"O! Don't cut my throat, sir," I pleaded in terror. "Pray don't do it, sir."

"Tell us your name!" said the man. "Quick!"

"Pip, sir."

"Once more," said the man, staring at me. "Give it mouth!"

"Pip. Pip, sir."

"Show us where you live," said the man. "Pint out the place!"

I pointed to where our village lay, on the flat in-shore among the alder-trees and pollards, a mile or more from the church.

The man, after looking at me for a moment, turned me upside down, and emptied my pockets. There was nothing in them but a piece of bread. When the church came to itself – for he was so sudden and strong that he made it go head over heels before me, and I saw the steeple under my feet – when the church came to itself, I say, I was seated on a high tombstone, trembling, while he ate the bread ravenously.

"You young dog," said the man, licking his lips, "what fat cheeks you ha' got."

I believe they were fat, though I was at that time undersized for my years, and not strong.

"Darn Me if I couldn't eat em," said the man, with a threatening shake of his head, "and if I han't half a mind to't!"

I earnestly expressed my hope that he wouldn't, and held tighter to the tombstone on which he had put me; partly, to keep myself upon it; partly, to keep myself from crying.

"Now lookee here!" said the man. "Where's your mother?"

"There, sir!" said I.

He started, made a short run, and stopped and looked over his shoulder.

"There, sir!" I timidly explained. "Also Georgiana. That's my mother."

"Oh!" said he, coming back. "And is that your father alonger your mother?"

"Yes, sir," said I; "him too; late of this parish."

"Ha!" he muttered then, considering. "Who d'ye live with – supposin' you're kindly let to live, which I han't made up my mind about?"

"My sister, sir – Mrs Joe Gargery – wife of Joe Gargery, the blacksmith, sir."

"Blacksmith, eh?" said he. And looked down at his leg.

After darkly looking at his leg and me several times, he came closer to my tombstone, took me by both arms, and tilted me back as far as he could hold me; so that his eyes looked most powerfully down into mine, and mine looked most helplessly up into his.

"Now lookee here," he said, "the question being whether you're to be let to live. You know what a file is?"

"Yes, sir."

"And you know what wittles is?"

"Yes, sir."

After each question he tilted me over a little more, so as to give me a greater sense of helplessness and danger.

"You get me a file." He tilted me again. "And you get me wittles." He tilted me again. "You bring 'em both to me." He tilted me again. "Or I'll have your heart and liver out." He tilted me again.

I was dreadfully frightened, and so giddy that I clung to him with both hands, and said, "If you could kindly please to let me keep upright, sir, perhaps I shouldn't be sick, and perhaps I could attend more."

He gave me a most tremendous dip and roll, so that the church jumped over its own weather-cock. Then, he held me by the arms, in an upright position on the top of the stone, and went on in these fearful terms:

“You bring me, to-morrow morning early, that file and them wittles. You bring the lot to me, at that old Battery over yonder. You do it, and you never dare to say a word or dare to make a sign concerning your having seen such a person as me, or any person sumever, and you shall be let to live. You fail, or you go from my words in any partickler, no matter how small it is, and your heart and your liver shall be tore out, roasted and ate. Now, I ain’t alone, as you may think I am. There’s a young man hid with me, in comparison with which young man I am a Angel. That young man hears the words I speak. That young man has a secret way pecooliar to himself, of getting at a boy, and at his heart, and at his liver. It is in wain for a boy to attempt to hide himself from that young man. A boy may lock his door, may be warm in bed, may tuck himself up, may draw the clothes over his head, may think himself comfortable and safe, but that young man will softly creep and creep his way to him and tear him open. I am a keeping that young man from harming of you at the present moment, with great difficulty. I find it very hard to hold that young man off of your inside. Now, what do you say?”

I said that I would get him the file, and I would get him what broken bits of food I could, and I would come to him at the Battery, early in the morning.

“Say Lord strike you dead if you don’t!” said the man.

I said so, and he took me down.

“Now,” he pursued, “you remember what you’ve undertook, and you remember that young man, and you get home!”

“Goo-good night, sir,” I faltered.

“Much of that!” said he, glancing about him over the cold wet flat. “I wish I was a frog. Or a eel!”

At the same time, he hugged his shuddering body in both his arms – clasping himself, as if to hold himself together – and limped towards the low church wall. As I saw him go, picking his way among the nettles, and among the brambles that bound the green mounds, he looked in my young eyes as if he were eluding the

hands of the dead people, stretching up cautiously out of their graves, to get a twist upon his ankle and pull him in.

When he came to the low church wall, he got over it, like a man whose legs were numbed and stiff, and then turned round to look for me. When I saw him turning, I set my face towards home, and made the best use of my legs. But presently I looked over my shoulder, and saw him going on again towards the river, still hugging himself in both arms, and picking his way with his sore feet among the great stones dropped into the marshes here and there, for stepping-places when the rains were heavy, or the tide was in.

The marshes were just a long black horizontal line then, as I stopped to look after him; and the river was just another horizontal line, not nearly so broad nor yet so black; and the sky was just a row of long angry red lines and dense black lines intermixed. On the edge of the river I could faintly make out the only two black things in all the prospect that seemed to be standing upright; one of these was the beacon by which the sailors steered – like an un-hooped cask upon a pole – an ugly thing when you were near it; the other a gibbet, with some chains hanging to it which had once held a pirate. The man was limping on towards this latter, as if he were the pirate come to life, and come down, and going back to hook himself up again. It gave me a terrible turn when I thought so; and as I saw the cattle lifting their heads to gaze after him, I wondered whether they thought so too. I looked all round for the horrible young man, and could see no signs of him. But, now I was frightened again, and ran home without stopping.

Biographies

by Bill Laar

Florence Nightingale

She was tall and slender and moved lightly and gracefully, no matter how exhausted she might be. Her face was delicate, but firm and determined and, it seemed, often ready to break into a smile.

Her dress was plain and simple: a small cloak over a neat white blouse and a long plain skirt that rustled softly as she moved. They were never clothes for balls or parties or relaxation, but for long hours of punishing work, with her sleeves rolled up, and no ornaments or jewellery to get in the way of scissors and bandages.

Of course, what we most remember her for were her constant patrols in the night. Then she would dress in a longer, warm cloak, a bonnet on her head, the lamp always in her hand, throwing a soft, warm light along the wards. She would bend over her patients, listening intently for their breathing, looking at them from dark, compassionate eyes in the lined face. Then she would glide away to the next ward, her shadow lengthening along the wall as she moved out of our sight.

Goliath

Our hearts missed a beat when we first saw him. He seemed to block out the sun. His gigantic bearded head was half concealed in an iron helmet, but we could see the savage eyes, the scarred cheeks and the snarling teeth.

He seemed like a moving wall of armour. He wore a brazen breastplate, iron gloves, iron leg protectors and massive boots that shook the ground as he walked. He clanked with every step he took; scattering small rocks and stones before him as he lumbered forward. At his side hung a sword so massive that no two of us together could have lifted it. In his other hand he carried a lance like a small tree, and slung over his shoulder was a shield that could have stopped a runaway chariot.

But most terrifying of all was his voice. Our hearts quaked and the dogs in the camp yelped and ran for shelter as he thundered, "Come, Israelites and fight like men!"

Jeanne d'Arc

Jeanne was born, the daughter of peasants, in a little French village named Domrémy, in the early 15th century. At first she seemed little different from the other boys and girls in the village, working from an early age on the land, helping to look after the animals, to plant the seeds and crops and to reap the harvest when the time came.

She grew into a strong and powerful young woman, due to her healthy working life; she was loved in the little village for her good humour and her kindness to everyone, whether young or old. But soon her neighbours began to look at her in a different light, to wonder about her and, in some cases, to think she might be mad. This was because Jeanne claimed that she could hear supernatural voices in her head urging her to take up arms, to lead the people of France in driving out the English who ruled stretches of the land, and to crown the Dauphin, the heir to the throne, King of France.

Jeanne, through the strengths of her beliefs and convictions, the vivid descriptions of her "visions" and, what seemed to the simple people of the countryside, her power to work miracles, was accepted as leader of a small and rather ramshackle French army setting out to capture the great city of Orléans. The task appeared impossible, but inspired by her courageous leadership and, her apparent total resistance to physical harm, the army of superstitious soldiers overcame the city.

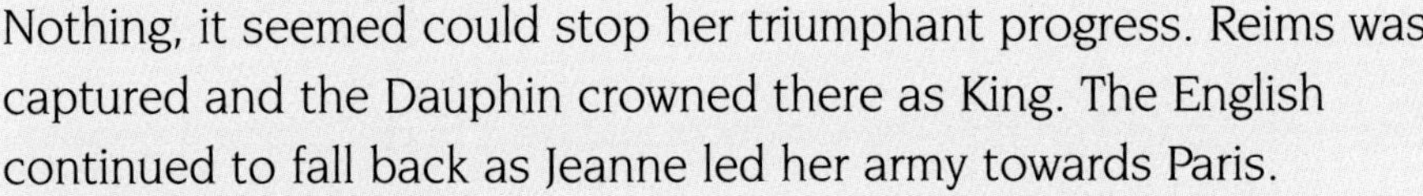

Nothing, it seemed could stop her triumphant progress. Reims was captured and the Dauphin crowned there as King. The English continued to fall back as Jeanne led her army towards Paris.

But the amazing story was moving to a tragic end. Jeanne was wounded and her sword broken in a battle near Paris, and her followers and soldiers began to doubt her invincibility. At the same time powerful nobles, jealous of her success and fearful of her growing power, decided she could be dispensed with now the task of vanquishing the English was accomplished. They cynically betrayed her to the English and, in 1431, accused of witchcraft and condemned as a witch, Jeanne endured an agonising death, burned at the stake.

After her death, stories, legends and myths multiplied about her. She became a national heroine and in 1920 she was canonised, that is, declared a saint. She remains one of the great and most remarkable heroines, not merely of France, but of the whole world.

Mahatma Gandhi (1869-1948)

Mahatma Gandhi was an Indian who studied in London and became a lawyer. Gandhi first went to work in South Africa where there were many Indians living and working. He was horrified by what he saw as the unfair way in which his fellow countrymen and women were treated. They were prevented from being appointed to important jobs, no matter how clever or well qualified they were and had to live in poor, unhealthy housing. Gandhi worked as a lawyer, often without payment, to help impoverished oppressed Indians.

Gandhi went back to live in India which was then part of the British Empire. Gandhi wanted India to be free to run itself and he set up a political party to bring this about. But he refused to use any force or violence. Gandhi believed that all living things, from the smallest insect to the most important human, were sacred and should never be harmed. He believed in trying to persuade people to see his point of view and would not fight or strike back no matter how badly he was treated.

Gandhi also believed that the world would be a better place if people lived simply and did not worry so much about material things and possessions. He himself dressed in the simplest of clothes; to people who did not know him or did not bother to try to understand what he was saying, Gandhi often looked a slightly comical figure. But he was really a man of great power and what is often called "vision". That is, he thought deeply about things and suggested good solutions to difficult problems. He was also very determined, as the following example will show.

Salt was particularly important to the people of India, because of the need to keep meat fresh and edible in a fiercely humid climate. But salt was extremely expensive because its ownership was completely controlled by the British government in India. Gandhi wanted to show that the people of India had a right to find their own salt. So he led thousands of Indians in a 200-mile march to the sea to collect the precious commodity, simply to show the world that Indians had a right not only to salt, but to be free and independent. Gandhi was imprisoned several times for breaking the law in this way. But he never allowed violence to be committed by his followers.

In the end Britain agreed that it was right to give India its freedom and Gandhi played a leading role in setting up the new state.

However, there was great conflict between Indian people themselves, mainly because Hindus and Muslims, followers of the two great religions of the country, could not agree about how the country should be governed and how it should be divided between them.

Gandhi was broken-hearted by the quarrel. He wanted peace for India and was sure that if people talked together they could settle their differences. He was horrified at the idea that the disagreements could be settled by violence.

But violence was already too far gone to be stopped. As Mahatma Gandhi, the man who probably did most to free India and make her independent, was walking to a prayer meeting one day in 1948, a Hindu, who could not accept Gandhi's vision or idea of peace between the two great religions, stepped out of the crowd and shot him dead.

But Mahatma Gandhi is still remembered years later as a symbol of peace.

The Final Whistle for the Milltown Cannonball

Football supporters, not to mention a wider public less interested in the game, were saddened to learn of the death yesterday, after a long illness at his home in the North East, of Jack Ripley, the international footballer, known throughout his long career as "The Milltown Cannonball".

It is over thirty years since Jack Ripley kicked a football as a professional, yet his name remained instantly recognisable, as the stories of his football skill and achievement are known even to a generation of young followers of the game who have only ever seen him as a fleeting figure in old flickering newsreels and ancient TV replays of games. Two pictures will always jump first to mind when the name "Jack Ripley" is uttered: the sight of that massive figure bearing down on the Brazilian goal and letting fly with the shot that brought England its first ever World Cup, and the bandaged head rising above everyone to nod home the winning goal for Milltown in the famous "David and Goliath" Cup Final of 1958.

* * *

Jack Ripley spent all his career at tiny, unglamorous Milltown, taking them, through his prodigious goal-scoring feats, from the old Third Division to the heights of First Division success. Great clubs, both in Britain and abroad, battled to sign him, but he remained faithful to his northern roots, to the town where he was born and grew up, and to the people who idolised him.

Standing by the large bronze statue of Ripley that guards the entrance to the Milltown United ground (now sadly fallen on hard times as the team struggles vainly to win a place in the Premier League), an elderly fan, wiping his eyes, voiced the opinions of many, not merely in the town, but outside as well, when he said "We'll never see the likes of him again; he was the greatest goal scorer this country has ever known. No wonder they called him Cannonball. I tell you I've seen him hit a ball that fractured the crossbar and bounced back to the centre spot." Other fans chimed in to remind me that "The Cannonball" could have earned a fortune by moving to larger, more wealthy clubs, but remained loyal to the club that gave him his first chance. "When I think," said a woman supporter, her eyes brimming with tears, "what these young slips of kids earn today, before they've played twenty games, and what Jack got for all he did, it makes me wild. He were worth three of any of them were 'The Cannonball'."

Ripley was discovered as a fourteen year-old playing in local school football and was playing league football for Milltown within two years. Powerfully built and with an electrifying turn of speed, he was able to compete with men from the beginning. But it was his devastating shooting and heading that brought Ripley undying fame. He broke scoring records all over England and it was not long before he was leading his country to spectacular success. The high point of his dazzling career was undoubtedly the 1962 World Cup series when he rounded off a series of brilliant performances with his thrilling final hat trick and, of course, the winning goal, replayed a thousand times on TV.

But many older Milltown fans may treasure even more the courageous winning goal he scored, despite injury, in the 1958 final against the mighty Alltop United.

For all his power and strength and the ferocity of his shooting, Jack Ripley was noted for his sportsmanship. Never booked, and never sent off, he was truly not only one of the great stars of the game, but one of its true gentlemen as well.

Jack Ripley is survived by his wife Sheila and grown-up family of two sons and two daughters.

* * *

The funeral will take place tomorrow in Milltown. All shops, factories and businesses will close for the occasion and the town will come to a halt as their beloved "Cannonball" is carried to his final resting place.

* * *

Death of Distinguished War Hero

The death is announced of General Sir James Gordon Coburn-Smith, one of the most decorated soldiers in the British Army, at his home in Westbourne at the age of ninety two.

General Coburn-Smith came from an old military family; an ancestor fought at Waterloo. He himself saw his first military action at the tender age of seventeen when, having falsified his birth certificate to gain under age admission to the army, he led a handful of men in a valiant defensive action, allowing almost his entire battalion to escape from the trap into which the enemy had lured them.

His extraordinarily cool leadership, at so young an age, and his personal bravery, which proved such an inspiration to his men, brought him his first decoration for bravery. It was to be the first of many, culminating in the Victoria Cross awarded for his famous action during the First World War.

Coburn-Smith spent the years between the wars in military hot spots all over what was still a wide British Empire. After distinguished service in India he was brought back to Britain in time to prepare for the Second World War. His qualities and inspiring leadership were evident in the disaster of Dunkirk, where his battalion was the last off the beaches after a fierce and stubborn resistance.

After that General Coburn-Smith, an expert in guerrilla warfare, played a leading role in training and managing Britain's commando forces. Churchill called him, "My hidden hammer". Coburn-Smith commanded the famous "Ironsides" Regiment during the invasion of Europe and led the first successful break-out from the beaches on D-Day. After that he was in the forefront of most of the great struggles leading up to the end of the war. Field Marshall Montgomery paid him the compliment of inviting him to be present as a witness on the occasion of the enemy's formal surrender.

Coburn-Smith held various senior posts in the Army before retiring in 1958. He maintained his interests, however, in Service Welfare and continued to play a leading organisational role in various army charities. Famous throughout the Services for his generous nature (his troops referred to him – behind his back of course – as "Old Uncle Jim") his work on behalf of retired and infirm veterans will be sadly missed.

Coburn-Smith also retained his interests in sport, and athletics particularly, until the end. A notable runner himself, he had been selected for the British Olympic Team of 1924, but was obliged to withdraw because of pneumonia. "That is one medal I would have loved to have won" he used to say, wistfully.

He is survived by his daughter Melissa, the well-known opera singer, and by his son Geoffrey, MP for Fairlehurst.

Report One:

The Tale (tail – get it?!) of a Cow

I have just heard that some time in the last few weeks a cow, belonging to a farmer somewhere in Oxfordshire, had a lucky escape from danger.

Cows as you know are quite large creatures and they can get into trouble if they go where they shouldn't. Well this cow – or according to some people it may have been a bull – was a bit of a wanderer. Cows are inclined to wander, and when they do, it often leads to trouble.

She – or he if it was a bull – decided to go for a stroll one day some time ago. How on earth she got out of the barn, or the pen or wherever she was – or he was, of course, if it was a bull – I don't know and can't find out.

Anyway, off she went and came to a river. I suppose you can guess what happened; that's right – she fell in and got stuck.

I'm not sure how long she was there, but it seems when people found out they came from all over the place to see her – or him, if it was a bull. In fact it must have been a bull, because bulls are more valuable than cows and maybe that's why so many people turned up.

Anyway, I believe they even showed it all on the TV, though I didn't see it myself.

The thing is, you'll be glad to hear they got her out in the end, though I'm not quite sure how they managed it. Some people said they think the farmer had to bring in a large crane to manage the rescue.

We hope to have a picture of the cow to show you in next week's edition.

Report Two:

Prize Bull Saved from Death Swamp

Large crowds watched in mounting tension yesterday as fire and specialist services raced against time to pull a prize bull from deadly quicksand.

The near tragedy began when a TV crew arrived at Mrs. Giles' farm in Cumnor, Oxfordshire to film "Bruiser", one of the most valuable bulls in Europe, for a major series on international animal stars.

However, Bruiser seems to have had an attack of show business temperament. No sooner were the lights on and the cameras rolling, than he decided to take off, like a runaway lorry, crashing through a fence and scattering the TV crew and equipment in all directions. Then, however, the story turned from comedy to near tragedy. Bruiser's charge took him through a fence and into a large patch of treacherous quicksand in a remote corner of the farm.

Immediately his massive weight began to drag him down to what seemed a certain and horrendous death.

While farm hands worked overtime to make a platform of sacking, wood and sand about the struggling animal, fire services and lifting crews raced to the scene.

For a nail-biting period the task seemed hopeless as Bruiser's great weight and frantic efforts to free himself, dragged him further downwards.

Many people in the large crowd that had gathered could not bear to watch. Others knelt and prayed.

After almost four hours of struggle the rescue crews finally succeeded in securing padded chains around the weary bull and Bruiser was slowly pulled to safety, amid scenes of wild excitement and relief in the crowd. "Another minute and I think it would have been too late," gasped mud-covered Fire Chief Alan Dawson, "I never thought I'd want to hug a bull but I could have done it when I saw Bruiser safe on firm ground."

As for Bruiser, he wobbled about for a while on rubbery legs and then trotted off back to his paddock as if nothing had happened. And to top it all, the TV crew got the whole thrilling story on film, so Bruiser is likely to become an even bigger star than ever.

"Bumble United Cheated of Victory"

Bumble United 0 : Bankrupt City 3

Looking at the score-line you would think there had been only one team in it, wouldn't you! And you'd be right; but it wasn't City – it was United.

United were clearly superior in every area of the field, without exception, and should have run out clear winners. That they did not was due to a few highly regrettable factors.

First of all there was the refereeing. Your reporter has seldom seen such a poor performance on the part of the man in the middle. The two goals he disallowed for United were clearly not offside. Then the penalty he awarded City for the accidental kick by United's star centre half Joe Basham, that saw their striker carried off with a broken leg, was extremely harsh.

City's goals were extremely lucky: the unfair penalty, the thirty yard drive that only scored because United's goalie was unsighted and the final, scored after a fluky seven-man passing movement.

The crowd protested loudly at the end of the game, not because of the Bumbles' display as one or two trouble-making fans suggested, (why don't these so-called supporters stay away altogether; United don't need them!) but because of the standard of refereeing.

Provided that United keep up this level of performance, have some decent luck for a change and meet fair referees then there seems no reason why they can't win the Championship.

I am a Wasp

I am a wasp
I am stuck in a sticky jar
I used to fly in the wind
buzz my wings in the sun
and hover in sweet places

but I am stuck in a sticky jar.

Up I fly
and my wings hit a tin lid
my hard yellow head knocks it
so down I glide for a flicker of a second
and my legs, my body
are in sweet water where there is no breath to
breathe.

I used to soar and swoop
I used to circle round and round
and settle on sweet things

but I am stuck in a sticky jar.

Above me the heat of the sun
pours through holes in the tin.
I buzz and crawl to them.
Isn't that the way I came in?
– but nearly there, my feelers hit tin.
The ragged cut edge of tin.
And who am I to dare to drag this weak waist
across that edge?

Beneath me, all about me,
is the smell of crushed strawberry.
It doesn't grow stronger if I buzz nearer.
It doesn't grow weak if I hover or move.
It's strong everywhere in smell
and nowhere to be found.

I used to *find* crushed strawberries –
or maybe melting chocolate, the hearts of fat plums.
I used to cut my way to the syrup of bruised bananas
in the gutters of the market.
I used to linger on the rims of glasses and bottles
to nibble at the crystals of lemonade, cherryade
and old orange pop.

All around me now
other wasps, even a bee and a blue-bottle
buzz up buzz down
and we're all swerving to miss each other's wings.

I turn back.
One is at my foot.
I twist to dodge him
but he is at my neck.
I snip at his scales –
he twists, a hairsbreadth from my eye.
A sting sticks, weaves to find
a soft spot to get in.
I cut back, take off
and my wing is flying in the sweet water
dragging me down.

I use my legs and run up over the backs
of wasps floating where water and glass meet.
They sink. I sink.
And the buzz in the sweet smell of the air
goes on and on

There is heat in the sun through the holes
in the lid of the tin.
The heat pours in.
Up above me, my eyes shadowy with the sugar
see a hole for the heat.

Into it comes the eyes, the feelers, the jaws,
the head, the legs, the chest, the –

Those of us in here could say:
Go back.

But those of us in here who could say
are no more than black and yellow scum,
dead froth bobbing on the water.

In through the hole comes the chest,
the wings, the waist, the body and the sting.

Too late,
you silly, sugar-sniffing, soft nibbling, sweet sucker.
That's the end.

by Michael Rosen

The Two Roots

A pair of pine roots, old and dark,
make conversation in the park.

The whispers where the top leaves grow
are echoed in the roots below.

An agèd squirrel sitting there
is knitting stockings for the pair.

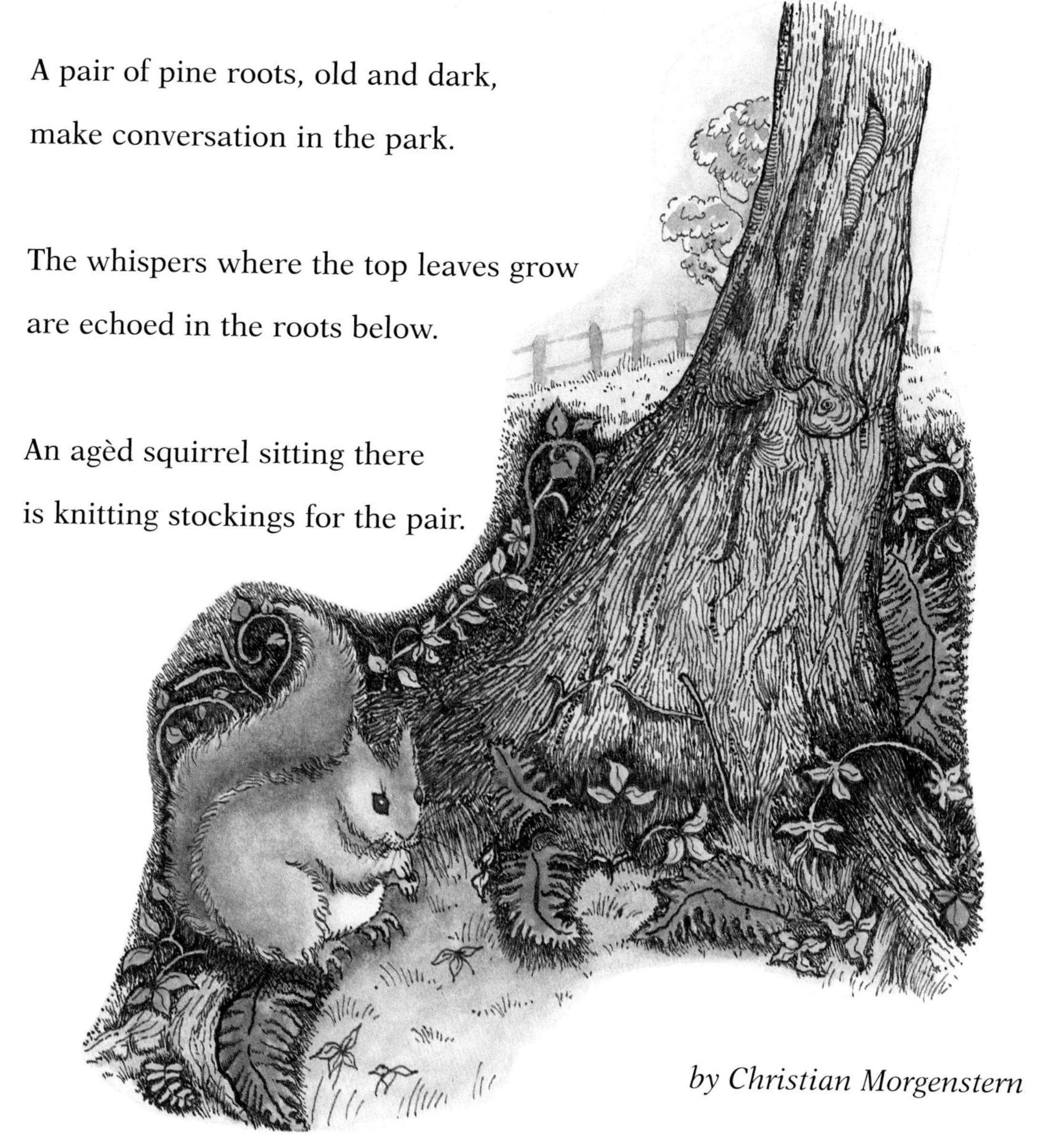

by Christian Morgenstern

At School

by Eleanor Allen

Elementary schools

In the 1920s most children went to elementary school from the age of five up to the leaving age of fourteen. The elementary schools were free. Children who went to other schools (small private schools, preparatory, secondary or public schools) either won a scholarship or had families who could afford to pay the school fees.

Unfortunately, elementary schools were going through a difficult time and, as a result, many of the children suffered. The school buildings tended to be very out of date. Many had been built in Victorian times, for Victorian methods of teaching, with just one large room to accommodate several classes of children. Even by the mid-1920s, many children were being taught in rooms which accommodated more than one class. Under those conditions, teaching had to be very strict and very formal. The first lesson of the day was scripture, followed almost entirely by "the three Rs" (reading, writing and arithmetic).

By modern standards, schools had very little equipment.

> "It was nearly all blackboard teaching. Very few text books were used and, except when writing compositions, we weren't encouraged to use our imaginations."
>
> "We were taught to read and do simple arithmetic, but no science and hardly any history or geography."

In 1922 it was made compulsory for all children to stay on at school until they were at least fourteen. Before that, children who were over twelve years old had been allowed to leave school if they found a job, or to "part-time", spend part of the day at work and part at school.

Difficulties arose because no proper provision was made for the extra numbers of older children who would be going to school. There was serious overcrowding, and not much thought had been given to what sort of lessons were appropriate for twelve to fourteen year olds. Sometimes they were given a partitioned-off corner of the schoolroom to themselves, but there were usually no rooms set aside where older children could go to receive instruction in a wider variety of subjects. Teachers often weren't trained to teach that age group and didn't know what to do with them. Many children were intensely bored. For clever children, the situation was often aggravated by the fact that they were allowed to jump standards (classes).

In mixed schools, boys and girls had separate playgrounds and went into the school through separate entrances.

Secondary schools

The only way in which a bright child could escape the boredom of the last years at the elementary school was by moving at the age of eleven to what was known as a secondary school.

A secondary school provided a wider range of subjects, such as Latin, French and science. But to get there, you had to have parents who could afford the fees, or you had to sit an exam to win a scholarship for a free place. Many clever children passed the exam but still couldn't go, even though the place was free. Their parents couldn't afford to buy the special uniform and extra items which these schools required. Often, parents needed their children to leave school and start earning wages as soon as they could.

Uniform

Most children at fee-paying schools, and some at elementary schools, wore a uniform. For boys it was usually a flannel shirt and a grey serge suit. Short trousers were usually compulsory up to the age of fourteen, and all boys had to wear braces to hold up the trousers because they had baggy, unfitted waists.

Both boys and girls wore the traditional cap, beret or boater and a tie in the school colours.

Girls usually wore a white blouse with a "Peter Pan" collar, cardigan, gym-slip with box pleats (whose hem had to be precisely four inches above the knee), navy knickers, and black woollen stockings, which were much hated.

Summer uniform dresses were made with long sleeves. Boys from poorer families usually wore just short trousers and a jersey for school. Girls wore a skirt and knitted jumper, or a plain cotton dress in summer, which was "very often your sister's, cut down".

Lunches

Elementary schools didn't provide pupils with lunch and, except in very rare cases, didn't have dining halls. Children went home for lunch if they could.

> "I always walked home for lunch. It was about two miles each way so, in all, I walked eight miles a day to and from school, in all weathers. But eight miles wasn't unusual in those days..."

Children who couldn't get home for lunch ate their sandwiches in a classroom.

> "As most of the children came such a long way and brought sandwiches for lunch, a large kettle was boiled on the schoolroom stove, and either the teacher or an older girl made Oxo or cocoa for their lunchtime drinks..."

But not all schools were so hospitable.

> "At my school they ate in the cloakroom – hunks of bread and cheese, bread and jam, that sort of thing. They only ate in the classroom in really cold weather. They wouldn't have wanted to – they were always desperate to escape from the classroom!"

Lavatories

Schools did provide lavatories, but usually they were outside. Many schools, especially those in the countryside, didn't have flush toilets. Pupils, and teachers too, had to cope with old-fashioned earth closets.

Even schools which did have flush lavatories didn't always provide wash-basins. "Now wash your hands" was a rule they didn't bother too much about applying in those days.

"I can remember great excitement when water was finally laid on to three wash-basins. We had to teach the infants how to wash their hands..."

Discipline

Discipline was strict, whether you went to a free elementary school, or to a fee-paying school. Speaking in class, except to the teacher, was usually absolutely forbidden and could even get you the cane. Corporal punishment was given out for what would be considered quite minor offences today. Although, on the whole, pupils respected and liked their teachers, many felt that punishments were too severe at times.

"Punishment at our school for misbehaving included caning, rapping the knuckles with a ruler, lines, and being sent to Coventry. Most teachers were strict, but kind – though I remember one who was disliked by all the pupils in her class as she persistently pinched their arms and tugged their hair at the least provocation..."

"In the junior school, you were stood in a corner until you got tired and asked to sit down. In the upper school, the cane was used quite a lot – for next to nothing, in fact! Being late, work not as good as it should be, talking in class... I think the whole set-up was completely wrong."

School Games

Many elementary schools had no Games fields and their pupils never got the chance of a proper Games lesson. It was different at the fee-paying public schools and secondary schools. At public schools in particular, being good at sport was more admired than being good at lessons.

Boys played rugby, or sometimes had a choice of rugby or rowing in winter and cricket in summer.

Girls played hockey or lacrosse in winter and tennis in summer, though some tough-spirited girls' schools were starting to play cricket, too. Hard-playing girls were very much admired in the 1920s. The hockey team and lacrosse team were the "bloods" (the fashionable "in" set), as were the First XV and First XI in boys' schools.

Until the 1930s there were no teachers who were specially trained in either Games or PE, so all members of staff who were not too infirm were expected to lend a hand.

Drill

Most schoolchildren in the 1920s, even at the better equipped schools, didn't have the benefit of gym with special apparatus such as ropes and wallbars. Such things were for specialist gymnastics only.

PE usually took place in the playground or, if the weather was bad, in the school hall. It was known as "drill" because a lot of the exercises were rather like army drill. Pupils were arranged in rows and, on sergeant major type commands from the teacher, they had to carry out a series of vigorous exercises.

"Feet astride – place!

Hips – firm!

Trunk forward – bend!

Trunk forward – stretch!

Trunk upward – stretch!"

Drill wasn't so different from modern "keep fit" and the aims were much the same; healthy bodies with correct posture, good physical co-ordination and mental concentration. Everybody was very fitness conscious in the 1920s, because there had been such a need for healthy fighting men in the War.

Pupils usually did drill in their ordinary school clothes. Boys had to remove detachable collars and tie their braces round their waists like belts. Under their school skirts, girls were supposed to wear sensible navy knickers which were "not too ample" and ended just above the knee. Suspenders for holding up stockings were thought more suitable for drill than garters, which cut off circulation.

A "handkerchief drill" was recommended to start. It involved everybody producing a handkerchief and giving their nose a good blow, so that they could breathe really deeply. But, for obvious reasons, teachers usually seem to have missed it out!

Noah's Ark

by Roger McGough

It began
When God popped His head
Through the clouds and said:

"Oh you wicked, wicked children
What a mess this place is in
All the violence and corruption
It really is a sin.

I turn my back for five aeons
(For I've other work to do)
Keeping the universe tidy
And I get no thanks from you.

You've grown selfish and conceited
Your manners are a disgrace
You come and go just as you please
You'd think you owned the place.

A telling-off's not good enough
You've grown too big for your flesh
So I think I'll wash my hands of you
And start again afresh."

He turned full on the tap in the sky
Then picked out the one good man
Pure of heart and strong in arm
To carry out his plan: Noah.

"What I need," explained God
"Is an arkwright to build an ark, right away."
Said Noah, "If I can sir."
"Of course you can, now get stuck in
I won't take Noah for an answer."

"I want a boat three storeys high
Aboard which you will bring
Not only your wife and family
But two of every living thing."

"Even spiders?" asked Noah
(who didn't really like them)
"Even spiders," said God
(who didn't either).

"Cats and dogs and elephants
Slugs, leopards and lice
Giraffes and armadilloes
Buffaloes, bed bugs and mice.

Antelopes, ants and anteaters
(though better keep those last two apart)
Bears from Koala to Grizzly
Horses from Racing to Cart.

Fish will be able to fend for themselves
And besides, a wooden ark
Is not the sort of place to keep
A whale or an angry shark.

And don't forget our feathered friends
For they'll have nowhere to nest
But vermin will determine
Their own survival best.

Flies, maggots and bluebottles
Mosquitoes and stingers that bite
Will live off the dead and the dying
So they'll make out all right.

That seems to be all for now, Noah
The rest is up to you.
I'll see you again in forty days
Until then God Bless and Adieu."

He disappeared in a clap of thunder
(Either that or he banged the door)
And the wind in a rage broke out of its cage
With an earth-splintering roar.

And no sooner was everyone aboard
Than the Ark gave a mighty shudder
And would have been crushed by the
onrushing waves
Had Noah not been at the rudder.

Right craftily he steered the craft
As if to the mariner born
Through seas as high as a Cyclops' eye
And cold as the devil's spawn.

And it rained, and it rained
And it rained again
And it rained, and it rained
And it rained, and then …
… drip …
… drop …
… the last …
… drip dropped …
… to a …
… stop.

Noah at the helm was overwhelmed
For both cargo and crew were unharmed
Then the wind turned nasty and held its
breath
So the Ark became becalmed.

Hither and thither it drifted
Like an aimless piece of jetsam
"Food's running out," cried Mrs Noah
"We'll perish if we don't get some."

"Maybe God's gone and forgotten us
We're alone in the world and forsaken
He surely won't miss one little pig
Shall I grill a few rashers of bacon?"

"Naughty, naughty!" said Noah sternly
(For it was the stern that he was stood in)
"I'm ravenous, but bring me a raven
I've an idea and I think it's a good 'un."

As good as his word, he let loose the bird
"Go spy out for land," he commanded
But in less than a week, it was back with its
beak
Completely (so to speak) empty-handed!

Next he coaxed from its lovenest a dove
"We're depending on you," he confided
Then gave it to the air like an unwrapped
gift
Of white paper that glided away.

Then the Ark sat about with its heart in its
mouth
With nothing to do but wait
So Mrs Noah organized organized games
To keep animal minds off their fate.

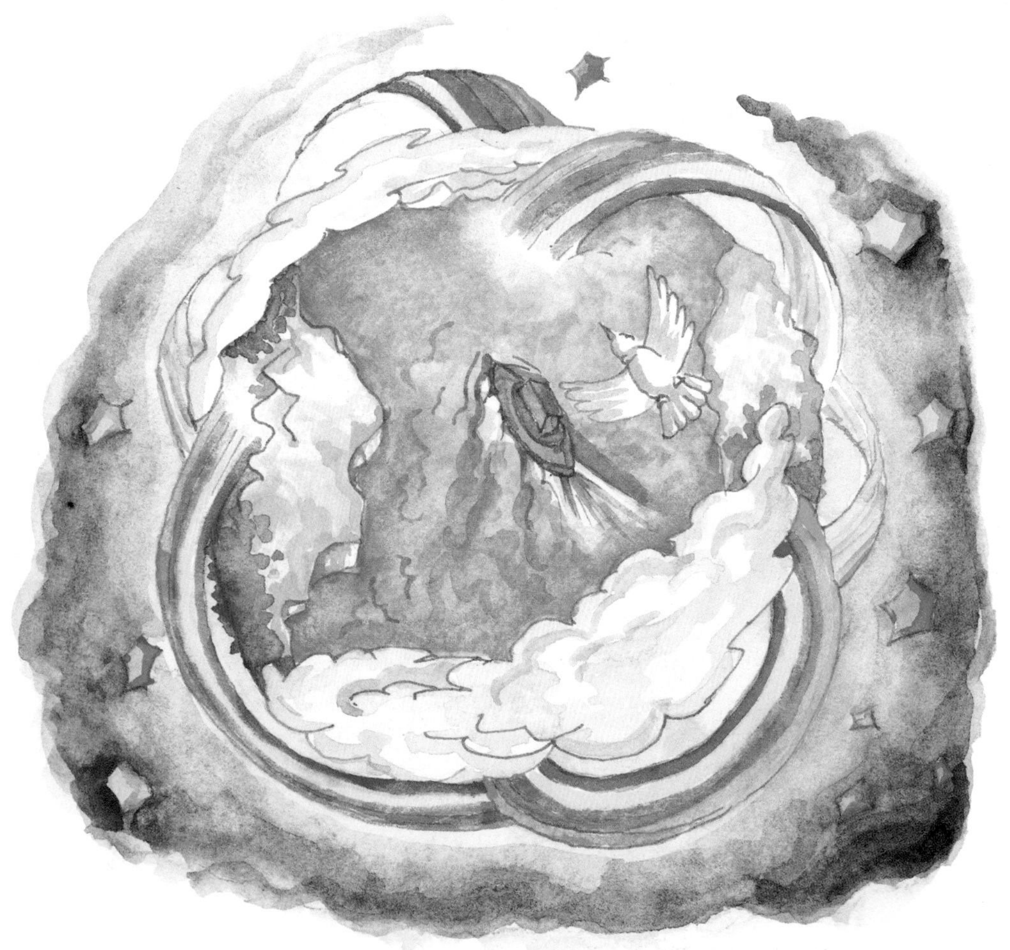

Until one morn when all seemed lost
The dove in the heavens was seen
To the Ark, like an archangel it arrowed
Bearing good tidings of green.

"Praised be the Lord," cried Noah
(and Mrs Noah cried too)
And all God's creatures gave their thanks
(even spiders, to give them their due).

Then God sent a quartet of rainbows
Radiating one from each side
To the four corners of the earth
Where they journeyed and multiplied.

And as Noah set off down the mountain
To be a simple farmer again
A voice thundered: "Nice work there
  sunshine."
Here endeth the story. Amen.

From Professor Branestawm's Dictionary

by Norman Hunter

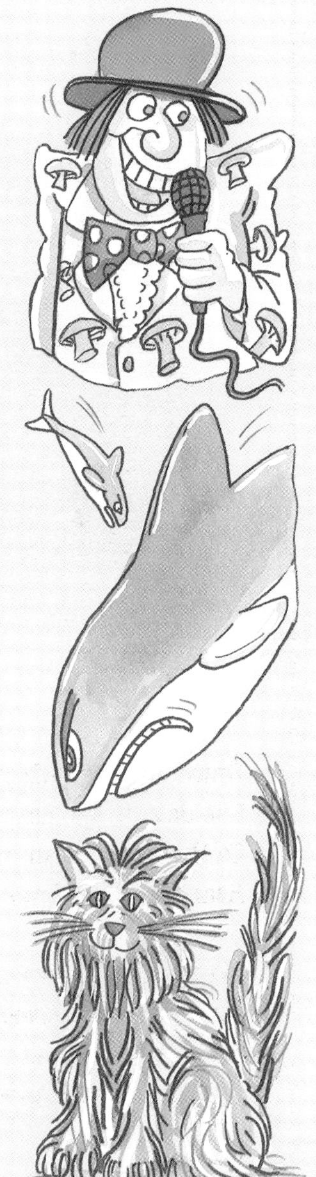

Aaron	What a wig has.
abandon	What a hat has.
abundance	A waltz for cakes.
accord	A piece of thick string.
addition	What a dinner table has.
aftermath	The next lesson after arithmetic.
already	Completely crimson.
boycott	Bed for a male baby.
buoyant	Male insect.
copper nitrate	What policemen get paid for working overtime in the evenings.
cross purposes	Bad-tempered fish.
dozen	Opposite of what one does.
during	Did you use the bell?
enchant	A female chicken's song.
fungi	A comedian.
furlong	The coat of a Persian cat.
hyacinth	Familiar greeting for Cynthia.
jargon	The vase is no longer here.
khaki	A thing for starting a motor car.
knapsack	Sleeping bag.
liability	Capacity for telling untruths.

macadam	The first Scotsman.
offal	Terrible.
out of bounds	A frog too tired to leap.
oxide	Leather.
pasteurise	Across your vision.
ramshackle	Handcuff for a male sheep.
raucous	Uncooked swear word.
rheumatic	An apartment at the top of a house.
robust	A line of knitting that has come undone.
sediment	What he announced he had in mind.
shamble	Imitation male cow.
statue	Enquiry as to whether it is yourself.
urchin	The lower part of the lady's face.
versatile	Poetry on the roof.
vertigo	In which direction did he proceed?
Windsor	Did you succeed at your game, guv'nor?

Haiku

Spring rain falls –
under silver trees
a crystal stream

Tyrannosaurus Rex

By Stanley Cook

A Flamingo

A Flamingo
is a long
coooooooooool
drink
of
something
pink

By J. Patrick Lewis

Cat

A toe-nibbler
A dark-dreamer
A paw-padder
A floor-scratcher
A warm-sleeper
A night-creeper
A fur-cleaner
A flea-finder
A mouse-hunter
A house-minder
A secret-hoarder
A china-breaker
A four-foot-lander

by Rachel Myers

Haiku

Snowy morning –
one crow
after another.

Yellow rose petals –
thunder –
a waterfall.

Winter downpour –
even the monkey
needs a raincoat.

How pleasant –
just once **not** to see
Fuji through mist.

Do not forget the plum
blooming
in the thicket.

Mouth

A good-gobbler
A wide-opener
A constant-eater
A yawn-helper
A noise-bringer
A finger-sucker
A lip-smacker
A teeth-clicker
A loud-shouter
A sharp-whistler

by Anadil Hossain

The Sands of Dee

by Charles Kingsley

"O Mary, go and call the cattle home,
And call the cattle home,
And call the cattle home,
Across the sands of Dee!"
The western wind was wild and dank with foam,
And all alone went she.
The western tide crept up along the sand,
And o'er and o'er the sand,
And round and round the sand,
As far as eye could see.
The rolling mist came down and hid the land:
And never home came she.

"Oh! is it a weed, or fish, or floating hair-
A tress of golden hair,
A drowned maiden's hair,
Above the nets at sea?
Was never salmon yet that shone so fair
Among the stakes on Dee."
They rowed her in across the rolling foam,
The cruel crawling foam,
The cruel hungry foam,
To her grave beside the sea:
But still the boatmen hear her call the
cattle home
Across the sands of Dee.

Newspaper Report

A tragic accident at the weekend robbed a family of their youngest daughter. Full details were not available to us at the time of going to press, but the facts seem to be as follows:

The young girl's mother asked her to drive home the cows from the edge of the sea late on Friday evening. When she did not return within an hour, and because a mist was falling, her father and some friends set out to find her. They spied her body eventually caught in the staked fishing nets and were obliged to row out and recover it. The young girl was buried that evening in the local churchyard.

Typewriting Class

by Gareth Owen

Dear Miss Hinson
I am spitting
In front of my top ratter
With the rest of my commercesnail sturdy students
Triping you this later.
The truce is Miss Hinson
I am not hippy with my cross.
Every day on Woundsday
I sit in my dusk
with my type rutter
Trooping without lurking at the lattice
All sorts of weird messengers.
To give one exam pill,
"The quick down socks...
The quick brine pox...
The sick frown box...
The sick down jocks...
Humps over the haze bog"
When everyone kows
That a sick down jock
Would not be seen dead near a hazy bog.
Another one we tripe is;

"Now is the tame
For all guide men
To cram to the head
Of the pratty."
To may why of sinking
I that is all you get to tripe
In true whelks of stirdy
Then I am thinking of changing
To crookery classes.
I would sooner end up a crook
Than a shirt hand trappist
Any die of the wink.
I have taken the tremble, Miss Hinson
To trip you this later
So that you will be able
To understand my indignation.
I must clothe now
As the Bill is groaning
Yours fitfully...

Letter from a Soldier to his Mother

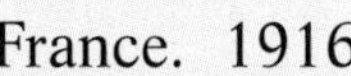

France. 1916

Dearest mother,

I have just finished my final round of the trenches. It is the most beautiful night you can imagine. The night is full of calm and lovely stars, a breeze whispers, and apart from softly muttered commands along the lines, the occasional whinnying of a nervous horse, the far off barking of a dog, it is absolutely peaceful. Yet we know that tomorrow will be very hard. When we advance in the first light of dawn we are likely to meet desperate resistance. Everyone knows it. All around me as I sit in the dugout and write by the sad, exhausted light of a candle, men everywhere are doing the same thing: composing letters home, to parents and family, to their wives and children, to lovers and friends.

For many it will be the last letter they ever write. It may well be mine. I have a cold feeling about me now, for all the beauty of the night. I can write that knowing that by the time you receive it everything will be all over, one way or another.

I wish you could know what is in my heart, but it's hard to find the right words in a muddy trench, with the dawn just over the horizon and so much still to prepare.

You know, dearest mother, that words were never a gift with me. So if the last words I shall write to you come out a bit like a poem, however poor, it's my love talking and not me suddenly getting grand ideas about myself.

As I await the dawn and what it brings,
death lying out there in the frosty fields,
I think it would not matter much at all,
Could I but see your dear face one more time.
There would be no fine speeches I'm afraid,
I am not made like that as well you know.
No good with honeyed words or speeches grand.
I just would want to touch your cheek and say
You have been more to me than all the world
To have the chance to talk for one more hour
Of other times that fill my mind tonight,
So ordinary then it seemed,
But now like dreams of Heaven to me
On this the eve of death.
Of all the expeditions that we had,
Of rambles by the wood and by the sea.
And how you made me think that I could learn
To play that complicated violin.
And made me brave enough
For all my stammer,
To talk and joke and flirt with pretty girls.
But as I write it is my hand that's stammering now.
And will not write the things I want to say.
But I know well that in your heart you know,
You who have known and loved me best of all,
All that I want to say.
Just remember, down all the years to come,
Whatever happens in the awful dawn
That if I fall, I'll face with smiling face
And courage high
And at the very end will think only of you.

2 Corinthians 11

21 But if anyone wants some brazen speaking – I am still talking as a
fool – then I can be as brazen as any of them, and about the same
things.*
22 Hebrews, are they? So am I. Israelites? So am I. Descendants of
Abraham? So am I.
23 The servants of Christ? I must be mad to say this, but so am I, and
more than they: more, because I have worked harder, I have been
sent to prison more often, and whipped so many times more, often
almost to death.
24 Five times I had the thirty-nine lashes from the Jews;
25 three times I have been beaten with sticks; once I was stoned;
three times I have been shipwrecked and once adrift in the open
sea for a night and a day.**
26 Constantly travelling, I have been in danger from rivers and in
danger from brigands, in danger from my own people and in
danger from pagans; in danger in the towns, in danger in the open
country, danger at sea and danger from so-called brothers.
27 I have worked and laboured, often without sleep; I have been
hungry and thirsty and often starving; I have been in the cold
without clothes.
28 And, to leave out much more, there is my daily preoccupation: my
anxiety for all the churches.
29 When any man has had scruples, I have had scruples with him;
when any man is made to fall, I am tortured.
30 If I am to boast, then let me boast of my own feebleness.
31 The God and Father of the Lord Jesus – bless him for ever –
knows that I am not lying.
32 When I was in Damascus, the ethnarch of King Aretas put guards
round me, and I had to be let down over the wall in a hamper, in
order to escape.

* The needs of controversy oblige Paul on several occasions to appeal, as he does here, to his past life as a faithful Jew.

** For the most part nothing further is known of these hardships.

Moby Dick

by Herman Melville adapted by Geraldine McCaughrean

Chapter 1

The Tattooed Harpooner

There is a whale in the sea, as white as a ghost, and it haunts me. It haunts me on winter nights, when the sky tumbles like a grey sea, and drifts of snow hump their backs at me. It haunts me in summer, when the sun overhead turns the grass sea-green, and the almond blossom rears up white over my head.

Sometimes, when I'm afloat in sleep, like a drowned sailor, he swims towards me – a nightmare all in white, jaws gaping, and I wake up screaming and salt-water wet with sweat. Somewhere out there in the bottomless oceans lives Moby Dick, a great white winter of a whale, and I shiver still at the thought of him. Even in summer.

Call me Ishmael. It might be my name. There again it might not. In my devout, church-going part of the world, it is usual for parents to name their children after characters in the Bible. Maybe mine did. There again, a man can always choose a new name, later in life, to suit his nature and experience. I call myself Ishmael, like that despised son of Abraham cast out into the wilderness places of the world. He may have lived apart from other men, but God was with him in the wilderness, even so, and heard him when he cried. *God hears*. That's the meaning of Ishmael. A man could be called worse. "Ahab", for instance.

That Ishmael in the Bible, he galloped about the wide world and never cared to settle down. I'm like that. I suppose that's

why, finally, I took it into my head to go whaling. Five times I went to sea with the merchant navy, and then, for a change, I decided to go whaling. So I stuffed two shirts into a carpet-bag and went to Nantucket, because that's where you go to find a whaling ship.

It was late and bitter cold when I arrived, and the dark so dense that I could barely see where I was going. The creaking of an inn-sign led me to the door of a dilapidated inn – The Spouter. Scribbled across the lintel in black letters were the words, Landlord: Peter Coffin. (A superstitious man might have taken that for a bad omen, but a man can't help his surname, can he?) In I went. "Do you have a bed for the night?"

"If you don't mind sharing it with a harpooner," said Peter Coffin, with a grin, and others nearby spluttered in their beer or looked me over and sniggered.

For all I had not been whaling before, I knew well enough about harpooners. They are generally very *big* men, not given to frill-fronted shirts or frock coats or taking tea with the ladies. I was nervous, no denying it. "Which one is he?" I asked, peering round the bar. "Maybe I'll look him over before I get under a blanket with him."

"Not back yet. He's out trying to sell his head," said the landlord, polishing a tankard.

I thought it must be the start of a joke. "Oh, yes?"

"Yes. He's sold the other four already, but he's out trying to get rid of the fifth... He may be a cannibal, but he pays regular. I don't judge a man beyond that."

It was too late at night and I was too tired for such nonsense. So I took myself off to bed. But as I shed my top clothes and scrambled under the warm covers, I was feeling more and more nervous of who would come through the door and get into bed beside me. A madman, by the sound of it. Selling his head, indeed!

Beside the bed leaned the man's harpoon – a hollow metal spear with several ferocious barbs at the tip. I'm no weakling, but I would have been hard put even to lift it, let alone heave it at a passing whale. Just as I was dozing off, I heard footsteps on the stair. Best pretend to be asleep, I thought, so it was through my lashes that I first glimpsed Queequeg.

In one hand he held an Indian tomahawk – a lethal-looking axe – and in the other a shrunken human head.

His own face was hardly less ugly than the one in his fist, for it was tattooed with purple scrolls and black squares, and a single lock of hair swirled like a whirlpool in the centre of his forehead. When he took off his clothes, his body, too, was chequered purple-and-black, while columns of green frog tattoos trooped up and down his legs.

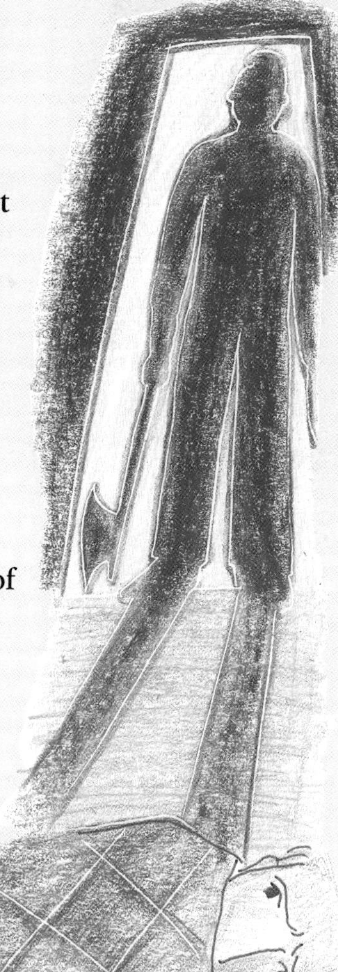

Out of a leather bag, he pulled a small brown object – I thought it was a human baby, at first, but it was a woodcarving of a crouching, hunched little man. Setting it down, he began to pray to it, his lips moving in a silent chant, his breath vaporous in the cold air.

"What a heathen! To pray to a carved idol!" I thought, as prim and supercilious as a Sunday-school spinster.

Then suddenly, Queequeg blew out the lamp, so that the room was plunged into darkness, and jumped into bed right on top of me.

"Whaahh!" I shrieked, rolling hard over against the wall.

"Who there?" His huge hands began to feel me like a blind pianist exploring a piano keyboard. "Who you? What you do in my bed?"

"Coffin! *Coffin!*" I yelled.

"You speak or I finish you!"

"PETER COFFIN!"

The landlord burst into the room, thinking to find a fire or a ghost. His lamp splashed us with yellow light. But when he saw me curled up like a hedgehog, and Queequeg trying to prise me open, he stood in the doorway and laughed out loud.

"Save me! Don't let him take my head!" I heard myself squealing.

"Bless me! What a row! Sorry, Queequeg: this fellow was in need of a bed, so I said he could share yours. Hey! You! Queequeg won't do you no harm sailor! Gentle as a moose, our Queequeg. Stop your racket and let the man get some sleep."

An embarrassed silence filled the darkness after Peter Coffin had gone. "I'm sorry," I said. "A misunderstanding."

"No matter," came his voice out of the darkness. "You Christians give me plenty big frights some times."

It turned out that he had not hunted the shrunken heads himself. He had bought them in New Zealand, to resell as curiosities to ghoulish Americans. He himself was a South Sea islander – a nobleman at that! His father was High Chief of the Kokovoko islanders. And shall I tell you something? That Queequeg proved a deal more civilised than many a man I've met before or since. By the time we had told each other our life histories and talked about the joys and terrors of the sea, I had made a friend I thought would last me a lifetime.

"Yojo says, you find us a whale ship," said Queequeg next morning, pointing at the little carved idol. "We two sail round the world."

"I hope we can sign up together," I agreed.

But Queequeg, as I found out, did not simply *hope* for the future to bring him things. "We *will*," he said, as if nothing else was possible, come good or ill.

I searched Nantucket harbour for a ship which took my fancy, and settled on the Pequod the moment I saw her. Besides being a rugged, sound, weathered little vessel, her entire ship's rail

was studded with the teeth of whales she had taken, and in the place of the bowsprit, the lower jaw of a sperm whale projected five metres. The tiller, too, for steering the ship, was the jawbone of a whale. It was as if the ship were kin to the beasts it hunted, or was gradually changing from wood to whalebone, from ship into whale.

Eager for my great adventure to begin, I leapt up the gangplank and generously offered my services to the man in Quaker-black sitting at a table on deck. "Where do I sign, captain?"

"I'm not the captain. He's belowdecks, sick," snapped the man in black. When he looked up at me, he had the face of a hell-fire preacher, sizing me up, saint or sinner. "Starbuck's my name. First mate. Why dost thou want to sign?"

I was taken aback. "I'd like to see the seven seas," I said.

"Well, take a look yonder." He pointed at the sloppy grey wash of the fog-bound sea. "It all looks like that. Why put thyself to the pain of three years at sea and risk thy life whaling, to see more?"

"I've been on five voyages with the merchant navy—" I began.

"Call that going to sea? Merchant navy indeed!"

"And I've heard so much about the whaling, that I've decided to try my hand at it."

He gave me a look which seemed to write me off as a sinner determined to damn myself, then said, "One three-thousandth share of the takings. That's all you get," and turned the ship's register around, for me to sign.

"I have a friend," I said, my pen hovering over the paper.

"What manner of friend? A three-year-three-times-round-the-world kind of friend?" blared Starbuck the mate.

"A harpooner, name of Queequeg. From Kokovoko Island."

I thought he might refuse to have a heathen aboard his ship, but as I looked at the names signed above mine, hardly a one looked American: Tahiti, Manx, Tashtego, Daggoo...

"Islanders make the best whalers," said Starbuck. "Maybe because the whale's a kind of island himself... Let him show his worth, this friend of thine, and he shalt sling his hammock alongside thee," said Starbuck. "We sail on Christmas Day."

So, next day, I was back on the Pequod's quarterdeck carrying my carpet-bag, and with my three-year-three-times-round-the-world kind of friend, Queequeg. The captain was still nowhere to be seen, but a lot more of the crew were in evidence. When they saw Queequeg's black-and-purple peculiarity, they were all set to jeer and scoff. But after Queequeg had thrown one man into the water and dived in to rescue him from drowning, he got more respect.

"You see streak of paint on bollard? That is eye of whale," he said, weighing his harpoon in hand. (It was all we could do to see through the fog as far as the bollard on the dockside.) In a single, sudden, lithe movement, Queequeg raised and threw his harpoon. It hit the bollard with a thud, and vibrated with a single, hollow, eery note. When I ran ashore to fetch it back, I found the harpoon's barb had gouged away the fleck of paint altogether. "That whale pretty much dead now," boasted Queequeg from the bow.

I whistled with admiration. And it was as if my whistle woke the local ghosts, for a pale figure lurched out from between some stacked crates and bales, and came towards me cloaked in fog.

"I am Elijah!" he said, in a wavering howl.

"Good name for a prophet," I said, feeling my face adopt that polite smile people reserve for idiots and madmen. "Are you going to prophesy?"

"Have you seen him yet? Old Thunder?"

"Who?"

"Ahab, of course! The fiend Ahab!"

"Well, no, not yet. The captain's stayed belowdecks, so far. He's not been well, but we hear he'll be better before long."

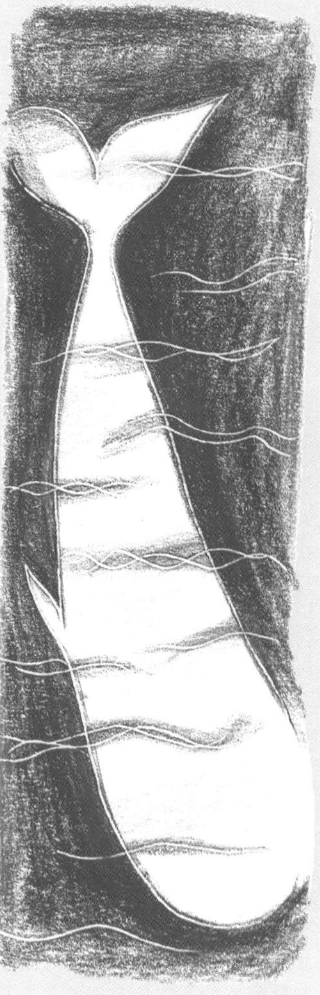

"The day Ahab gets better from what ails him, so shall this arm of mine!" Elijah shook the empty right sleeve of his coat. "Sail not on the devil's business! For verily I say unto you, Ahab is a devil. I sailed with him once, and I know what I know! Is he not named with the name of wickedness? Was King Ahab not the wickedest man in all the Bible, who slew the Lord's prophets and worshipped heathen idols?"

"He can't help what his mother called—"

"Have you not seen the demons he keeps in his ship's hold? His work is Satan's work, and his brain is Satan's brain, and he goeth nowhere but unto Hell! Sail not with Ahab! I sailed with him once, and I know what I know!"

For a moment, my hair stood on end. Then a horse-drawn cart rattling along the wharf drew between us, and when it had passed, Elijah was nowhere to be seen. I hurried back aboard, in time to see Queequeg's name wrongly written into the ship's register: "Quohog" it read. Against it was written "one-seventeenth" – his share of the profits.

On a whaling ship, a good harpooner is more valuable by far than the likes of me.

Chapter 2

The Gold Dubloon

Ships like the Pequod are not owned by one fat tycoon rubbing his soft hands in some New York counting house. Nor are they owned by their captains. Whole towns own them – a plank here, a nail there. Widows and retired sailors, clergymen and chandlers, thrifty shopkeepers and destitute orphanages may all own tiny shares in a single Nantucket whaler. So when it puts out to sea, a whole community of souls watches it go. They watch their investment sail over the horizon, and watch from the hilltops to see it sail home again: their means of survival. A lot was resting on the success of our voyage.

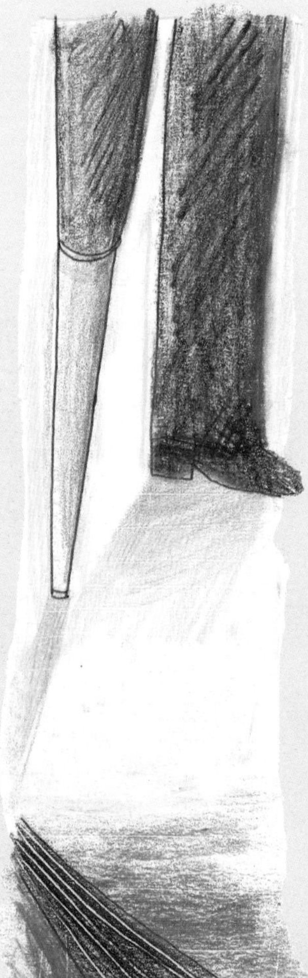

We sailed on Christmas morning, the sun still resting on the morning clouds like Jesus on his manger of straw. And still I had not set eyes on the mysterious Captain Ahab. He kept belowdecks, and the longer he remained invisible, the greater our awe of him grew. His cabin was like some holy shrine where no man entered – nor would have dared to enter, for fear of meeting God.

We heard him, though. At night, swinging in our hammocks, we could hear Ahab walking the deck overhead, up and down, up and down. A soft thud was followed by a sharp crack: a man's foot and then the sharp tap of a peg. For Captain Ahab had only one leg.

I heard Starbuck say to him once, "Wilt thou not rest, captain? Thou wakest the men from sleep with the clatter of thy leg."

The answer came back no louder than the growl of a sleeping bear: "Why should they sleep? Do I sleep? Besides... the sound of my whalebone leg will trample dreams of whales into their sleeping brains, and what business have they to sleep unless it's to dream of whales?"

King Kong

by Anthony Browne, from the story conceived by Edgar Wallace

What the Beast said was quite good sense, though it was not what one might call intelligent conversation. But every day Beauty observed some new kindness in him, and as she became used to seeing him, she also became accustomed to his ugliness.

Beauty and the Beast

Once upon a time in New York city the evening sky was growing dark and a thin veil of snow was falling. The streets were crowded; old men with shopping bags, couples out on dates, people going home from work. The city was a never-ending tide of human beings.

One person seemed to be swimming against that tide. He was Carl Denham, a film director, known as the craziest man in Hollywood. Denham always made his films in distant, dangerous places and rumours were spreading throughout the film world about his next film – it was to be his most ambitious yet.

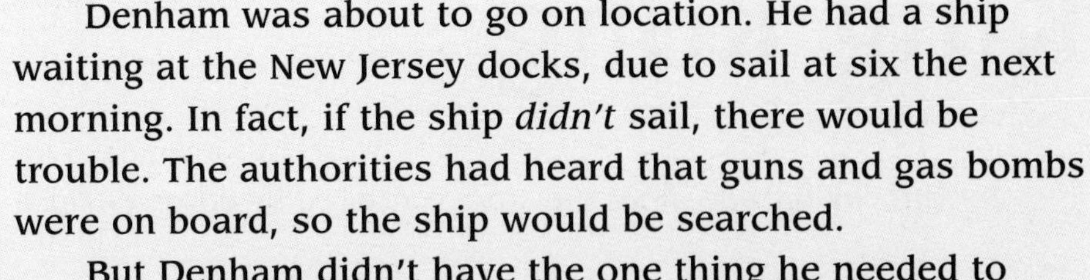

Denham was about to go on location. He had a ship waiting at the New Jersey docks, due to sail at six the next morning. In fact, if the ship *didn't* sail, there would be trouble. The authorities had heard that guns and gas bombs were on board, so the ship would be searched.

But Denham didn't have the one thing he needed to make his film. It was going to be the best picture he'd ever made, but it needed a young, beautiful woman. He'd tried every acting agency in New York, and they had all turned him down. "You take too many risks," they said, "and you won't even tell us where you're going. No actress will take that job."

That was why Denham was walking the streets of New York, looking for the right face for his film, the face of Beauty. He looked into thousands of faces; faces in shops, faces on park benches, faces in cafés, faces in queues. Sad faces, happy faces. But not one of them was the right face, *the* face, for his greatest ever film.

Denham was tired, and there wasn't much time left. He stopped at a store to get something to eat. That was when he saw the hand. It was a very beautiful hand... and it was about to steal an apple.

"Gotcha!" screamed the shopkeeper. "You little thief! I'm callin' the cops!"

"No!" cried the woman. "I didn't take it. Let me go."

"That's true," Denham butted in. "She didn't touch the apples." He gave the shopkeeper a dollar. "Here, take this, and shut up!"

The woman looked up at Denham. "Thanks," she said.

It was only then that Denham saw her face. He was astounded – it was the face he had been searching for!"

It was the face of Beauty.

Half an hour later Denham and the woman were sitting in a café. She had just finished her first proper meal for weeks. She told him that her name was Ann Darrow, she was down on her luck with no money and no job. Denham couldn't stop looking at her. She was a film director's dream – he'd never seen anyone so beautiful.

"Ever done any acting?" he asked.

"I've been an extra over on Long Island a few times. The studio's closed down now."

"I'm Carl Denham," he explained. "Ever heard of me?"

"Y-yes," said Ann. "You make moving pictures. In jungles and places."

"That's me. And *you're* going to star in my next picture. We sail at six!"

Ann gaped at him.

"Don't just sit there, Ann," Denham said. "Come on! We've got to buy you some new clothes and get you to the hairdresser."

The next morning Ann Darrow slowly opened her eyes. What was different?

It was the first morning for a very long time that she had woken up without feeling hungry. Ann saw a bowl of apples next to her bed and remembered what had happened. She was in a cabin, on a ship called the Wanderer. Her room was gently rocking up and down, and the engines hummed under her feet – so they were already on their way.

Then she saw all the boxes – dress boxes, hat boxes and shoe boxes. To someone as poor as Ann they were the most magical sight in the world.

Ann spent over an hour getting ready. She couldn't believe her luck; yesterday she had been dressed in rags, and so hungry that she'd been ready to steal – today she was dressed like a princess, fed like a queen, *and* she had a job! There was just the slight nagging worry that Denham

hadn't said where they were going, but Ann convinced herself that she could trust him... more or less.

She left the cabin and set out to explore the ship. A man was shouting orders at the crew. He was the first mate, Jack Driscoll, and he didn't notice her as one of the sailors dropped a rope. "Don't put it there!" Driscoll yelled. "It goes over here." He swung back his arm and hit Ann in the face.

"What are *you* doing up here?" he asked gruffly.

"I – I just wanted to see..."

"Oh, you must be that girl Denham picked up last night... I should warn you, I don't think much of women on ships. Still, I am sorry I hit you. Hope it didn't hurt."

"Oh, it's okay," said Ann. "I'm sort of used to it."

For Ann the days just glided by; she loved life aboard the Wanderer. The rest, fresh air and good food made her feel like a new woman. Work on the film was going well, she spent hours each day in front of Denham's camera. The director tested her face from every possible angle and found her perfect. Ann was a little concerned that he kept asking her to scream as though she'd seen something terrible, but she was having so much fun that she pushed this disturbing thought to the back of her mind.

Ann and Jack gradually became very close friends. Jack wasn't used to women but he found Ann easy to talk to. As they got to know and like each other, Jack started to worry about what would happen to her when they reached their destination. The ship had already sailed through the Panama Canal, past Hawaii, Japan, the Philippines and Sumatra, and still Denham hadn't told them where they were going. Jack decided it was time to find out, so he went to confront Denham.

"Hey, Denham!" Jack said. "You've got to let us know what's happening. Where are we heading? What crazy plans have you got this time?"

Denham raised an eyebrow. "What's this Jack? You going soft on me?"

"Course I'm not," Driscoll said. "It's Ann..."

"Oh!" said Denham. "You've gone soft on *her*." He frowned. "As if I haven't got enough problems without you falling in love."

"Who said anything about...?" Jack blushed.

"I always thought you were a real tough guy, Jack." Denham went on. "But if Beauty gets you..." He laughed. "It's just like my movie. The Beast is a tough guy, tougher than anyone – he can lick the world. But when he sees Beauty, she gets him. Think about it, Jack."

Driscoll stared angrily at Denham and the director laughed. "Come on, Jack. Let's go see the skipper. It's time I gave you both some answers."

They found Captain Engelhorn in the chart room looking at a map.

"We're *here*, Denham," he said, pointing. "You promised some facts when we got to this spot, so tell me where we're going."

"Southwest," snapped Denham.

"Southwest?" said Engelhorn. "But – there's nothing there!"

"Nothing but *this*!" said Denham. He took a piece of paper out of his pocket. "I got this map from an old Norwegian sea captain. He's a man I trust, not the sort to make up tales, so I know this is real."

"That wall," said Denham, "is higher than twenty men, and hundreds of years old. The natives of the island don't know when the wall was built, or who built it – but they keep it strong, just the same."

"Why?" asked Jack.

"Because there's something on the other side," answered Denham. "Something they fear." He lowered his voice. "Have either of you ever heard of... Kong?"

"Why... yes," Engelhorn replied uneasily. "The Malay people talk about him. Some kind of god or devil, isn't he?"

"A monster," said Denham. "He holds the island in a grip of fear. I'm going to find that beast and put him in my picture!"

Jack gulped. The Beast... Denham's movie was going to be about Beauty and the Beast! The image of Ann Darrow's face came into his mind and Jack Driscoll was suddenly afraid.

A few days later the ship was wrapped in a blanket of fog, and slowed down to a crawl. Denham, Driscoll and Ann were on deck with the captain, impatiently waiting for their first glimpse of the island. From down below came the voice of a sailor measuring the depth of the water. "Thirty fathoms!" he called "Twenty-five fathoms! Twenty fathoms! Ten!"

"We're closing in fast," said Engelhorn. "Driscoll, tell them to drop anchor."

Jack gave the order, and they heard the anchor splash into the ocean. At the same moment they heard another, chilling sound.

"Drums!" said Driscoll.

As they listened, a wind came up and the fog parted like a curtain. There, right in front of them, was the island, less than a quarter of a mile away.

"Skull Mountain!" shouted Denham. "D'you see it? And the wall! Look at that wall!" His eyes were wild with excitement.

"Get out the boats!" he screamed. "Everyone to the island."

Life of the Nation

by John Coldwell

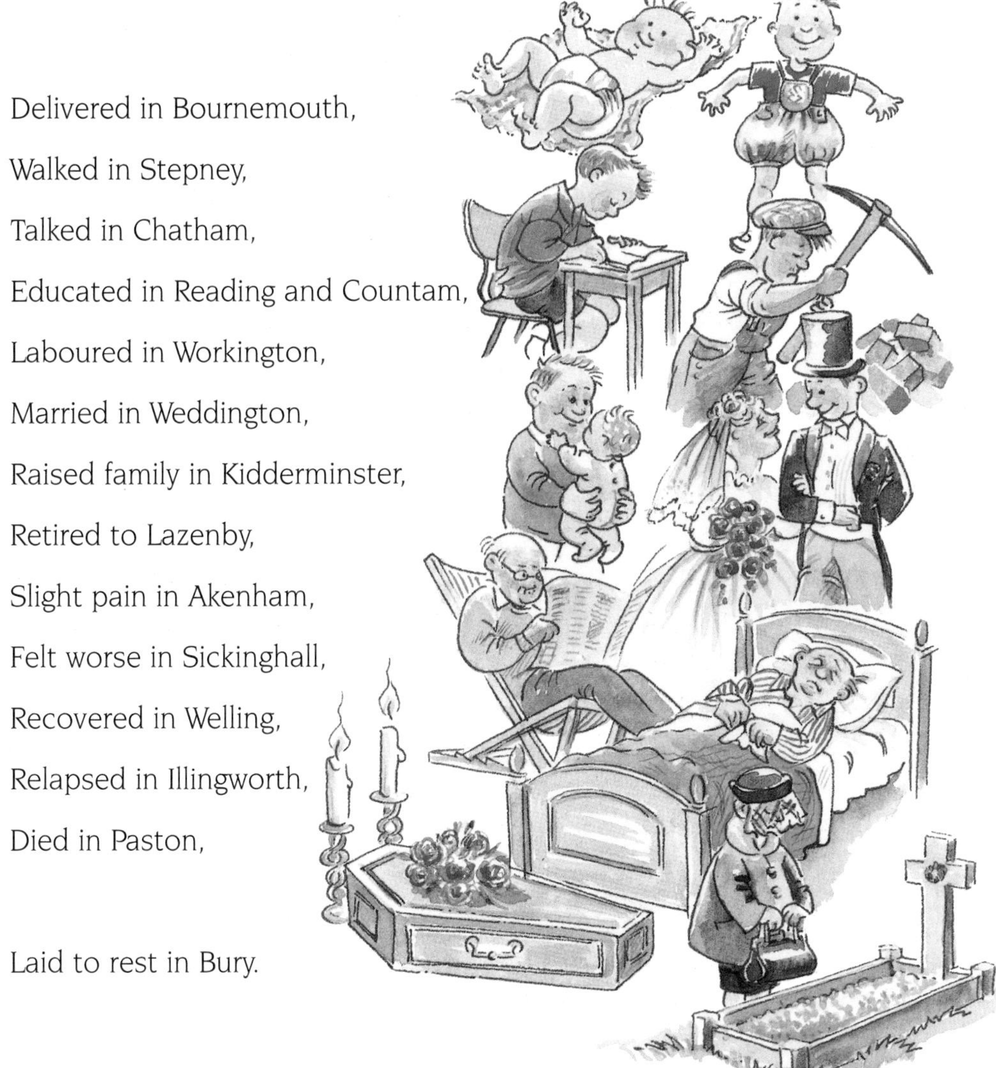

Delivered in Bournemouth,
Walked in Stepney,
Talked in Chatham,
Educated in Reading and Countam,
Laboured in Workington,
Married in Weddington,
Raised family in Kidderminster,
Retired to Lazenby,
Slight pain in Akenham,
Felt worse in Sickinghall,
Recovered in Welling,
Relapsed in Illingworth,
Died in Paston,

Laid to rest in Bury.

National Insurance Contributions
Contributions Agency
Midlands Region

April 29th

Dear Mr Jones,

It has become necessary to discuss with you your National Insurance contributions. We have not received a reply to our letter of March 12th indicating to you the necessity for completing the standard questionnaire. This was sent to you at the end of January. I have to remind you that you are obliged by law to provide the information we requested.

Consequently it is now urgent that you contact us and inform us about your arrangements for completing the official documentation.

Alternatively it is possible for us to visit you on the following dates and times. If these are not convenient, please let us know immediately.

To arrange a convenient time to call, either contact us by:

- telephone,

  or
- filling in Part 4 of this form using block capitals and returning it at the address shown overleaf.

We will need at least five working days notice from the date when you send this form.

Your reply Please fill in the necessary details.	What is the address where we can visit you? Postcode
What date can we visit you?	
What would be a convenient time?	Signature Date

The Planning Department
City Hall
Aberdeen

Dear Mrs Granger

It has been brought to our attention that there are indications of a commercial business being conducted on your premises.

The indications are as follows:

> Significant numbers of people come regularly to your house, and stay for brief periods and then leave.
>
> A range of commercial vehicles regularly stop at your house for the purpose of delivering materials and equipment compatible with a hairdressing business.
>
> We have evidence of advertisements placed by you in the local press and "Hairdressing News" suggesting that you have set up in business as a qualified hairdresser at No 17 Jasmine Avenue, and are seeking paying customers.

We must make it clear that such a business would infringe the terms of your lease, and put you in breach of By-law 193 of the Local Government Act. This sets out unreservedly that all building in your area is residential in nature and the establishment and maintenance of any commercial business is not permitted.

It must also be pointed out that the regular and frequent presence of commercial vehicles outside your house is likely to impede the Public Highway in contravention of By-law 141b (1943) and constitutes an offence.

We accept that there is every possibility that the reports we have received are unfounded. We look forward to your written assurance on this matter.

Should no assurance by received from you within two weeks of the receipt of this letter then an inspector from this Department will make a formal inspection of your house.

In replying to this letter please contact Mr J Driver at the above address.

Yours sincerely

K Ainsworth

Chief Planning Officer

Truckers

by Terry Pratchett

Part 1

The sky rained dismal. It rained humdrum. It rained the kind of rain that is so much wetter than normal rain, the kind of rain that comes down in big drops and splats, the kind of rain that is merely an upright sea with slots in it.

It rained a tattoo on the old hamburger boxes and chip papers in the wire basket that was giving Masklin a temporary hiding place.

Look at him. Wet. Cold. Extremely worried. And four inches high.

The waste-bin was usually a good hunting ground, even in winter. There were often a few cold chips in their wrapping, sometimes even a chicken bone. Once or twice there had been a rat, too. It had been a really good day when there had last been a rat – it had kept him going for a week. The trouble was that you could get pretty fed up with rat by the third day. By the third mouthful, come to that.

Masklin scanned the lorry park.

And here it came, right on time, crashing through the puddles and pulling up with a hiss of brakes.

He'd watched this lorry arrive every Tuesday and Thursday morning for the last four weeks. He timed the driver's stop carefully.

They had exactly three minutes. To someone the size of a nome, that's more than half an hour.

He scrambled down through the greasy paper, dropped out

of the bottom of the bin, and ran for the bushes at the edge of the part where Grimma and the old folk were waiting.

"It's here!" he said, "Come on!"

Part 2

It had been a dreadful summer. Grimma organised those who could still get about into midnight raids on the litter-bins, and Masklin tried to hunt.

Hunting by yourself was like dying a bit at a time. Most of the things you were hunting were also hunting *you*. And even if you were lucky and made a kill, how did you get it home? It had taken two days with the rat, including sitting out at night to fight off other creatures. Ten strong hunters could do anything – rob bees' nests, trap mice, catch moles, *anything* – but one hunter by himself, with no one to watch his back in the long grass, was simply the next meal for everything with talons and claws.

To get enough to eat, you needed lots of healthy hunters. But to get lots of healthy hunters, you needed enough to eat.

The Ministry of Defence
Section 3. Area 9
Oakleigh
Shirehampton

To the Town Council, Oakleigh

Recent events in relation to the area of land commonly known as "The Small Moor" on the outskirts of the town have persuaded us to address you formally, both as a plea and a warning. The letter is written in the interests of the health and safety of all the residents of the town and surrounding countryside.

You will be aware from newspaper coverage that "The Small Moor" has recently been subjected to a series of break-ins by groups of people for the purpose of picnicking, parties and general expeditions and exploration. We wish to make it clear that apart from damage to fences, little harm has been done otherwise.

This letter is therefore not so much a complaint as an attempt to protect the public from its own actions.

The land, fenced off from the open common known as "The Big Moor," is the <u>sole</u> property of the Ministry of Defence.

Members of Her Majesty's armed forces regularly <u>conduct manoeuvres</u> and training exercises over the territory. Large <u>vehicles</u>, including tanks and heavy guns, are used in these operations. <u>Live</u> ammunition is used on occasions.

It will be clear from these facts that the area represents <u>serious potential danger</u> to people, and especially children, who enter there without permission or authority.

We appeal urgently, therefore, to all the <u>inhabitants</u> of the region to avoid "The Small Moor" at all times and at all costs. There is <u>ample</u> attractive open ground, on "The Big Moor" for example, to provide for the public's <u>recreation</u>. We are confident that most people will <u>respond positively</u> to our appeal.

We must, however, <u>formally</u> warn the public, through you, the Town Council, that we shall <u>be obliged</u> to deal rapidly and firmly with those who continue to <u>trespass</u> on this <u>prohibited</u> land. They will be <u>apprehended</u>, <u>detained</u> and handed over to the local police. We must stress that such an action would be taken <u>reluctantly</u>, but <u>resolutely</u>, in the best interests of all.

We thank you for your attention in this matter. We have no doubt your <u>concern matches ours</u>.

Yours faithfully

Brigadier Hammer

Officer commanding Section 3. Area 9

P.S. On a lighter and more <u>informal</u> note, we enclose details of our Grand Open Day and Military <u>Tattoo</u>, when <u>everyone</u> is invited for a marvellous FREE day of fun, <u>hospitality</u> and adventure.

See the side of the Army we like to show: **happy and welcoming**.

Self-certificate

And Sickness and Invalidity Benefit Claim form

SC1

SPECIMEN

1 About you

PLEASE USE BLOCK LETTERS

If you cannot fill this form in yourself, ask someone else to do so and to sign it for you

Surname: Mr/Mrs/Miss/Ms
First names
Present address
Postcode

Date of birth

National Insurance number

CLOCK/STAFF/WORKS NUMBER

2 Details of sickness

Give details of your sickness. Words like 'illness' or 'unwell' are not enough

PLEASE USE BLOCK LETTERS

If you cannot fill this form in yourself, ask someone else to do so and to sign it for you

Please say briefly why you are unfit for work

- Is your sickness due to an accident which happened while you were working for an employer?

Tick one box YES ☐ NO ☐

- Is your sickness due to a prescribed industrial disease caused by conditions at work, while you were working for an employer?

Tick one box YES ☐ NO ☐

NOTE: This does not apply if the accident or prescribed disease occurred while you were self-employed.

FORM SCI (1988)

SPECIMEN

3 Period of sickness

If you do not fill in this section or if you fill it in wrongly, any payment of benefit due to you may be delayed.

Everyone to fill in	Date you became unfit for work	day			19
Do not complete if you are unemployed	Date you last worked	day			19
	Time you finished work	time am/pm			
Night shift workers only	When did your shift begin — time am/pm	day			19
Everyone to fill in	Do you expect to be unfit for work for more than 7 days? YES ☐ NO ☐ If you ticked 'YES', go to part 5				

4 Returning to work

			date	month	year
	Last day of sickness before starting or seeking work	day			19
	Date you intend to start or seek work	day			19
Night shift workers only	Shift will begin at time am/pm	and end next day at time am/pm			

5 If you are claiming Sickness or Invalidity Benefit

Go to part 6 'Your work' — do not sign below

If you are using this form for Statutory Sick Pay

Stop here. Sign below, and send this form to your employer

Signature Date

Remember, if you are sick for a second week, your employer may want a sick note.

6 Your work

Are you?:-

Tick one or more boxes

Employed ☐ Unemployed ☐ A student ☐
Self employed ☐ Other ☐

What is your usual job?

Please turn over the page

7 Your employer and SSP

Before your present illness began, have you in the last 8 weeks been off work sick for at least 4 days in a row?

Tick one box YES ☐ NO ☐

If you ticked '<u>YES</u>', please give the name and address of the employer you were working for.

8 Your doctor

Doctor's name and address

9 In hospital

Have you been a hospital in-patient since you became unfit for work?

Tick one box YES ☐ NO ☐

If you ticked '<u>YES</u>', please state the name and address of the hospital

10 You and your family

Phone number where we can ring you during the day ☐

Tick one box Are you? single ☐ married ☐ widowed ☐ divorced ☐

You can claim extra benefit for your spouse or a person looking after children.

- A SEPARATE CLAIM MUST BE MADE. If you want a claim form sent to you, tick the box or boxes below:–

SPOUSE ☐, PERSON LOOKING AFTER CHILDREN ☐,

CHILDREN ☐ (see the '**NOTE**' below).

NOTE: You can only claim extra money for children if you are a man over 65 or a woman over 60 or if you are claiming Invalidity Benefit.

SPECIMEN

11 Other benefits

- **Tick any benefits that you are getting or that you have already claimed.**

Tick one or more boxes

Income Support	☐	Unemployability Supplement	☐
War Widow's Pension	☐	Job Release Allowance	☐
Youth Training Scheme Allowance	☐	Invalid Care Allowance	☐
Enterprise Allowance	☐		

- **Are you getting any other Social Security benefit, pension or allowance or waiting to hear the result of a claim for one.**

Tick one box   YES ☐   NO ☐

If YES, state which

- **Is anyone getting extra benefit for you as a dependant?** NOTE: Also tick 'YES' if they are waiting for the result of a claim for extra benefit.

Tick one box   YES ☐   NO ☐   If 'YES' please state:

His/her name

Address

Postcode

Name of benefit

- **Have you received any money for training or rehabilitation in the past 8 weeks?**

Tick one box   YES ☐   NO ☐

If 'YES', where was it from?

12 Declaration

Remember: if you knowingly give wrong or false information you may be prosecuted.

I declare that I have not worked during the period of sickness which I have stated and that the infromation given is correct and complete.

I claim benefit

I agree to my doctor giving medical information relevant to my claim to a doctor in the Regional Medical Service

Signature   Date

If you have signed on behalf of the person claiming, tick the box ☐

Send the form immediately to your local Social Security office to avoid losing any benefit

TOWN & COUNTRY PLANNING ACT 1990

NOTICE OF PUBLIC INQUIRY
At THE COUNCIL CHAMBER, COUNTY HALL, OXFORD
REASON FOR INQUIRY

Appeal by DOLTON & SONS LTD
Relating to the application to the Cherwell District Council for

DEMOLITION OF SITE BUILDINGS AND ERECTION OF 4,000 sq m OF B1 OFFICE BUILDING WITH CAR PARKING FOR 130 SPACES, LANDSCAPING AND ALTERATIONS TO ACCESS.

AT THE GRAIN SILO, GOSFORD, KIDLINGTON

An Inspector instructed by the Secretary of State for the Environment, Transport and the Regions will attend at the place, date and time shown above to hear the appeal, and will also consider two planning applications, called-in by the Secretary of State, for park and ride facilities.

Members of the public may attend the inquiry and, at the discretion of the Inspector, express their views. If you, or anyone you know is disabled and is concerned about facilities at the inquiry venue, you are advised to write to, or contact the council to confirm that suitable provisions are in place.

Planning Inspectorate Reference:
APP/C3105/A/98/291530
Government Office References:
GOSE/103/003/OXON/001,
GOSE/103/003/OXFO/003
Contact point at the Planning Inspectorate:
Mrs A Edmonds, Room 12/22, Tollgate House, Houlton Street, Bristol. Tel: 0117 987 8858.

150685

Excerpt from a contract between an author and a publisher

11. Copyright

11.1 The copyright notice in the Work shall remain the property of the Author and the copyright notice to be printed in every copy of the Work shall be in the Author's name, with the first year of publication together with, where appropriate, an acknowledgement of the cover or jacket designer's copyright

11.2 If the Publisher considers that the copyright in the Work has been or is likely to be infringed it shall on giving notice to the Author be at liberty to take such steps as it may consider necessary for dealing with the matter and if the Publisher shall desire to take proceedings it shall, on giving the Author an undertaking to pay all costs and expenses and to indemnify the Author against all liability for costs, be entitled to use the Author's name as a party to such proceedings but to control settle or compromise the same as the Publisher deems fit. Any profit or damages which may be received in respect of any infringement of the copyright shall after deduction of all costs and expenses be divided equally between the Author and the Publisher

11.3 The Author undertakes to do any and all acts and execute any and all documents in such manner and at such locations as may be required by the Publisher in its sole discretion in order to protect perfect or enforce the Author's copyright or any of the Subsidiary Rights or any of the other rights granted to the Publisher pursuant to this Agreement

12. Moral Rights

12.1 The Author hereby asserts the moral right to be identified as the author of the Work in relation to the Publication Rights and the Subsidiary Rights. The Publisher hereby undertakes:

12.1.1 to print on the reverse of the title page of every copy of every edition of the Work published by the Publisher in the United Kingdom the words "the right of [the Author] to be identified as the author of this work has been asserted by him/her in accordance with the Copyright, Designs and Patents Act 1988"

12.1.2 to make it a condition of contract with any licensee concerning any edition of the Work to be published in the United Kingdom that a notice of assertion in the same terms as above shall be printed in every edition published by such licensee

12.1.3 to set the name of the Author in its customary form with due prominence on the title page of every copy of the work published by the Publisher and to make it a condition of contract that a similar undertaking is made in respect to any editions of the Work licensed by the Publisher

12.2 The Author acknowledges that no casual or inadvertent failure by the Publisher or by any third party to comply with this provision shall constitute a breach by the Publisher of this Agreement or the Author's rights and in the event of any breach of this Clause 12 the Author shall not have the right to seek injunctive relief and the sole remedy of the Author shall be a claim for damages

12.3 The assertion by the Author of his moral rights and the obligations of the Publisher pursuant to this Clause are without prejudice to the rights granted to the Publisher by Clause 8.2

The Ghost Train

Sydney J. Bounds

Billy Trent ran down the lane towards the common, sandy hair poking like straws from under his cap, eyes gleaming with excitement. The common blazed with coloured lights, post-box red and dandelion yellow and neon blue. The evening air throbbed with the sound of fairground music and his pulse beat in rhythm.

He reached the entrance and passed beneath a banner that read:

BIGGEST TRAVELLING FAIR IN BRITAIN!

A jolly, red-faced man dressed as a clown called to him. "On your own, son? Enjoy all the fun of the fair."

Billy nodded eagerly, too excited to speak, for the fair came only once a year and he'd saved hard for the occasion. Almost a pound's worth of change clutched tight in his pocket, he darted between the coconut shy and a hamburger stand, chair-o-planes and swing-boats. He paused, fascinated, in front of the merry-go-round with its pairs of magnificent horses going round and round and up and down. He stared up in awe at the big Ferris Wheel revolving in the sky, trying to make up his mind which to try first.

There were dodgem cars, and a snaky switchback ride. Music played, fireworks exploded in cascading showers of light. The smell of candy floss tempted him. For Billy it was the best night of the year, until...

In a shadowy empty space behind the fortune teller's tent, he found himself between two youths dressed in jeans and leather jackets studded with stars.

The big one with the scarred face gripped Billy's arm: "Hi, kid, we'll give you a break – you can pal up with us tonight. It's more fun sharing things. I'm Ed, and my mate here answers to Higgy."

Higgy, fat and pimply, sniggered in a way that gave Billy gooseflesh. "Hi, pal, glad to meet yuh. Ed and me's broke, and that ain't much fun, so I hope you've got plenty of cash. We're all pals together, see?"

Billy shook his head, mute. He had a sinking feeling in his stomach and his hand tightened round the coins in his pocket as he stared up at the two older boys. He decided he didn't like either of them.

Ed's big hand tightened on his arm till it throbbed with pain. "Now come on, share the loot – reckon we'll all go on the dodgems first, okay?"

Billy gasped desperately. "You're hurting me. All right, I'll pay for you to have one ride, if you promise to leave me alone after that."

Big Ed laughed meanly. "That's no way for a pal to talk. Share everything, that's our motto, ain't it, Higgy?"

"You bet. Now then, kid, hand it over."

As Billy slowly brought his hand from his pocket, Ed relaxed a fraction, grinning at Higgy. Instantly Billy twisted like an eel, slipped from Ed's grasp and ran off as hard as he could go.

"Little perisher," Ed shouted angrily. "Just wait till I get my hands on 'im – I'll break 'is flaming neck!" With Higgy at his heels, he gave chase.

Billy pushed his way into the fairground crowd, panting, looking for someone – anyone – he knew. But they were all strangers, intent on enjoying themselves and oblivious to his trouble. The music blared loudly and bright coloured lights flashed.

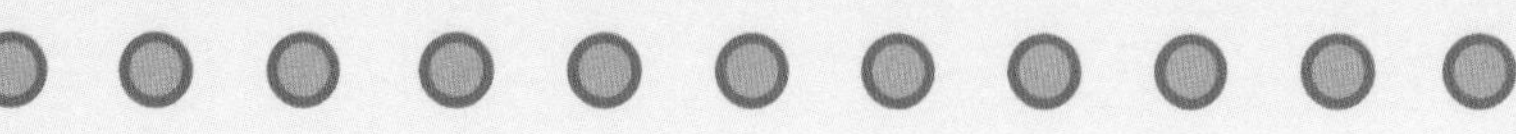

Billy glanced back; the two youths were still after him, and Ed's scarred face looked savage. He ran behind a wooden hoarding and found himself trapped between the Wall of Death and the switchback ride. It was dark and he could see no way out. The roar of motor–cycle engines was deafening; even if he shouted, no-one would hear. He hunted for somewhere to hide as Ed and Higgy turned the corner and spotted him.

Dim blue lights spelled out:

GHOST TRAIN

Billy could just make out the shape of the miniature steam engine with six open carriages in the gloom. The carriages were empty. There seemed to be no-one about, not even at the pay desk.

As the train began to move towards the dark mouth of the entrance tunnel, Billy ran forward and sprang into the carriage nearest the engine. He crouched low, but...

"There he is!" Ed shouted, pointing. Higgy right behind him, he put on a spurt and they reached the train in time to scramble aboard the last carriage.

The Ghost Train gathered speed as it rumbled into the tunnel. In the darkness, Billy gulped as he looked up to see the luminous skeleton-figure of the engine driver grinning back at him. But he was too scared of his pursuers to be really frightened.

Then Ed and Higgy started to climb over the empty carriages towards him.

The track wound and the carriages swayed and rattled. Cobwebs brushed Billy's face. An eerie green glow illuminated the tunnel and a tombstone beside the track; the stone lifted and a cowled figure rose with a dreadful wail.

It was night-black again and a woman's scream echoed. In a phosphorescent glow, a headless phantom stalked towards the engine, vanished. Chains clanked and something evil-smelling dripped from the roof. A bat-thing swooped, hissing.

The dark came again. Then a lightning flash revealed a fanged monster.

The train rattled on through the blackness. A red glow from a fire showed three witches stooped over a cauldron; as the train passed, the nearest lifted her death's-head and cackled with laughter.

Suddenly Billy was aware that the two bullies were no longer interested in him. The skeleton-driver of the Ghost Train had left his engine and was moving steadily back along the carriages towards them. Ed's face had lost its savage look. Higgy's eyes no longer gleamed with malice.

As a bony arm extended, skeletal finger pointing, they backed away. Empty eye-sockets stared sightlessly at them, jaws gaped in a toothless snarl. A hollow voice intoned: "Beware!" And, scared stiff, Ed and Higgy scrambled back to the last carriage.

The ride ended and Billy got away smartly. As he mingled with the crowd, he saw Ed and Higgy – their faces as white as chalk – hurrying towards the exit. They'd had enough.

Billy looked again for the Ghost Train, but he could not find it now.

Left alone, he enjoyed all the fun of the fair. He went on one ride after another until he'd spent his money. He was very happy as he turned to go home.

On his way out, the clown called to him again. "What did you like best, son?"

Bill Trent paused and thought. "The Ghost Train," he said.

The clown's jolly red face paled. "But there's no Ghost Train

now! Used to be one, with Old Tom driving, dressed all in black with a skeleton painted on. Then one day a youngster fell off the train and Tom dived after him. Killed he was, saving the lad. After the accident, the boss scrapped it – so you must have dreamed that."

But Billy was quite sure he hadn't.

Papa Panov

adapted by Leo Tolstoy from the original by Reuben Saillens, re-told by Anne Isles

Papa Panov is a well-loved figure in his village, but none of his family is near and Christmas on your own can be a very lonely time. As Papa Panov prepares for Christmas, he receives a very special promise, but things don't turn out quite as he expected they would...

This traditional story, based around the story of the Nativity, the birth of the Christ child, was first told in the French version by Reuben Saillens, but was most famously re-told by Leo Tolstoy.

Chapter 1

Many years ago, and many miles away, in a small village in Russia, the light of Christmas Eve was beginning to fade. Papa Panov began to clear away the leather and nails which filled his shoemaker's shop. Christmas was here and it was time to stop work.

As he cleared up, Papa Panov smiled gently, remembering Christmases from years ago. He thought of the toys he had secretly carved and painted for his children in the evenings. He remembered his wife carefully wrapping the toys; tying up the parcels with colourful pieces of wool. He remembered the joy reflected in his wife's eyes as she watched their young children open their presents, full of excitement, their voices full of laughter.

Papa Panov turned back to his workbench sadly. He still loved Christmas time, but now he had no one to share it with. His wife had died several years ago, and now his children were grown up and lived far away with their own families. All he had to look forward to was a day full of memories.

Chapter 2

But it was not like Papa Panov to feel sorry for himself. That was probably why people liked him so much. He always had a smile for his neighbours in the little village. Papa Panov had always missed his children once they had grown up and moved away. He still made little toys out of the scraps of leather that were left over from making shoes and gave them away to the village children. This is how he got the nickname "Papa" Panov.

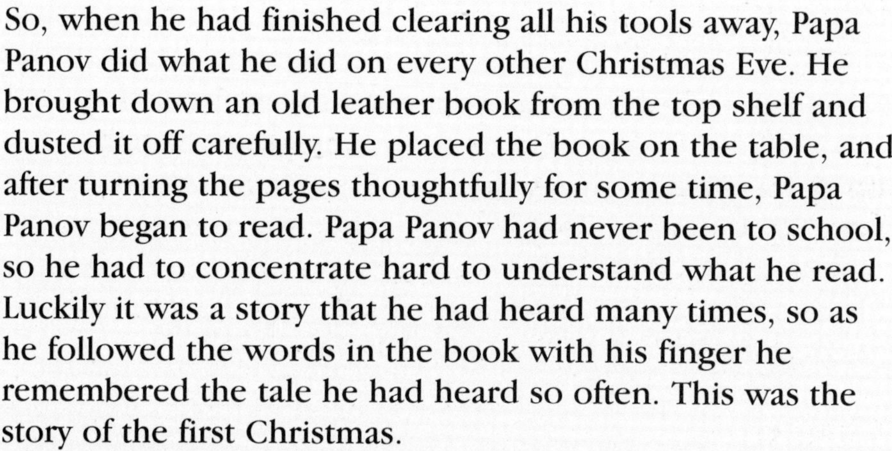

Chapter 3

So, when he had finished clearing all his tools away, Papa Panov did what he did on every other Christmas Eve. He brought down an old leather book from the top shelf and dusted it off carefully. He placed the book on the table, and after turning the pages thoughtfully for some time, Papa Panov began to read. Papa Panov had never been to school, so he had to concentrate hard to understand what he read. Luckily it was a story that he had heard many times, so as he followed the words in the book with his finger he remembered the tale he had heard so often. This was the story of the first Christmas.

Chapter 4

He read about Mary and Joseph struggling to get to Bethlehem on a donkey. He read how they searched the town for somewhere to stay, but could only find a stable. Papa Panov looked around his room; it wasn't much but it was comfortable. He had his stove to keep him warm; a comfortable bed with a faded patchwork quilt which his dear wife had made; a chair to sit in and a table to eat at. All in all, Papa Panov thought as he looked around him, I am very lucky. As the light of his candle flickered, Papa Panov read on. He read about the visitors who had come to see the baby Jesus; the wise men who had been watching the star. Papa Panov thought about the gifts that these visitors had brought and sighed. The wise men had brought expensive gifts, the sort he could never afford to give. He looked around his little room again, and then got up and started searching through one of his cupboards. At last he found what he was looking for; a faded box, which contained the most beautiful little pair of shoes, you can imagine. He had worked for hours to make those shoes. They were made of the softest leather and were covered in the most intricate patterns that Papa Panov's old fingers had been able to fashion. He had made these shoes for his first grandchild, but his family lived so far away that he had never been able to give them the gift, and now his grandchild was too big to wear them.

"Yes, that is what I would give to the baby Jesus" he found himself saying. Carefully he wrapped the shoes up again. By now it was late, and Papa Panov's eyes were beginning to close. The crackling fire was warm and his chair comfortable, and as he sat there with his thoughts and memories, gradually he fell asleep. "I am so lucky," he murmured to himself.

Chapter 5

Papa Panov had been sleeping for some time, when suddenly he heard a voice.

"Papa Panov!" The voice was clear and strong. "Papa Panov!"

Papa Panov fumbled around the table for his glasses. The candle had burnt down low and he could see nothing. "Papa Panov, I know that you are lonely, and I know that you wished to see me today, and I know the present that you wanted to give me. I will come to see you, but be sure you look out for me, for I will not say who I am." Papa Panov struggled to put on his glasses, but as he peered around the room, he could see no one.

That was Jesus - he thought, and a little shiver ran up and down his spine - that was Jesus! I may not have a family coming to visit me for Christmas, but Jesus himself is coming to visit me! Papa Panov was so excited he began to clean and tidy his little room all over again. He polished the coffee pot, he smoothed down the quilt and looked at his larder with some concern. Would he have enough food to share with his very special guest? However, he seemed to remember that his guest had a knack for providing food and drink.

Chapter 6

Somehow night turned into morning, and the Christmas bells began to ring out. Papa Panov stood at his window holding his mug of coffee tightly. He couldn't stop his mind from racing. What would his guest look like? A man from Palestine would look very obvious in the middle of a Russian winter, but what had Jesus said? "Be sure to look out for me, for I will not say who I am". Papa Panov stared out of the window again. What was that? In the distance Papa Panov saw the figure of a man beginning to appear. Papa Panov cleared the frost from the window in front of him with impatience. A man, all alone, this had to be Jesus. But as the figure came into view Papa Panov realised with disappointment that this was just the old road sweeper, who made his way around all the local villages. Like Papa Panov he had no family, so for him today was much like any other day.

Papa Panov sighed with irritation, but as he watched the icy wind blowing the snow in little flurries, and saw how the road sweeper shivered, he thought of the pot of coffee on the stove. I am lucky, he thought, and somewhat reluctantly he opened the shop door and called out to the roadsweeper. Jesus would be along soon, but in the mean time, he could share a little coffee with the old road sweeper.

The road sweeper stamped the snow off his worn old shoes in Papa Panov's doorway and eagerly welcomed a cup of coffee. As he stood by the stove and warmed himself, his face glowed and melted into a smile. Papa Panov looked at the little pools of melted snow on the floor around the road sweeper and thought of how he had cleaned up his room for Jesus, but there wasn't much point in being cross, it was Christmas after all. Having warmed himself with the coffee the roadsweeper was soon on his way again.

Papa Panov once more stood at his window looking and waiting. As he looked the children began to play on the frozen cobbles outside his shop on their way to church. There too was Nicolai who baked the bread, there was Nicolai's wife Natasha. He saw the old people and the young people, the rich and the poor. In fact he saw everyone. He waved and shouted "Happy Christmas" to them all - but where was his special visitor?

Death's Murderers

from "The Pardoner's Tale" (*The Canterbury Tales*)

by Geoffrey Chaucer, retold by Geraldine McCaughrean

The man Snatch was slumped over a table at the Tabard Inn in Southwark – (you may know the place). He had wetted his brain in beer, and it weighed heavy. The clanging of the church bell registered dully in his ears. "Who are they burying?" he asked.

Old Harry, the landlord, who was wiping tables close by, said, "Don't you know? I wondered why you weren't at the funeral – him being a friend of yours. It's Colley the Fence. Caught it last Wednesday and gone today. Him and his wife and his two boys."

"Caught what?" demanded Snatch, grasping Harry's arm.

"The Black Death, of course!"

Then another customer chimed in. "Ay, they do say the Plague came to Combleton over yonder, and Death laid hands on every man, woman and child and carried 'em off."

"Where? Carried them off where?" demanded Snatch, fighting his way through drink-haze like a ghost through cobwebs.

"Who knows where Death carries men off to," said a deeply hooded character sitting in the corner of the bar, "but he sure enough comes for every man in the end. And he's taken twice his share recently, thanks to the Plague."

Tears of indignation started into Snatch's eyes. "I don't see what gives Death the right to go carrying off anyone!" he slurred. "And if you ask me, it's about time some brave soul stood up to Death and put an end to his carryings-on – his carryings-off I mean. Dip! Cut! Where are you?" And he stumbled off into the sunlight to look for his two closest friends.

Dip was at home in bed, but not for long. Snatch knocked him up and called him into the street. They met with Cut coming home from a card-game and cursing his empty pockets.

Snatch threw an arm over each friend's shoulder. "Have you heard? Old Colley the Fence is dead. Death carried off him and all his family in a couple of days. Let's take an oath, friends, not to rest until we've tracked down this 'Death' fellow and stuck a knife between his ribs. Think what the mayor and parish would pay if we brought in Death's dead body. Besides – how many purses do you think he's emptied on the dark highway, eh? Death must have made himself quite a walletful by now."

Cut fingered his sharp penknife – the one he used for cutting purposes. Dip felt his fingers itch at the promise of rich pickings. "We're with you, neighbour Snatch!" they cried, and off they reeled, not the sum total of one brain between the three of them.

They looked for Death in the graveyard, but decided he must be out hunting the living instead. They looked for Death in the fields, but he had always gone before they arrived, leaving the flowers doomed to wither and the leaves, sooner or later, to fall.

Then, as the daylight failed, they saw a small figure on the road ahead. "We've caught him up!" cried Snatch, and they fell on the man, with flailing fists.

"Wait a minute! This isn't Death at all!" said Cut, letting his penknife fall. "He's just some silly old duffer. Look at him – he's older than Methuselah!"

The old man peered at them out of the dark recesses of his hood. His face was as white and bony as a skull, with purse-string lips and eyes sunk deep in red whorls of wrinkled skin. His hands were as brown as vinegar-paper, and his back hunched over like a turtle's shell. "What do you want with me? Don't I have enough to put up with? Can't you leave a poor blighted old creature in peace?"

"You're no good to us!" Dip said in disgust. "We wanted Death, not some wrinkled old prune on legs!"

A bitter laugh creaked out through the creature's gappy ribs. "*You* want Death! Ah, not half as much as I do! I'm the one poor beast alive that Death can't carry off. I'm condemned to live for ever and to creep about the Earth in this worn-out old body, getting older and older and older. As for Death – I've just left him under that oak tree yonder. If you hurry, you'll find him still there."

Cut's knife was raised again. "So! You've had dealings with him. We'll kill you anyway!"

The fossil of a man let go a sigh that seemed to break through his brittle skin. "Aaah, I wish you could rob me of this tedious burden, Life. You should pity me, even if you have no respect for my old age. But don't bother to batter on this prison my soul calls a body: you can't free me from it." He shuffled out from under their raised blades, muttering, "You're the lucky ones – you might die today!"

"Get to bed with the maggots and mould, you old relic of the Devil," Snatch cursed. "We're on our way to kill Death. Then no one will have to die any more!" As soon as the old man was out of sight, the three accomplices forgot him completely.

Under the oak tree, there was no sign of Death. But there was a pot of money as big as any crock of gold at the rainbow's end.

Cut tipped the jar over with his foot, and the wealth of seven life-times spilled out on to the grass. They looked around. No one was even in sight. And there had been no attempt to hide the gold. It lay there, just inviting them to keep it. Snatch and Dip and Cut were suddenly rich!

"Rich! We're rich, rich, rich!" As the gold coins spilled out of the jar, so all thought of their plot to kill Death dropped out of their minds.

"Dip, your legs are youngest," said Snatch. "Run into town and fetch us some wine. We've got to celebrate luck like this!"

"Why is it always me?" Dip threw a sulky look at the gold but was given only one coin to buy the makings of a party.

"We'll both stay and guard it, don't you worry," Snatch assured him. "Be quick, lad. When you get back we'll decide what we're to do with it all – what mansions we'll build, who to bribe, what monks we'll pay to have done in. We don't have to do our own dirty work from now on, boy! We'll be the Three Kings of the Footpads."

Full of such thoughts, Dip set off into the dusk to buy cakes and wine. The sun was behind him, and his shadow stretched long and spidery ahead, so that he was all the time stepping into his own darkness.

Snatch and Cut watched him

go, then sat down on either side of the pot of gold. They counted the coins. Somehow it always came to a different number: 848 or 916 or 772. Snatch scowled. "Of course you realise we can't divide it three ways."

"We can't?"

"You take my word for it. It won't share out evenly."

"It won't?"

"Two ways, yes. Not three. One of us will have to take less."

"Oh!"

Cut decided at once that since Dip was the youngest, he should take the smallest share. They both nodded to themselves and settled back to counting the gold. This time there seemed to be 999 – or 783, or perhaps 870. But it did not change the opinion that Dip should have less.

"Of course it won't go far between the *three* of us," Snatch mused. "Not with the cost of living how it is. And you know how Dip squanders money."

"No?"

"He'll soon have spent all his, and he'll be asking to borrow from us."

"But I can't spare any of mine!" said Cut anxiously.

"No more can I. There's little enough to share out between two, let alone three." They lapsed into silence, and above them the oak's heavy branches groaned while the gold coins clinked between their fingers. "Supposing..." said Cut, "just supposing Dip was to meet with an accident on his way back from town..."

"So many footpads these days..." said Snatch nodding sadly. "So many ruffians and murderers."

Meanwhile, Dip was watching his shadow move ahead of him on the roadway like a black plough. How big it was – much bigger than him. When he had his share of the money, he would be a bigger man in every way. No more creeping through the crowds at fairs, cutting purses and catching the pennies that dropped. He could walk tall and stately, in fur-trimmed robes, and people would touch their forelocks and step aside. Beggars would fight for the chance to plead with him. And if he felt like it, he could drive them away with a pelting of money, and see them grovel in his wake. Ah, but if he was going to start giving money away, there would be less for the true necessities – drink and women and gambling. In fact he could think of so many good uses for the gold that it seemed a pity Cut and Snatch had been with him when he had found the jar. Really, the more he thought about it, the less fair it seemed that they had bunked in on his good fortune.

As he reached the outskirts of the town, he noticed an apothecary's sign hanging over a door. He did not remember ever having seen it before, but he knocked without hesitation.

"What's your trouble, young man, that you rouse me from my bed?" An ancient, hairless head poked out of an upstairs window, grotesque and vaguely familiar with its parchment-yellow shine.

"Rats," said Dip, his head muffled up in his cloak. "The rats are eating me out of house and home."

"Here. One drop of this will finish them off. Have it for free." The ancient apothecary must have had the poison in his pocket, for he dropped it down at once, into Dip's outstretched hands. "It couldn't be simpler," he called as the boy hurried off to the inn.

Dip bought three bottles of wine. Every last drop of the poison went into two of the bottles. The third he marked carefully to be sure of telling it apart. Then he was off to collect his rightful share of the golden hoard – every last coin of it.

In the pitch dark of late evening, he stumbled over Cut and Snatch snoozing under the oak tree in the deep grass. "Thought you'd forgotten us," said Snatch with a sort of grin.

"I wouldn't forget my two old friends, now would I?" Dip opened his bottle of wine and took a swig. "Have a drink, why don't you?" Cut and Snatch knelt up and groped for the wine, their hands brushing Dip's face in the dark. They moved to either side of their good friend...

Along the road came the sudden noise of the plague cart rattling out of the town towards the lime pits in Ring-a-Rosey Hollow. They all three watched its creaking progress beneath the light of the coachmen's torches. Its white cargo of dead bodies joggled against one another like restless sleepers. A limp arm dangling through the cart rails swung to and fro, for all the world as if it was beckoning them...

"We took an oath to kill old Death," said Cut, remembering.

"We'll get round to it some time," said Snatch, drawing his dagger. "One thing at a time."

He plunged the knife into the back of Dip's neck. It met with the seam of his hood, and the lad looked round in astonishment in time to make out the shape of Cut, outlined against the moon. Then Cut's sharp penknife caught him under the ribs and he sprawled, cursing, to his death, among the gnarled roots of the oak tree.

"It's done," Snatch panted, and his throat felt suddenly dry. "Let's drink to our partnership, Cut. Where did he put the bottles?"

By feeling along the ground, they found the three bottles in the long grass. The opened one had emptied itself into the ground, but the others were intact. A bottle apiece, Cut and Snatch sat with their backs to the oak tree, and drank to their new-found fortune.

In the morning, Death came back for his pot of gold. He wrapped it in the miserable rags of his decaying cloak, close to his gappy ribs. The three corpses under the tree made no move to stop him, and he left them to a wealth of flies and crows before continuing his endless journey. The gold weighed light in his arms. Though his bones were dry and his muscles were like the withered tendrils of a grapeless vine, his strength was greater than that of any man.

The Fall of Troy

from Black Ships Before Troy, *Rosemary Sutcliff's re-telling of the* Iliad

Helen, the wife of the Greek King Menelaus, left him and went to the city of Troy with Paris, a Trojan nobleman. The Greek army layed siege to Troy in an attempt to recapture Helen and avenge the insult to Menelaus. Many great warriors, including Odysseus, king of Ithaca, supported Menelaus in his war against the Trojans, but the siege lasted for many years and Troy still held out against the Greeks. In the 10th year of the siege, the Goddess Athene gave Odysseus an idea: they should build a huge wooden horse, big enough for many warriors to hide inside. Then they would pretend to give up the fight, depart from their camp, and sail for home, leaving the wooden horse behind as a gift to the Trojans. The horse would be taken inside the city walls, but the Greek fleet would secretly return to Troy, and on its arrival the warriors inside the horse would come out and, opening the city gates to their comrades, attack Troy from within. One man, Sinon, would be left in Troy to tell the warriors when the fleet returned. Menelaus agreed to this idea, and promised Odysseus he would give him whatever Odysseus asked for if the plan was successful. One Trojan was suspicious, and said he didn't trust the Greeks, especially when they came bearing gifts, but the people of Troy were taken in by the plan and accepted the gift of the horse.

All day the people rejoiced, singing and dancing in the streets, decking their temples with branches of oak and myrtle in readiness for a sacred festival next day. And when all was done and darkness fell, they went to their own places and lay down to sleep.

By then, covered by the quiet darkness before moonrise, the fleet was returning from Tenedos as swiftly as the rowers could send their ships through the water. And crouched close in the airless space within the horse's belly, Odysseus and his fellows waited with straining ears and breath in check, while high on the temple wall Sinon strained his eyes seaward for the signal from the High King's ship, to tell him that the fleet was close in shore and the time had come to let out the hidden warriors. And all around, Troy lay quiet in sleep.

At last the signal came: a red blink of fire, far over in the darkness out to sea. Sinon's heart stumbled within him and began to race. He dropped from the wall and made his way to where the great horse stood, its shape blotted against the sky that was silvering towards moonrise. Standing beneath it, he cried out once, like a shore bird but not quite like a shore bird, to those listening within.

Then Epeius drew back the pine-wood bars, and a trapdoor fell open in the horse's side. A rope came spooling down from it, and one by one the warriors, Menelaus and Odysseus and Diomedes and the rest, came dropping to the ground.

They stole down like armed shadows from the high place to the city gates. They slew the gate guards and flung open the broad gates to their fellow Greeks swarming up towards them. Then terror came upon sleeping Troy. The dark tide of warriors poured through and became a river of flame, as men kindled torches at the guardhouse fires and ran to burn the houses of the city.

Men, half-waking and half-armed, straggled out to meet them and were cut down. The night was full of the screams

of women and children. The air grew thick with the sounds of battle, and fire went roaring through the city as it goes through a cornfield when a high wind is blowing.

But Odysseus had no part in all this. Indeed no man had seen him since the war-band came out from the horse's belly.

Diomedes, with Automedon and a growing band at his heels, had found the king's palace and overcome the guards in the outer court. They were flinging firebrands up on to the roofs, where defenders were tearing up the heavy coloured roof-tiles to hurl down upon them. Guarding their heads under their shields, they charged the main doors with war-axes and gilded beams torn from lesser buildings. The door-leaves burst open, tearing the bronze-sheathed hinge-posts from their sockets, and the men spilled through into the courts and chambers and colonnades beyond, cutting down the guards who stood against them.

No bolts or bars nor desperate courage of drawn swords could hold them back. They stormed up one passageway and down another, until they came at last to an inner court where stood an altar to the gods of the home, with an ancient bay tree bending over it as though to shield it from the fiery sky. And there the queen and the princesses had gathered, clinging about the twisted trunk like doves that have swooped to shelter from a storm. But there was no refuge for them, nor for Priam the aged king himself, who knelt praying to the gods before the altar.

A young warrior, drunk with fire and killing, seized him by his long white hair and dragged him backwards on the altar steps, and drove his sword through the old man's body so that his life-blood fouled the sanctuary where he had so often made offerings to the gods.

And they bound the royal women, despite all their screams and struggling, and dragged them captive away.

All through the city was fire and killing and the crashing down of walls and roofs as, after ten years' siege, mighty Troy was put to the sword.

But Helen had not been with the rest of the royal women, and Menelaus had gone striding off through the palace courts where rags of burning timbers fell from the sky, seeking the house of Deiphobus, for he guessed that, with no other of the king's sons still living, that was where she would be.

He knew when he had found the right house, for in the entrance he came upon Deiphobus lying sprawled in his armour, the spear that had killed him standing upright in his breast. A chain of crimson footprints that started in the pool of his blood led on through the portico and into the darkness of the hall beyond.

Menelaus followed them like a hound on the scent; and so found Odysseus, leaning as though weary against one of the central pillars of the great chamber with the light of burning roofs glinting through the high windows upon his armour, and a trickle of his own blood oozing darkly out from his sleeve.

"Where is Helen?" Menelaus demanded, standing in the doorway, his sword naked in his hand. "If you are hiding her—"

Odysseus raised his head. "Earlier today you swore to give me the thing that I asked for. Whatever it might be."

"Ask then, and the thing is yours," Menelaus said. "I am not an oath breaker, though now is surely not the time—"

Odysseus said, "I ask for the life of Helen of the Fair Cheeks, that I may give it back to her in payment for my own life, which she saved for me when I came here seeking the Luck of Troy."

There was a long stillness in the great chamber, a hollow stillness amid all the outcry of the sacked city beyond the walls. Then Helen, with her pale robes gathered close about her, stole from the dark corner where she had been hiding. She fell at her lord's feet, her golden hair outflung all about her, and reached her hands beseechingly to touch his knees, with no word spoken.

Menelaus stood looking down at her, remembering that she had betrayed him to go with Paris, and left his hearth desolate and his child without a mother. And if it had not been for his promise to Odysseus he would have slain her in that moment. But he had made the promise, and because of it he held back.

As he stood looking down at her, he began to remember other things from the time that they had shared together before Paris came. Pity and love stirred again in his heart. His drawn sword slipped from his grasp and fell ringing upon the pavement. He stooped and gathered her up, and her white arms went round his neck even as he coughed in the smoke of burning Troy.

When dawn came, Troy lay in ashes, the temple of Athene and the great horse with all the rest. The gold and silver, the ivory and amber were being shared among the Greek war-host. Priam lay dead before his household altar; the scorched bodies of his slain warriors lay piled in the fallen streets waiting for the dogs and the birds of prey. And the women were being herded to the ships of their new masters.

Hector's baby son lay dead beneath the ramparts from which he had been thrown in the fighting, as Andromache was thrust aboard the ship of a new prince of the Myrmidons. Princess Cassandra was carried to the great ship of Agamemnon himself. Only Helen, who, after Discord with her golden apple, had been the cause of it all, was led with honour, as a queen and not a slave, to the ship of her husband Menelaus.

The long siege was over, and in the young light of morning the ships of the great fleet were run down into the shallows. The rowers sprang aboard and took up their oars; and leaving the boat-strand empty save for the shore birds crying, and the smoke of Troy still rising behind them, they set their prows toward the home beaches that they had left so many years ago.

Treasure Island: A Synopsis

Jim Hawkins, a boy of about twelve, lives with his mother on a lonely and desolate stretch of the English coast. Billy Bones, an ex-pirate, comes to stay at the inn. He possesses a map to a great hoard of treasure stolen by the notorious Captain Flint, and buried by him before his death, on an island in the Spanish Main.

Other pirates are looking for the map. When Bones dies suddenly, Jim discovers the map and gives it to Squire Trelawney and Dr Livesey. The Squire fits out a ship to sail in search of the treasure and Jim goes along as cabin boy.

By chance Jim discovers that many of the crew are pirates, former shipmates of Billy Bones who have served under the terrible Flint. They want the treasure and are ready to murder anyone who gets in their way. Their leader is the cunning Long John Silver.

When they reach the island, Jim meets Ben Gunn, an old sailor who has been marooned there for three years. He has discovered Flint's treasure and hidden it in his cave. Jim and he return to the ship to discover that the pirates have mutinied, forcing the Squire and his party to barricade themselves in an old stockade on the island.

Jim tells them about Ben Gunn, who has gone back to his hiding place.

The pirates attack the stockade but are beaten off after a fierce struggle.

Then Jim goes back and frees the ship, killing the pirate sentry in the process. On his return he finds that the Squire's party has abandoned the stockade and handed over the treasure map to Silver.

The pirates set out to look for the treasure, taking Jim with them: when they discover the treasure is gone, they turn on Silver – and Jim – and prepare to kill them. But Dr Livesey and company had set up an ambush. Two pirates are killed, Silver is captured and three pirates escape. The treasure is loaded on board the ship, the three surviving pirates are abandoned, and the Squire's party sails for home. But Silver escapes when they briefly dock in South America.

Back in England the treasure is shared out and Jim, the Squire, the Doctor, Ben and all their friends settle down to contented lives.

Treasure Island

by R.L. Stevenson, retold by Virginia Bowen

The old inn called the Admiral Benbow was pulled down long ago, but there was a time when it was the best known inn on the coast, in spite of being a wild and lonely place. It was kept, at one time, by a Mr and Mrs Hawkins, who had one son - a young lad called Jim. After a while, Mr Hawkins died, and his wife and Jim kept on the inn and tried to make a living from it.

One day, while Jim was out in the inn yard, an old man walked up the road to the Admiral Benbow. He looked at the inn, and he looked at Jim, then he looked back along the way he'd come.

"Many people here?" he asked.

"No, sir," said Jim.

"Good," the man replied. "That suits me. Don't like too much company. And I'll be obliged to you if you'll keep a sharp look out for a sailor with only one leg. It'll be worth a silver coin every month to you, if you're sure to keep a sharp look out."

The man's name was Billy Bones, and he had been a sea captain. He was a fearsome looking man, with a bristling black beard and a bad-tempered look. He sang shanties, swore oaths, and told terrible stories about his life at sea. His worst stories were about pirates, and Jim's mother began to think he might have been a pirate himself. She

was too afraid of him to ask him to pay for his room, and the captain stayed on at the inn, month after month.

In fact, Billy Bones had been a pirate. Not only that, but he had double-crossed his former shipmates, and stolen the map of the island where they had buried the treasure they had stolen. One day, though, the other pirates found out where Bones was living. When he realised they were on his track, he was so frightened that he had a heart attack, and died.

Jim and his mother were afraid too. They didn't know what the pirates might do. Quickly, they searched the chest in Bones' room. Mrs Hawkins found a bag of silver, and began to count out what Bones owed her for the room. Suddenly, they heard someone at the door of the inn. They hurriedly grabbed the money and papers from the chest, and raced off to hide in a secret room in the attic.

Soon, the pirates burst into the inn and searched all over it, looking for Billy Bones' room. They flung open the door, and rushed in. The chest was still open! They pulled everything out of it, scattering the contents all round the room. When they couldn't find the map, they were furious.

"The papers have gone!"

"Find the boy!"

Just then, a whistle was heard from the lookout the pirates had stationed outside. A troop of soldiers was marching over the hill towards the inn. Quick as a flash, the pirates scattered, and disappeared into the countryside around the inn. The soldiers searched for them, but the pirates had got away.

"They were looking for these papers," said Jim to the officer in charge. "They could be something important."

"Well, I don't know," mused the officer. "Perhaps we'd better take them to the squire."

Jim and the officer went to the Hall, where Squire Trelawny lived. They were shown into the dining room, where the Squire was having dinner with Dr Livesey. Jim explained what had happened, and the Doctor opened the packet of papers. Inside was a map of an island. Next to a cross on the map were the words "Captain Flint's treasure buried here".

The squire and the doctor looked at each other.

"If we were to get a ship ourselves..." murmured the squire.

"We have a head start on the pirates, anyhow," said the doctor. "After all, we have the map."

Jim raised his eyes to the squire.

"Can I come with you? Please?" he implored.

"All right," said the squire. "It is your map, isn't it?"

Squire Trelawny hired a ship, the Hispaniola, and set about finding a crew to sail her. Somehow, the pirates found out about the Squire's plan, and signed up as members of the ship's crew. They were led by Long John Silver, the one-legged sailor Bones had warned Jim about. The pirates planned to wait until the treasure was found and then kill the squire, and loyal members of the crew.

One night, when the ship was very close to the island, Jim overheard Long John Silver trying to persuade the other sailors to join the pirates. Quickly, he hurried to Doctor Livesey, and told him what he had heard. The doctor

instantly realised what this meant. He hurried Jim off to the squire and the Hispaniola's captain.

"We've sighted the island now," said Captain Smollett. "We can't go back. We'll have to find out how many of the men we can count on, and be ready for trouble."

Soon, the Hispaniola was anchored in one of the island's bays. It was very hot, and Captain Smollett gave the crew permission to go ashore. Jim went with them. He roamed about the island, exploring it and dreaming about what he would do when they had found the treasure. Suddenly, he heard angry voices nearby.

"You've no choice," hissed Long John Silver to a sailor. "Join with us, and be rich, or die."

"I'll not join with you," retorted the sailor, and he bravely turned and walked away.

Long John snarled angrily, whipped his crutch from under his arm, and flung it at the sailor so hard that it knocked him down and killed him instantly.

Jim was frozen with horror for a second. Then he turned and raced away as fast as he could. He stumbled blindly through woods and bushes and over streams until he tripped over a log and lay panting. A movement made him look up in terror, then he remembered the gun he was carrying, and pulled it out.

"Don't shoot," said a voice, and a wild-looking old man stepped from behind a tree. "Don't shoot. I'm only Ben Gunn. Three years I've waited for someone to come. Ever since my shipmates went and left me here to die. Who are you, and how did you come here?"

Jim told him how he had found the map, and how the squire had hired a ship to come to the island.

"I know where the treasure is," Ben Gunn said. "I'll make you rich if you'll take me with you."

Meanwhile, Dr Livesey had taken some of the men to look for Jim. As they searched the island, the doctor found a stockade, a log house on a hill, surrounded by a strong fence. Suddenly, they heard a scream, as the pirates attacked another of the sailors. "The trouble has started," thought the doctor, "but at least we can barricade ourselves in here. We must fetch the others so they will be safe."

The captain and the squire's men moved to the stockade, giving up the Hispaniola to the pirates, who hoisted the Jolly Roger. Jim saw the Hispaniola's flag flying above the log house. He rejoined his friends and told them about Silver killing the sailors, and about meeting Ben Gunn. Just then, Long John Silver came up to the stockade, and offered to let them go free if they gave up the map, but they refused to give in.

A fierce battle followed between the pirates and the squire's men, and men on both sides were killed. After a long struggle, the squire's men held the stockade, and the pirates returned to the woods. Dr Livesey treated the men who had been injured, then took the map and left the stockade.

Jim took two pistols and slipped into the woods. He knew that Ben Gunn had built himself a small rowing boat, or coracle, out of thick sticks and goat skins. Jim used the boat to row out to the Hispaniola. There was only one, wounded pirate left on the ship. They fought, and the pirate flung his dagger at Jim, pinning him to the mast through the shoulder. With the shock, Jim's pistols went off, and the pirate was killed. Bravely, Jim pulled the dagger out, and climbed shakily onto the deck. He raised the anchor, and let the boat drift round to another part of

the shore. He dropped the anchor and waded ashore, thinking that at least the ship was theirs again.

Jim set off back to the stockade. Nobody was on watch, and he was able to slip in without anyone seeing him. Suddenly, someone called his name. It was Long John Silver! One of the pirates grabbed Jim and held him tight.

"You'll have to join us, now," said Silver. "Your pals have gone and left you. If you don't join with us, we'll have to kill you."

"You won't get away with it," said Jim. "One day you'll all be tried for piracy."

One of the pirates drew his knife, but Silver stopped him.

"I'm in charge here," he snarled.

The pirates muttered among themselves. Finally, one said, "We want a new leader. So far all we've done is work and fight. Where's the treasure?"

To Jim's astonishment, Long John Silver quieted the angry pirates by producing the map of the island. They cheered him loudly. "Now we'll all be rich!" they shouted.

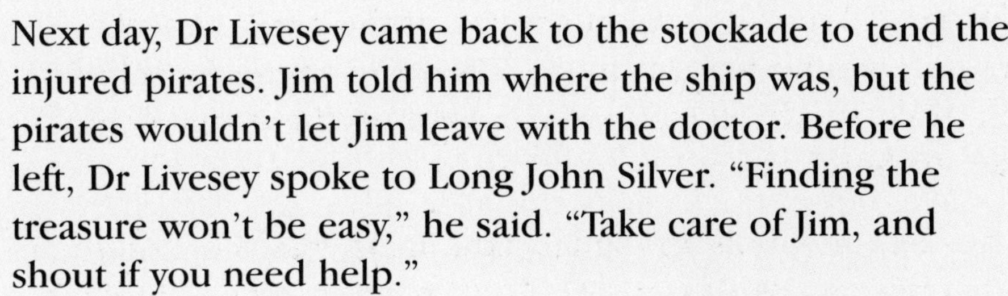

Next day, Dr Livesey came back to the stockade to tend the injured pirates. Jim told him where the ship was, but the pirates wouldn't let Jim leave with the doctor. Before he left, Dr Livesey spoke to Long John Silver. "Finding the treasure won't be easy," he said. "Take care of Jim, and shout if you need help."

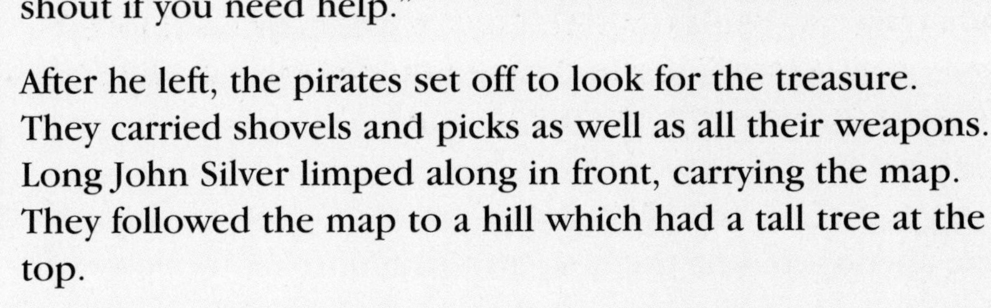

After he left, the pirates set off to look for the treasure. They carried shovels and picks as well as all their weapons. Long John Silver limped along in front, carrying the map. They followed the map to a hill which had a tall tree at the top.

“Is this the one?” they asked. One pirate gasped as he saw a skeleton in the grass on the hillside. “It’s Captain Flint’s ghost!” he shrieked. Long John Silver wasn’t afraid. “Flint probably left it to scare people away from the treasure,” he said. They went on to the top of the hill, and rushed up to the tree. At the foot of the tree was ... a huge hole! Someone else had got there first. The pirates roared in disbelief, and Long John Silver secretly handed Jim a pistol. “Stand by, Jim,” he said. “There’ll be trouble now.”

One of the pirates found a single coin, and held it up. “Is this all there is?” he roared. “Down with Long John Silver!”

Suddenly, two shots rang out, and two of the pirates fell. Dr Livesey and Ben Gunn appeared, both holding guns. The remaining pirates fled.

“After them!” shouted the doctor. “We mustn’t let them reach the boats.” He led them back to the beach, with Long John limping behind, and found the two boats belonging to the Hispaniola. They knocked a hole in one, and pushed out to sea in the other. As they rowed out to the ship, Dr Livesey explained that Ben Gunn had found the treasure while he was marooned on the island, and had dug it up and taken it to his cave. “Once we knew that,” said the doctor, “I knew it wouldn’t matter if the pirates got the map. It was no use any more. Then you saved the ship for us. Now we are all safe, we can load up the treasure and sail for home.”

They left one man on the Hispaniola, to guard it, and then went back to Ben’s cave. The squire and Captain Smollett were glad to see Jim safe. That night they all had a huge feast to celebrate finding the treasure.

The next day, they loaded the treasure onto the ship, and sailed for home, leaving the remaining pirates on the island. When they reached South America, the Squire and Captain Smollett hired a new crew. While they were there, Long John Silver managed to steal a bag of gold and escape. He knew he would be hanged for piracy if he went back home. The others all returned safely, and shared out the rest of the treasure. Jim never forgot his adventures on Treasure Island.

The True Story of the Three Little Pigs and the Big Bad Wolf

Why is it that, as soon as they start school, innocent little kids have to be told that ridiculous story about the three little pigs and the big bad wolf? I suppose it is something to do with the Government's spin doctors! Well, I can tell you that we, the famous group, "Wailing Wolfie and the Red Hot Porkers", have decided it is time people knew the true facts.

The old yarn, that I wanted to harm the pigs, that I went round blowing down their houses, is just a mischievous rumour. What I wanted from the beginning was to play with them; to play music I mean!

You see, although I say so myself, I've always had a fantastic voice. I can move, in the shake of a tale, from a deep throbbing purr to a high piercing whine or an ear-splitting howl. I can perform anything the audience wants: romantic ballads; rattling raps; hilarious hops or jungle bungles. And as for my dear

friends and partners, the pigs, they have to be the greatest backing group of all time. There's Priscilla on drums, Prunella on electric guitar and Peregrine on banjo and double bass. Whenever we play we bring the house down!

Well, of course, that was the trouble when we first played together. There we'd be, swinging sweetly and softly, the crowd buzzing, and me crooning melodiously, then I'd get carried away with the excitement, the applause, and the music and, before long I'd be howling, huffing, puffing and blowing as only a wolf can. Well, you can imagine what happened: flying furniture and dancers blown everywhere, including, sometimes, I regret to say, my dear piggy partners in the band.

On a few occasions my puffing and blowing really did bring down the walls and roof in those flimsy new discos made of straw and wood. Can you imagine how embarrassed I felt standing there in the middle of all that destruction.

That's why we became the first group ever to play all our concerts in the open air. Give yourself a treat and come and see us sometime. And hey! Persuade those dopey teachers to stop telling those sweet little kids that crazy mixed up story of the nasty wolf and the three petrified pigs. We love each other, daddy-o!

"I have found a kernel of wheat," said the Little Red Hen. **"Now who will help me plant this wheat? Where is that lazy dog? Where is that lazy cat? Where is that lazy mouse?"**

"Wait a minute. Hold everything. You can't tell your story right here. This is the endpaper. The book hasn't even started yet."

"Who are you? Will you help me plant the wheat?"

"I'm Jack. I'm the narrator. And no, I can't help you plant the wheat. I'm a very busy guy trying to put a book together. Now why don't you just disappear for a few pages. I'll call when I need you."

"But who will help me tell my story? Who will help me draw a picture of the wheat? Who will help me spell 'the wheat'?"

"Listen Hen—forget the wheat. Here comes the Title Page!"

Title Page.

(for The Stinky Cheese Man & Other Fairly Stupid Tales)

PUFFIN BOOKS

This book is dedicated to our close, personal, special friend:

(your name here)

—J.S. & L.S.

I know. I know.
The page is upside down.
I meant to do that.
Who ever looks at that
dedication stuff anyhow?
If you really want to read
it—you can always stand
on your head.

INTRODUCTION

A long time ago, people used to tell magical stories of wonder and enchantment. Those stories were called Fairy Tales.
Those stories are not in this book. The stories in this book are almost Fairy Tales. But not quite.
The stories in this book are Fairly Stupid Tales.
I mean, what else would you call a story like "Goldilocks and the Three Elephants"? This girl walking through the woods smells Peanut Porridge cooking. She decides to break into the Elephants' house, eat the porridge, sit in the chairs, and sleep in the beds. But when she gets in the house she can't climb up on Baby Elephant's chair because it's too big. She can't climb up on Mama Elephant's chair because it's much too big. And she can't climb up on Papa Elephant's chair because it's much much too big. So she goes home. The End.
And if you don't think that's fairly stupid, you should read "Little Red Running Shorts" or maybe "The Stinky Cheese Man."
In fact, you should definitely go read the stories now, because the rest of this introduction just kind of goes on and on and doesn't really say anything. I stuck it on to the end here so it would fill up the page and make it look like I really knew what I was talking about. So stop now. I mean it. Quit reading. Turn the page. If you read this last sentence, it won't tell you anything.

JACK

Up the Hill
Fairy Tale Forest
1992

SURGEON GENERAL'S WARNING: It has been determined that
these tales are fairly stupid and probably dangerous to your health.

Speech Against Foxhunting

Ladies and Gentlemen,

You have given me a very rough reception and I don't blame you for that. I know how you feel about people like me who try to have foxhunting banned.

However, please allow me to speak for just a few minutes. You may feel angry but I can tell you that I feel very nervous here.

If you are so sure that you are right and I am wrong, then perhaps you could at least let me be heard. I won't take long. Thank you. I appreciate your kindness.

First let me say that I am totally against people who try to stop foxhunting by harming horses and dogs or your cars and trailers. My friends and I will never break the law, no matter how strongly we feel.

We want to persuade you by giving you sensible reasons for our opinions, because we know that you are sensible, civilised, law-abiding people.

We think that foxhunting is cruel for two reasons:

> Even if the fox escapes it must be a terrifying experience to be chased for miles by riders on horseback and a pack of dogs. Can we imagine how we would feel being chased for our very lives?
>
> Often the fox does not escape and dies an agonising death, even if it is quick.

You all say you love animals. Can you really say that when you think of a beautiful creature like the fox dying like that? If you really love animals, could you stand by and watch?

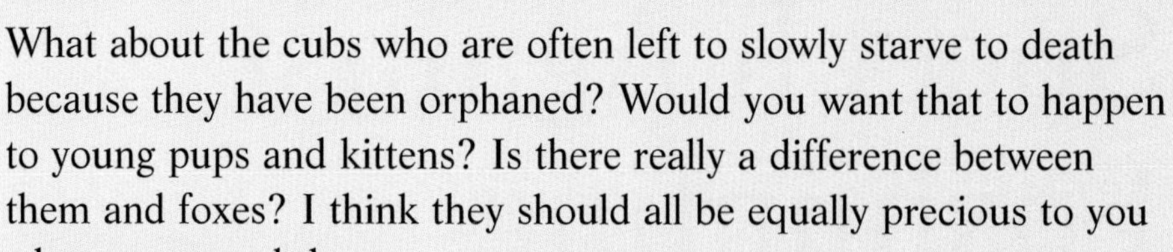

What about the cubs who are often left to slowly starve to death because they have been orphaned? Would you want that to happen to young pups and kittens? Is there really a difference between them and foxes? I think they should all be equally precious to you whoever created them.

You say that foxes do a great deal of damage to crops and poultry. If country people like you who love everything about the countryside say that is so, then I accept it absolutely. Mind you rabbits do even more damage and you don't hunt them with hounds and horses, do you? However if, as you say, foxes do damage, I accept your argument that their numbers must be kept down. Some foxes must be killed.

I am pleading with you not to do it in a cruel way, after a long, distressing chase.

I suggest you shoot the foxes that have to be destroyed. You could do it quickly so it would be all over in a split second and the fox would not have to suffer.

You say that if foxhunting is banned the people whose work is in hunting will lose their jobs. I suggest that they could be trained to keep a check on fox numbers and to do the shooting.

I believe that, in fact, you would kill more foxes in that way and keep the numbers down more efficiently than hunting does.

I understand how exciting it must be to hunt. I don't object to that at all, only to the killing of the fox in that way. You could still have all the fun of hunting by having drag hunts instead. People who take part in drag hunting say it is just as thrilling as a foxhunt, and does not harm anyone or anything.

Thank you for listening to me so politely. You have been very kind.

If I can say one last thing.

I love the countryside; I was born there and wish I could live there. I love horses. I regularly rode a pony when I was younger. However, I am forced to come to the city for my living. I know how hard you all have to work in the country for your living. I know you feel the Government and people in London don't worry or care about you. I think that is wrong and that it is a shame. But I have to say that when people in cities see on TV foxes being hunted to their death it turns them against you. It turns the Government against you. It's unfair, I agree, but you should think about it when you refuse to give up hunting.

Thank you for listening to me. My best wishes to you for your lives and work.

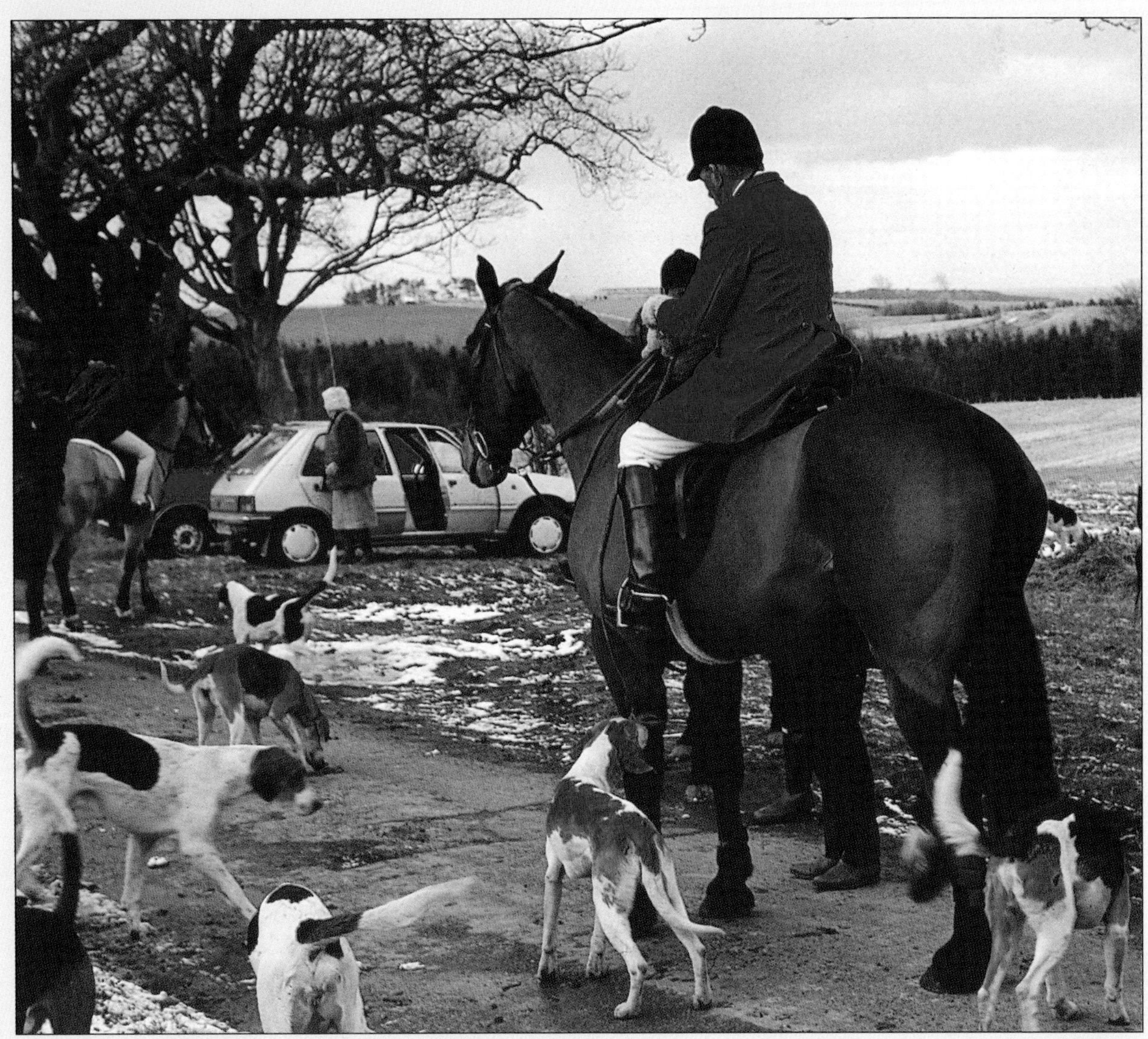

Letters of Complaint

11, Coombe Road
Belltown
Downshire
4 December 1997

To the Managing Director
Falldown Football Club

Dear Sir

I am writing on behalf of a number of supporters to complain about your decision to introduce yet another club strip. We hope you and your directors, and the manager, will listen to what we have to say. We would be happy too for you to circulate our letter to the players.

We are not important people but we are true and faithful supporters of the Club. We go, not only to all the home games, but some of us travel to away games as well. I myself have only missed one away game so far this season and that was when our baby was born, (I'll be bringing him up to be a Falldown supporter, I promise you). I was sorry I missed that game, because that was a great win away from home against a side in the top three in the division. Could I say here that I think we won that game because the manager decided to play Mickey Potts in the middle of the field. Then he went and played him in the back four again and we haven't done half as well since.

Anyway, as I said at the beginning, we are really upset about the new strip. Let me tell you why. This is the fifth new strip in the last eighteen months. First you changed the old strip when you had the new club logo put on. In fact we didn't mind that at all, because we liked the logo and we all thought the old strip was becoming a bit boring. But then straightaway you got a new away strip as well. We know you have to have a different away strip and with the new logo and we can all see why you needed two new shirts. But do you know what they cost? Well, of course you do; what am I thinking of – you're the top Director aren't you. Anyway for the new strips that was £64 – £32 each, PLUS another fiver for your favourite player's name and five on top of that for his number. That's £84 for two strips.

But that's only part of it! I have two lads who are as keen as I am on the club. I've been bringing them to the games since they were babies. Well, they have to have every new strip as well. Otherwise they couldn't show their faces in school with the other kids. Do you know what it costs me for three of us on Saturdays? Well, sorry, of course you must, you're the top Director aren't you! I have to work an extra day and a half a week in overtime so we can afford to go to football. And it's going to be harder now with the new baby. By the way, I've just bought him his first little shirt. He looks smashing! And, do you know, he swings his right leg like anything in the cot. Reminds me of our old centre forward "Bomber" Steele.

Anyway, to get back to the strip. As I said, there were two new ones, with the logo and then, in no time at all, <u>two more</u>. Mind you, we supporters were delighted in a way. We had to have a new strip to play in the semi-final of the Cup. Will you ever forget it! Best season of all time for us supporters! And we should have got to the Final. There's no doubt about it. That last minute goal of theirs was yards offside. Mind you, I think the manager made a mistake that day playing Tommy Green up front. So, we had three new strips all in a few months and then came a FOURTH one because the club was invited to play in that Tournament in Italy at the end of last season.

And now a couple of months into the new season there's another one, because the new Director, him with all the money, doesn't like the logo. And I suppose you'll have a new away strip to go with it.

Well, I must tell you, we are getting tired of it. No, no, I don't mean we are getting tired of the Club. We'll always love the Club. It's just that we can't keep on buying the strips, not with the kids to buy for as well. We'd be glad if you could stop for a while, at least until next season. Mind you, if we could have another good run in the Cup – or better still, have a chance of promotion – then none of us would mind forking out for a new strip to celebrate.

So, I hope you will take notice of this letter because it is being written on behalf of a lot of supporters. Maybe you could also mention my suggestions about Mickey Potts to the manager. Must stop now. There goes the baby and it's my night to look after him. His mother does overtime on Wednesday nights – expensive business these new babies. Still, the way he's kicking out, one day maybe I'll watch him play for dear old Falldown United.

~~Best wishes for the future~~

Yours ~~since~~ faithfully

Joe Keen

(a lifetime supporter)

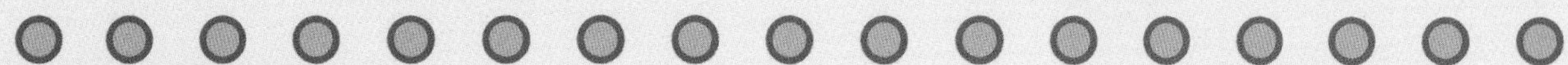

11 Lavender Close
Lakeside
Downshire

To the Editor
"The Belltown Times"

Dear Sir

I would be grateful for a little space in your letters column to comment on the matter of the Falldown United Football Club strip. I can tell you that what I have to say will be echoed by hundreds – maybe more – of the club supporters. I am confident, too, that this newspaper, which has always stood up for ordinary people, will share my views.

The club has now had five different strips in less than two seasons. It is only fair to say that two of the strips are for away games and supporters do not need to buy them. However, many supporters, and young people and children especially, feel they must have all the club strips. My son tells me that at his school you cannot call yourself a true Falldown supporter unless you have the most up-to-date strip.

This, of course, puts enormous pressure on parents every time the club decides to change what the first team is wearing. Families, especially those with more than one child, simply cannot afford such expense.

On top of the fact that you keep on changing the strip, it is much too expensive. The shirts cost three times more than they are worth. They are nothing more than cheap T-shirts, which, I know, can be bought in this very town, for less than £10. Add to that about £6, at the most, for the cost of the player's name and number. In other words we are paying over £40 for a strip that costs about £16.

So the club is making an enormous profit out of loyal supporters

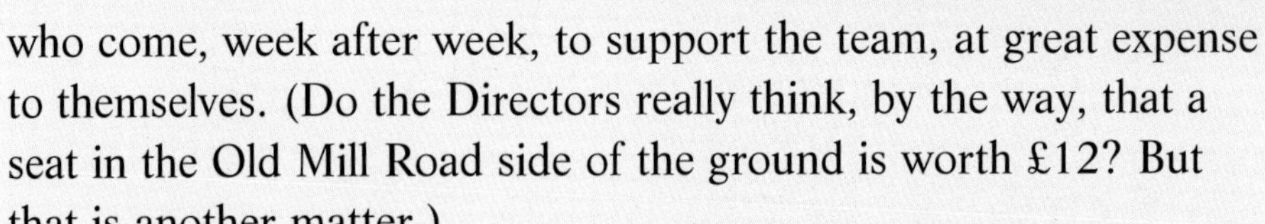

who come, week after week, to support the team, at great expense to themselves. (Do the Directors really think, by the way, that a seat in the Old Mill Road side of the ground is worth £12? But that is another matter.)

Most supporters would be only too happy to pay as much as £20 for a strip if they thought it was helping the club they love, and helping to buy good players for the team. But what the Directors are charging is outrageous.

The fact is: there is no need whatsoever to change the strip so often. How can the club justify the latest change, not long before the end of a very disappointing season. I believe it has been done for one reason only – to make up some of the money that is being lost through the latest fall in attendance at home games.

And we know why the gates are falling – the poor quality of the football. Perhaps the Directors would do better to think of ways of improving our present record than thinking up ways of squeezing even more money out of long-suffering fans.

The solution is simple. Stop this nonsense of constantly changing the strip. We can't afford it. Let's stick with the present one for the next five years at least. Yes! We will be happy to buy a new one if we get to the Cup Final or win promotion! At present there seems about as much chance of that as the Directors inviting us all to watch the next home game free.

We know the club has to make a profit. We know that unless they do they won't be able to buy the players we do badly need.

However, I genuinely feel that supporters would rather pay another pound or two for their tickets, at least for games against the "glamour" sides, than have the Directors rip us off with shirts we don't need and don't want.

Yours faithfully
A long-time supporter
(Name and address supplied)

New Regulations for Flat-dwellers

The Government is considering introducing a law to prevent people from keeping pets in flats, apart from guide dogs, police dogs in training and small fish. People who have pets already will be allowed to keep them, but after such pets have died may not acquire new ones. The Government states that its decision comes after wide consultation with people throughout the country; they believe that a majority of people will support their decision, which is based on considerations of:

- public order and tranquillity
- public health and hygiene
- animal welfare

This decision has caused bitter arguments across the country. Some people support what the Government is planning; just as many more people oppose it.

The following is an article in a newspaper by a writer who summarises both sets of arguments, highlights their strengths and weaknesses and lets us know his personal opinion.

The article

This decision by the Government has really put the cat among the pigeons. It is something that everyone has an opinion about. It has caused friends to fall out. It has led to public demonstrations and sit-ins.

At the same time there have been numerous counter-demonstrations by people who think that banning pets from flats is the greatest idea since sliced bread.

Where does the truth really lie? Who is right?

Let us look at the arguments for both sides and try to arrive at a cool, balanced judgement.

Let's look first at the arguments of those who oppose the ban. They say:

> We should learn a lesson from the fact that many unique and wonderful creatures world-wide have been made extinct, or are in danger of being made extinct, because of the way in which humans treat the environment. If the Government is allowed to bring in the anti-pet law then similarly the future of domestic animals could be threatened.
>
> Many domestic animals pay for themselves because in order to keep them their owners have to buy licences.

The livelihood of many people is dependent upon domestic pets: the makers of animal foods; veterinary surgeons and their staff; catteries and dog kennels to name but a few.

They bring incalculable pleasure, joy and comfort to people old and young.

Young children also have pets and have to care for them, learn to be organised, sensitive and responsible in doing so.

For many elderly and defenceless people pets such as dogs are their guardians, and their only security against unwelcome intruders.

Above all domestic pets are absolutely essential to the happiness and welfare of older people and people living alone. One old lady said, with tears in her eyes, "My dog is the only creature who has never stopped loving me, who is always thrilled to see me, who never gets tired of me. If they take away our pets they will take away everything worth having from us."

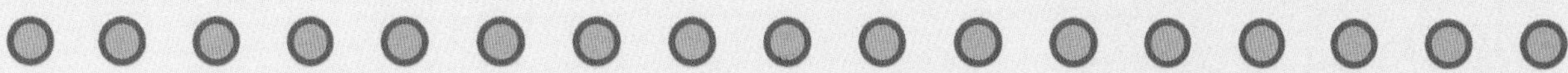

Well, after hearing those arguments you might think there was nothing else to be said, and that any sensible Government should forget the proposed new law immediately.

But it isn't quite so simple as that.

There are many people who think the new law is a good idea for these reasons. They say:

The law doesn't want to stop everyone from having domestic pets, only those people who keep them in flats. It is wrong to keep animals such as cats and dogs in flats, simply because:

a) flats are too restricted in space and too cramped for big animals;

b) animals need to be able to go out when they wish.

Very often big dogs have to stay inside all day, without real exercise if their owners are too old or afraid to go out.

Many animals are not suited to be domestic pets; for example, very large dogs, reptiles and large and dangerous insects. To keep such animals is often unhygienic and dangerous.

Some pets are simply a nuisance, with their incessant barking and crying, to other people living in the flats.

Finally people should remember two very important points:

All the pets currently owned by flat-dwellers will not be affected in any way. They can remain where they are at present to the end of their days. The new law only forbids the buying of new pets.

The law is being passed in the best interest of animals to prevent them from living out their days in flats that are totally unsuitable for them.

It is understandable that people who keep pets will feel upset. But they may find it a relief not to have the responsibility of caring for a new animal. There are many wonderful TV programmes about animals. They would make a very good substitute for keeping pets.

    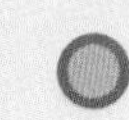    

Summary of Arguments

Now I shall clarify the strengths and weaknesses of both sets of arguments

First, those who oppose the new law. Strengths and weaknesses

+ I agree that many wonderful creatures have become extinct. But it is not logical to argue that the new law will help to make creatures such as cats, dogs and budgerigars extinct.

I agree that some people who make their living out of providing for pets would lose financially.

- However, I do not agree that animal licences bring money to the Government. It does not make a profit for the Government because it costs too much to collect.

+++ However, there is no doubt that domestic pets bring great happiness and companionship to many people, especially the old and the lonely. This is such a strong argument that I am giving it three plus marks.

++ The argument that domestic pets, such as dogs. make old people, and people living alone, more secure is also a strong one.

+ I agree, too, that the responsibility of looking after pets can be a positive experience for young people.

So, in my opinion, those arguing against the law scored seven positive points. But they lose one point because they are misleading people with an argument that is not absolutely honest.

So they total six positive points for their arguments.

Arguments for the law. Strengths and weaknesses:

++ I agree that flats especially those in high-rise blocks, are not ideal places for some domestic pets; certainly not for big dogs.

++ I agree too, that some creatures, e.g. certain reptiles and insects, should not be kept as domestic pets, and certainly not in more restricted environments, simply because they would be a potential danger if they were to escape.

++ Again, I accept that some domestic pets in flats, generally dogs, can be a nuisance to other people because of the noise they make.

+ We must accept the argument, too, that <u>some</u> domestic animals have hygiene problems where they are allowed to foul lifts and staircases

However, I do not feel that some of the arguments are in any way sound.

- Many people will not feel better about the law when their pets have died. Most of them will probably want to go out and buy a new pet almost immediately.

- The fact that the law does not affect pets already in flats is not a good argument; it is the fact that they cannot have pets in the future that is upsetting people.

The argument about TV animal programmes is probably not wrong, but it is a rather unkind one since such programmes are more likely to make pet owners sad over what they have lost, rather than <u>console</u> them. So I shall ignore it altogether as an argument.

So, those who support the law score seven positive points for good arguments and lose two for misleading ones. **This gives them a total of five points in all**.

So the issue is a difficult and **complex** one. Both sides have strong arguments to offer. But in my opinion what wins the **debate for those people who oppose** the new law is the **undeniable** fact that many old people and people who live alone would be **devastated** at the loss of opportunity to keep pets. That, it seems to me, **outweighs** any arguments on the other side.

Summaries

After the Goat Man

Figgy is an orphan who lives with his fierce, powerful and silent grandfather. People very quickly realise that Figgy's grandfather is not someone to cross or have an argument with. Figgy is not scared of his grandfather; he loves and trusts him and knows that in his silent, gruff way his grandfather loves him.

This feeling of being loved, makes up for the hard things, the deprivations in Figgy's life: the fact that he is an orphan who can barely remember his mother, that his grandfather's poverty means there is nothing in the way of toys or possessions and their odd life-style prevents him from having friends.

They live in a ramshackle old cabin built by his grandfather in the woods. Here in wild and natural surroundings the old man is happy, followed everywhere by the two goats who earn him, in the neighbourhood, the nickname of "The Goat Man". Figgy, in his harmless way, is allowed to run wild, roaming about and exploring, in ragged, cast-off clothing.

Then the blow falls. A great new highway is to be built, which means the woods and the old cabin will have to be demolished. For two years the old man fiercely resists, becoming quite famous in the local press as a result.

But in the end, after a bitter struggle, Figgy and his grandfather are forced out and rehoused in a modern home.

Figgy loves the conveniences, the running water, the gadgets in the home that will make their lives easier. But the old man retreats into silence and seems to have given up.

In despair Figgy goes roaming in the new neighbourhood and meets up with Ada and Harold.

Ada who lives with her father, a doctor, is herself a half orphan, her mother having recently died, while we hear only of Harold's mother and grandfather and nothing of a father. Ada is a gentle, loving girl; Harold on the surface is rather touchy and easily upset. He is spoilt at home where there seems to be no lack of money. But he has a great problem: he is seriously overweight, loves rich and fattening foods and has just been put on a severe diet by his mother. Because of his weight problem Harold is not good at sports or physical activities. He makes up for this by being a great day-dreamer, constantly thinking about glamorous and exciting jobs and occupations he will have when he is an adult: an astronaut; a news reporter on radio and TV, constantly reporting great disasters.

Figgy becomes friends with Ada and Harold, but is careful not to tell them much about his eccentric grandfather.

Then the old man suddenly arms himself with a gun, re-occupies his old cabin, hours before it is due to be demolished and refuses to come out. Figgy's secret is out and the kindly Ada insists the three of them go to persuade the old man to give himself up and come out of hiding.

On the way Harold and Figgy fall from Harold's bicycle and Figgy breaks his leg. While Ada looks after the agonised Figgy, Harold is forced to go and persuade the old man to come and help.

The cowardly Harold is terrified he will be shot. But he overcomes his fear because of his anxiety to help Figgy and persuades the old man to come back to the scene of the

accident. Harold is overcome with pity as he comes to understand the Goat Man's suffering at having, finally, to leave the old home he has loved. But he understands, too, that Figgy means more to the old man than anything, just as Figgy has realised that at moments of trouble the one who matters most to him in all the world is his cantankerous grandfather.

At the same time Harold realises that he himself can never really be a news reporter because he is too soft-hearted, cares too much for people, despite his rather abrupt manner, understands their suffering, and therefore could never calmly and coolly describe it in the way that reporters have to.

At the end the future is brighter for Figgy and his grandfather. Ada's doctor father says that he will arrange for them to live on a farm where they can be back at the heart of nature, and where the new friendship of the three young people, Ada, Harold and Figgy can continue to flourish.

Neither is the rest of the story just gloom and tension. In many ways it is wildly amusing thanks to Harold's stories of his many failed attempts to be heroic and important.

The Two-thousand-pound Goldfish

The story is about an American boy named Warren Otis and his older teenage sister Weezie, who live with their grandmother. Their fathers (they have different fathers) have gone out of their lives for ever and their mother has been on the run from the law for years because she has become involved in Civil Rights campaigns that have led to violence and death.

Warren is obsessed with films. His ambition is to be a film maker when he grows up and he spends most of his time devising, in his mind, weird and wonderful horror and science fiction film scripts. For a considerable part of the novel he is concerned with devising a plot about a two-thousand-pound goldfish, swimming about in the city sewers and emerging occasionally to slurp people to death.

The many plots Warren thinks up are highly amusing (e.g. Bossy the lethal cow who squirts radio-active milk over people) but in reality his life is a grim and deprived one. His grandmother has become sour and embittered by the actions of her daughter (Warren's mother) whom she treats as dead and refuses to talk about; she is cold and hostile to the brother and sister and does the minimum to care for them.

Warren, when he is not day-dreaming about film, spends his time longing desperately for his mother. He constantly imagines situations in which they will be ré-united, never to be parted again. He has seen countless images of her in various disguises on TV and newspapers as she moves from one wild and desperate deed to another. But the only real contact he has with her is in the shape of pathetic quickly, scribbled and rather selfish post cards ("love me; think of me; miss me!") she sends the children from various parts of America.

Then Warren discovers that just once in the blue moon his mother telephones his sister, by appointment at a particular phone booth. Just once, for a few brief moments, he manages to speak to her himself, for the only time since he had been an infant, and this only intensifies his desperate longing to be with her again. He and his sister do little to comfort each other; since there is such scant love in their lives there is none for them to spare on others.

Then their grandmother dies. Warren, confused and guilty, almost welcomes it, since he believes the funeral will bring his mother out of hiding.

But that doesn't happen and by the end of the novel Warren is at last facing up to the truth: his contact with his mother is never likely to be more than brief, secret phone calls and scribbled post cards.

But the future begins to look better. His mother's sister, his Aunt Pepper, a warm and generous person, comes to live with the children and Warren realises, as he hears his hard-working sister's plans for her career as a lawyer (her day dream to defend her mother one day) that he must work to bring his films to life, not just dream about them.

In some ways a grim story in a depressing setting; but alive with hilarious descriptions of Warren's film scripts.

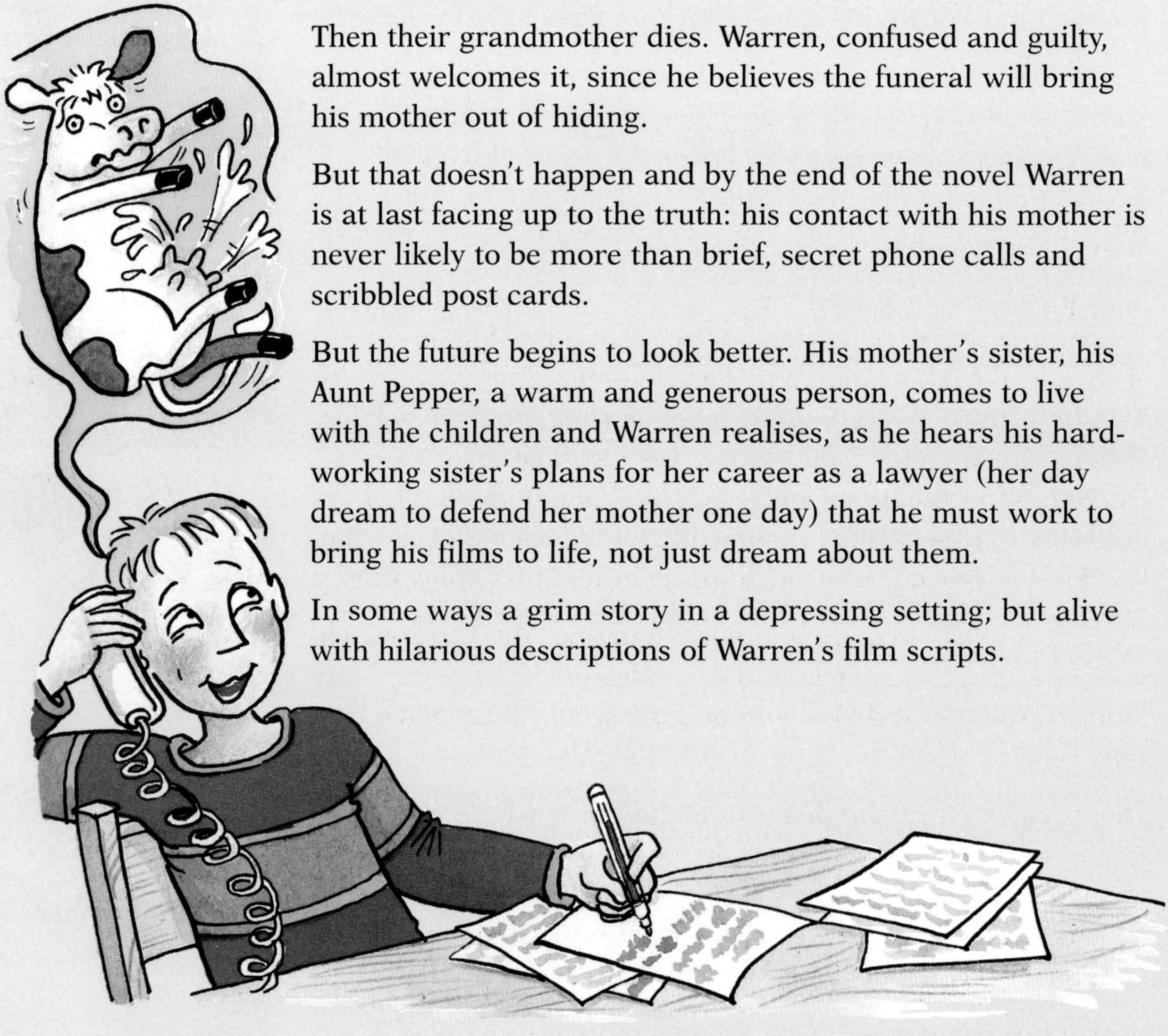

The Computer Nut

Kate lives with her mother, her doctor father and her teenage sister Cassie, who is mad about dogs and keen on boys.

Kate, who is rather spoilt and indulged by her parents (but in fact, underneath, is somewhat shy and uncertain) is obsessed by computers, when we first meet her. She is completing an art assignment on her father's machine when she receives, on the computer, a series of messages from someone claiming to be an alien and anxious to meet her.

At first Kate is convinced the messages are a hoax, designed as a practical joke by a friend or acquaintance. She is encouraged in this opinion by her well-intentioned but bungling friend Linda. Linda, in trying to prove their opinion about an unknown friend sending the message, puts Kate in embarrassing situations with two boys. One of the boys is odious; the other, Willie, is someone whom Kate thinks rather special. However, she is much too shy to let him know this.

Willie has a problem; in fact more than one. He is overweight and, as a result, is subject to a great deal of teasing. But he is much too gentle and kindhearted a person to react badly to this.

He also has a far from peaceful life at home where a large family means money is very scarce and he is constantly tormented by his three very young sisters. Despite the fact that he has little in the way of material possessions he is a generous person, warm and friendly, and slow to bear or keep a grudge.

He is very attracted to Kate but is too shy to let her know of his feelings. However, he becomes involved with Kate in the

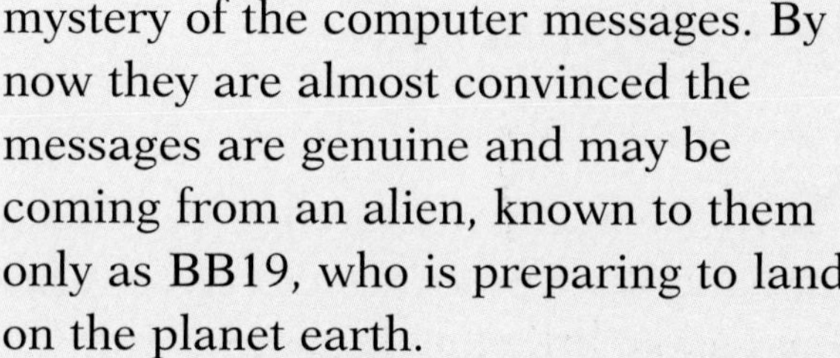

mystery of the computer messages. By now they are almost convinced the messages are genuine and may be coming from an alien, known to them only as BB19, who is preparing to land on the planet earth.

Keeping the secret to themselves, Kate and Willie prepare to meet him by night in a Burger Bar where he advises them he will be, in the form of an "earth-boy", wearing a "Wild and Crazy Guy" T-shirt. Willie who is still not fully convinced that someone is not playing a joke on them waits outside the Burger Bar while Kate ventures in. She meets up with BB19 and soon realises he is a genuine alien. Unfortunately all the other customers also suspect there is something strange about him, despite his perfect physical disguise, partly because of his mechanistic voice and partly because he insists on going round the tables telling strange and very unfunny jokes.

He explains his mission to Kate (or "Computer Nut" as he continues to call her). He has been sent to investigate Earth which, he tells Kate, is the only planet whose inhabitants laugh, and to discover whether he can master the technique of telling jokes.

He explains that he is going to walk into an American Football stadium and entertain the crowd by trying out his jokes on them. Kate and Willie, fearful of what the crowd may do if their football is interrupted, do everything they can to dissuade him, but all in vain. As they had anticipated, the venture turns out to be a disaster and only Willie's quick thinking saves BB19 from serious injury.

Downcast at his failure, the saddened alien leads them to a clearing where he is due to be "beamed up". Kate is equally sad to see the strange, gentle, well-intentioned alien leave

them. With his final attempt at a joke, BB19 actually makes Kate laugh and, happy that his ambition to be amusing, like earthlings, has at last been realised, he bids them a fond farewell.

A few days later Kate receives another message from outer space and is thrilled to realise her alien friend means to keep in touch. What she doesn't yet fully realise is that BB19 has brought her and Willie finally together.

This story is concerned with people's problems and obsessions, and with people who are isolated, "outsiders". But the problems are not the grim and desperate ones of *After the Goat Man* and *The Two-thousand-pound Goldfish*. However, like those books, *The Computer Nut* is full of fun, amusement and wit.

From After the Goat Man

A Plan

Without raising his head Harold looked over at Ada. His cheeks had gotten very pink and Ada's eyes were as blue as marbles. For a moment those seemed to be the only spot of colour on the porch. Neither Ada nor Harold spoke. The news bulletin they had just heard on the radio went, word for word, through both of their minds.

Figgy had been watching for some kind of reaction, and he noticed their expressions. He said quickly, "Maybe you read about my grandfather in the newspaper or something? Is that it?"

"Well, yeah," Harold said. "I did see his picture in the paper a while back."

One Sunday when the trouble first began, there had been a whole page of pictures of Figgy's grandfather in the Sunday newspaper. A photographer had posed Mr Gryshevich all over his land – in front of the cabin, by the creek where he fished, beneath the hundred-and-fifty-year-old tree behind the cabin.

The pictures were all alike and, as Harold had looked at them that Sunday morning while he was waiting for his sister to get through the comics, he had thought the photographer could have taken a cutout figure of the Goat Man and pasted it on different backgrounds and gotten the same results. No matter where the Goat Man stood he was stiff as a board, his eyes staring down at the ground.

It had made Harold a little sad. The pictures, he knew, would not help the Goat Man keep the cabin and the land, but would instead make people cry, "Get him out of the way of I-79. We want progress!"

Harold cleared his throat. "Look, Figgy. Ah, listen." He didn't think he was going to be able to continue. He realised suddenly that he liked to give out important news on the telephone but not to people's faces.

He hesitated, glanced at Ada for help, and she said, "Go on, Harold, *tell* him," in a low voice.

"Tell me what?" Figgy swung his head around quickly, looking from one to the other.

Harold hesitated again, and Ada said, "Go *on*."

"What are you going to tell me?" Figgy asked. "Is it something about my grandfather?"

"Yes. Well, it's nothing, really." Harold said, looking down at his feet. "It was just that we heard something on the radio about your grandfather. It was right before you got here."

"What?"

"Well, your grandfather has gone back to the old house, that's all, and he's locked himself in." Harold looked at Ada because he wanted to see if she thought he had told it as badly as he did. He thought maybe he wouldn't be a news reporter after all because it seemed to him that he had a desire to make a disaster seem unimportant. He didn't want people to worry. He imagined himself on the air. "And now," a voice would say, "with the news of the worst hurricane in the history of the United States, here is Harold V. Coleman."

And then he would come on and say, "Well, it's really nothing. It's just that this hurricane, or bad storm, whichever you want to call it, has knocked down a few houses and the water has ruined some trees and things. That's all. And now back to Walter Cronkite."

Reporting like that would make people feel a lot better, he thought, but he knew that a reporter should *enjoy* standing up to his neck in the rising waters. He should *love* holding the microphone out to a drowning man and asking, "Sir, how does it feel to be one of the hundred and twenty people who are drowning in this terrible hurricane?"

Figgy was staring at Harold. He said, "What did you say?"

"Your grandfather's gone back to your cabin."

"But he couldn't go back there. Our cabin's been torn down."

"No, it's *going* to be torn down. They were all ready to do it, I imagine, when he got there," Harold said. "Anyway I guess they can't tear it down with him in there. That would be murder."

Ada shot him a look from beneath her dark lashes. She said in a low voice, "He took a gun with him, though, Figgy, you ought to know that." Then she didn't look at either one of them.

Figgy said, "I know." Then he sighed and added. "Well, that's that." Then he realised he couldn't think of anything else to say. Neither could Harold or Ada, and a dark feeling settled over the three of them.

Finally Harold shrugged and said, "These things just happen, that's all." He thought that would be the way he would end his news programme. For a moment the thought of his own face on the television screen saying, "These things just happen, that's all, and a pleasant good evening to all of you," blocked out what was happening on the porch.

Figgy nodded quickly. Then he said, "Well, I guess I better go out there and see what's going on. My grandfather might shoot somebody or something. There's no telling what he might do, really. The cabin and the land are very important to him."

"But they gave him a new house, didn't they? And new land?" Harold asked.

"Yeah, but it's not the same."

Harold said, "But it's better and newer and everything, isn't it?"

Figgy shrugged his skinny shoulders. "It's just not the *same*."

There was another silence and then Harold asked, "Your grandfather didn't ever shoot anybody before, did he?"

"Not that I know of." Figgy said. "Anyway, he never *had* to shoot anybody. People just don't bother my grandfather much. They sort of know, see, not to fool with him. I know he wouldn't hurt *me*, and yet I wouldn't ever do anything to make him mad. That's just the way he makes me feel. You don't *want* to make him mad."

Harold looked at Figgy, and it was as if he were seeing him for the first time. Figgy was smaller than Harold had originally thought, thin and very dirty. Figgy looked back at Harold with his wide dark eyes and absently scratched at the mosquito bite with his rabbit's foot.

Ada said suddenly, "Listen, we'll all go out to the cabin with you." She put the top on the Monopoly game. "Won't we, Harold?"

"Well, yeah, sure," Harold said. He paused. "How are we going to get there, though? We can't walk. I know I can't." He glanced at Figgy apologetically. "I'm not very athletic."

"You don't have to be athletic to walk," Ada said. "Babies walk."

"Yes, but not for miles." Harold was self-conscious about his slowness at anything athletic. In his school in gym class when the boys were choosing teams for baseball or basketball, he was always the last to be chosen, he and Homer Ferguson who had bad ankles and was not allowed to run. He said, "We could take a cab."

Ada said, "Nobody but goops take cabs."

"Oh, well, sure," he agreed quickly, "but in an *emergency*—"

"We're going to walk. Just wait while I leave a note for my dad."

"Well, I better let my mom know too."

Harold got to his feet as Ada went into the house, and he started across the street. He knew all he would have to do was open the front door and call, "Mom, I'm going off."

"Not to the Dairy Queen, Harold," she would answer.

"All right," and that would be it. She never asked where he was going, and he thought that was because he was too big and slow to get far, like a box turtle he had once had. Harold could put the turtle down in the garden, go into the house, make a sandwich, watch something on television, talk on the telephone, and come back, and the turtle would just be coming out of its shell.

Biographies

William Wordsworth (1770–1850)

Wordsworth spent some time as a young man on a long walking tour in Switzerland and France. This helped to develop his already deep love of nature, his admiration of mountains, forests, fields, flowers and rivers. Back in England Wordsworth devoted his life to poetry. Some of his best loved poems are about nature, and about the ways in which human beings can live in a good and tranquil relationship with the earth, the sea and the sky, with growing things and living creatures.

Wordsworth thought that if all human beings could live in close contact with nature, and develop a strong relationship with natural things, then all things would be good and happy. He expressed this belief in his poetry, without always admitting that there could be obstacles and difficulties about all people managing to live like that. For this reason, for the rather dreamy ideals and beliefs he held, Wordsworth is known as a Romantic poet. While alive he came to be regarded as a kind of leader of Romantic poets in this country.

Wordsworth also wrote ballads. These are poems often written in an apparently simple way and sometimes set to music so they can be sung. Ballads always tell a story; so we can describe them as narrative poems. Some of Wordsworth's ballads are about simple, ordinary people living the kind of happy, untroubled romantic life that he felt they could if their days were spent in the countryside, by lakes and rivers in the heart of nature.

One of Wordsworth's poems, "The Daffodils" is one of the best known in the English language.

Wordsworth was appointed Poet Laureate before he died. He is regarded as one of the greatest of all English poets.

William Butler Yeats (1865–1939)

William Butler Yeats was born in Ireland but, as a young man, came to study in England. Although there was much that he found very attractive about the great city of London, he yearned for the tranquil and beautiful Irish countryside.

One humid day, while walking down a London street, he passed a shop where an artificial fountain of water was the central feature of a display. As Yeats watched the cool water gushing upwards and flowing over a collection of stones to form a little stream in the foliage in the window, he was suddenly overwhelmed with longing for the lakes, woods and rivers of his native country. He immediately returned home to Ireland and commemorated the event in one his most famous poems "The Lake Isle of Innisfree," which begins:

> "I will arise and go now, and go to Innisfree,
> And a small cabin build there, of clay and wattles made:
> Nine bean-rows will I have there, a hive for the honey-bee,
> And live alone in the bee-loud glade."

Yeats spent much of his life after that in Ireland. He was fascinated by folk tales, ghost stories, fairy tales and legends. He was also deeply interested in the religious beliefs and traditions of people in the Eastern world. Many of his poems are influenced by those interests.

Although he wrote some very complicated poems that are difficult to understand, Yeats never lost his enthusiasm for more simple poems such as the ballad you have been studying. And whether his poems are difficult and complex or about everyday things, they are all written with endless care and all composed in beautiful language. He would spend hours, and even days, thinking about the words and phrases that would express perfectly what he wanted to say.

Yeats was awarded the Nobel Prize for Literature in 1923. He is thought to be one of the great poets of the twentieth century.

Henry Wadsworth Longfellow (1807–1882)

Longfellow was one of the best known and best loved poets in English in the nineteenth century. He was a very clever scholar who excelled in modern languages, and was a professor of languages in both Europe and America.

He was a prolific writer, especially of narrative poetry. Some of his poems that tell stories of great or tragic events – "The Wreck of the Hesperus", "Paul Revere's Ride", and "The Village Blacksmith" for example – made him famous throughout the world. But he is probably best remembered today for the long narrative poem "The Song of Hiawatha". This was the fictional story of a young Indian warrior, Hiawatha, who was reared by his grandmother Nokomis on the shores of Lake Superior. He marries the beautiful Minnehaha ("Laughing Water") and has many wonderful adventures. Finally he dies and is carried off to the Isles of the Blest (Heaven) to rule the Kingdom of the Northwest Wind. The poem is written to a very strict rhythm, rather like the distant, insistent sound of Indian drums:

> By the shores of Gitche Gumee,
> By the shining Big-Sea-Water,
> Stood the wigwam of Nokomis,
> Daughter of the Moon, Nokomis.
> Dark behind it rose the forest,
> Rose the black and gloomy pine-trees,
> Rose the firs with cones upon them;
> Bright before it beat the water,
> Beat the clear and sunny water,
> Beat the shining Big-Sea-Water.

People loved the subject of the poem and were captivated by the drum-like chanting rhythm. In fact many people wrote imitations and also parodies of the poem.

Longfellow was loved and admired by many people during his life, not least because he was such a good and kindly man. However, his poetry is not read so widely today because it is thought to be too sentimental.

The Wreck of the Hesperus

by Henry Wadsworth Longfellow

It was the schooner Hesperus,
That sailed the wintry sea;
And the skipper had taken his little
daughter,
To bear him company.

Blue were her eyes as the fairy-flax,
Her cheeks like the dawn of the day,
And her bosom white as the hawthorn
buds
That ope in the month of May.

The skipper he stood beside the helm,
His pipe was in his mouth,
And he watched how the veering flaw
did blow
The smoke now west, now south.

Then up and spake an old sailor,
Had sailed the Spanish Main,
"I pray thee, put into yonder port,
For I fear a hurricane.

"Last night the moon had a golden ring,
And tonight no moon we see!"
The skipper he blew a whiff from his
pipe,
And a scornful laugh laughed he.

Colder and louder blew the wind,
A gale from the north-east,
The snow fell hissing in the brine,
And the billows frothed like yeast.

Down came the storm, and smote
amain
The vessel in its strength;
She shuddered and paused, like a
frighted steed,
Then leaped her cable's length.

"Come hither! come hither! my little
daughter,
And do not tremble so;
For I can weather the roughest gale
That ever wind did blow."

He wrapped her warm in his seaman's
coat
Against the stinging blast;
He cut a rope from a broken spar,
And bound her to the mast.

"O father! I hear the church bells ring,
O say, what may it be?"
"'Tis a fog-bell on a rock-bound coast!"–
And he steered for the open sea.

"O father! I hear the sound of guns,
O say, what may it be?"
"Some ship in distress, that cannot live
In such an angry sea!"

"O father! I see a gleaming light,
O say, what may it be?"
But the father answered never a word,
A frozen corpse was he.

Lashed to the helm, all stiff and stark,
With his face turned to the skies,
The lantern gleamed through the
gleaming snow
On his fixed and glassy eyes.

Then the maiden clasped her hands and
prayed
That saved she might be;
And she thought of Christ, who stilled
the wave
On the Lake of Galilee.

And fast through the midnight dark and
drear,
Through the whistling sleet and snow,
Like a sheeted ghost the vessel swept
Towards the reef of Norman's Woe.

And ever the fitful gusts between
A sound came from the land;
It was the sound of the trampling surf
On the rocks and the hard sea-sand.

The breakers were right beneath her
   bows,
She drifted a dreary wreck,
And a whooping billow swept the crew
Like icicles from her deck.

She struck where the white and fleecy
   waves
Looked soft as carded wool,
But the cruel rocks they gored her side
Like the horns of an angry bull.

Her rattling shrouds, all sheathed in ice,
With the masts went by the board;
Like a vessel of glass she stove and sank–
Ho! ho! the breakers roared!

At daybreak on the bleak sea-beach
A fisherman stood aghast,
To see the form of a maiden fair
Lashed close to a drifting mast.

The salt sea was frozen on her breast,
The salt tears in her eyes;
And he saw her hair, like the brown sea-
   weed,
On the billows fall and rise.

Such was the wreck of the Hesperus,
In the midnight and the snow!
Christ save us all from a death like this,
On the reef of Norman's Woe!

What has Happened to Lulu?

by Charles Causley

What has happened to Lulu, mother?
What has happened to Lu?
There's nothing in her bed but an old
rag doll
And by its side a shoe.

Why is her window wide, mother,
The curtain flapping free,
And only a circle on the dusty shelf
Where her money box used to be?

Why do you turn your head, mother,
And why do the tear drops fall?
And why do you crumple that note on
the fire
And say it is nothing at all?

I woke to voices late last night;
I heard an engine roar.
Why do you tell me the things I heard
Were a dream and nothing more?

I heard somebody cry, mother,
In anger or in pain,
But now I ask you why, mother,
You say it was a gust of rain.

Why do you wander about as though
You don't know what to do?
What has happened to Lulu, mother?
What has happened to Lu?

The Lion and Albert

by Marriott Edgar, 1880–1951

This piece of writing was composed for a comedian who intended to recite it as a monologue in a radio show. The idea came to the writer from a newspaper account of an alarming accident which fortunately did not prove fatal. The writer decided to change the setting of the piece to the North of England so that it could be recited in a Lancashire accent, which comedians in those days (almost seventy years ago) seemed to find amusing.

The first recital certainly proved a great success and the composition has been a popular party piece ever since.

There's a famous seaside place called Blackpool,
That's noted for fresh air and fun,
And Mr and Mrs Ramsbottom
Went there with young Albert, their son.

A grand little lad was young Albert,
All dressed in his best; quite a swell
With a stick with an 'orse's 'ead 'andle,
The finest that Woolworth's could sell.

They didn't think much to the Ocean:
The waves, they was fiddlin' and small,
There was no wrecks and nobody drownded,
Fact, nothing to laugh at at all.

So, seeking for further amusement,
They paid and went into the Zoo,
Where they'd Lions and Tigers and Camels,
And old ale and sandwiches too.

There was one great big Lion called Wallace;
His nose were all covered with scars–
He lay in a somnolent posture
With the side of his face on the bars.

Now Albert had heard about Lions,
How they was ferocious and wild –
To see Wallace lying so peaceful,
Well, it didn't seem right to the child.

So straightway the brave little feller,
Not showing a morsel of fear,
Took his stick with its 'orse's 'ead 'andle
And pushed it in Wallace's ear.

You could see that the Lion didn't like it,
For giving a kind of a roll,
He pulled Albert inside the cage with 'im,
And swallowed the little lad 'ole.

Then Pa, who had seen the occurrence,
And didn't know what to do next,
Said "Mother! Yon Lion's 'et Albert,"
And Mother said "Well, I am vexed!"

Then Mr and Mrs Ramsbottom –
Quite rightly, when all's said and done –
Complained to the Animal Keeper
That the Lion had eaten their son.

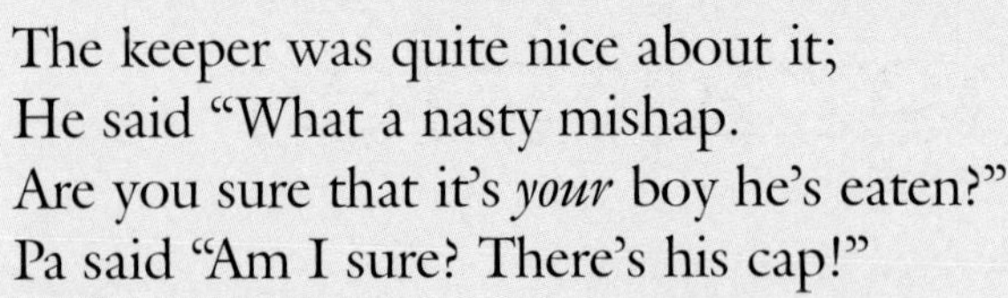

The keeper was quite nice about it;
He said "What a nasty mishap.
Are you sure that it's *your* boy he's eaten?"
Pa said "Am I sure? There's his cap!"

The manager had to be sent for.
He came and he said "What's to do?"
Pa said "Yon Lion's 'et Albert,
And 'im in his Sunday clothes, too."

Then Mother said, "Right's right, young feller;
I think it's a shame and a sin
For a lion to go and eat Albert,
And after we've paid to come in."

The manager wanted no trouble,
He took out his purse right away,
Saying "How much to settle the matter?"
And Pa said "What do you usually pay?"

But Mother had turned a bit awkward
When she thought where her Albert had gone.
She said "No! someone's got to be summonsed"–
So that was decided upon.

Then off they went to the P'lice Station,
In front of the Magistrate chap;
They told 'im what happened to Albert,
And proved it by showing his cap.

The Magistrate gave his opinion
That no one was really to blame
And he said that he hoped the Ramsbottoms
Would have further sons to their name.

At that Mother got proper blazing,
"And thank you, sir, kindly," said she.
"What, waste all our lives raising children
To feed ruddy Lions? Not me!"

Biographies

Robert Burns (1759–1796)

Scotland's national poet, Burns was the son of a poor farmer, William Burns, who struggled all his life on wretched poor land to make a living for his family. William was determined that his children should be educated (unlike the vast majority of poor people at that time) and despite the appalling poverty with which they had to contend he found enough money time and again to ensure that Robert and his brother Gilbert attended school. For a considerable period when there was no school nearby, William persuaded his neighbours that they should all contribute to pay for a teacher.

Robert and Gilbert worked at back-breaking farming work from a young age. But the education they had received, and the fact that books and reading were considered important by their parents in the home, made the boys enthusiastic about continuing with their learning.

Robert was particularly fascinated by literature and made some rather hesitant first attempts at writing poetry. Close friends encouraged him to continue with his writing, which began to be published locally.

But things were less happy in his personal and private life. His remarkable father died, worn out by the struggle to keep the farm going, his romantic life was not successful, and he found himself struggling as desperately as his father had to make a living.

He expressed his feelings, his anguish and despair, his disappointed love, his concern and compassion for people suffering as he did from want and deprivation in beautiful and moving poetry, written in the Scottish dialect.

For all the difficulties and disappointments of his life, Burns was a cheerful, generous and optimistic person, with a great understanding of the life and plight of others, and indeed of the natural world generally.

Like his father before him, he failed as a farmer, but was admired throughout Scotland for his poetry. He died at the early age of thirty-seven, probably worn out by the severe hardship of his life.

Robert Burns' poetry is difficult for many people outside Scotland to understand fully, partly because it is written in dialect, which is almost impossible in parts to translate into other languages, but also because some of the words and phrases are now archaic. However, despite the difficulty of many of his poems, their beauty, power and generosity of spirit shine through them, and people throughout the world continue to be moved and inspired by them today. Many people will have heard or read "To a Mouse"; "To a Mountain Daisy;" "The Banks O'Doon" and "A Red, Red Rose", while "Auld Lang Syne" is sung by people everywhere on occasions like New Year and final partings. Many of his phrases and sentences have become a permanent part of the English language.

William Allingham (1824–1889)

William Allingham was born in a remote, rural part of Ireland. Although he came later in his life to work in England as a customs officer (Robert Burns did similar work for part of his life) and settled down there for good, he always remained influenced by his early life in Ireland. At that time people, especially those in remote parts of Ireland, had a strong belief in fairies and spirits. They believed, for example, that grassed-over remains of Stone Age buildings were the homes of fairy folk, and would not venture near them at night for fear of disturbing fairy meetings and celebrations. William Allingham was an educated person and did not share such superstitions, but he was fascinated by them. He wrote a great deal of poetry for children (of which "The Fairies" is the most famous) and much of it has fairies and similar spirit creatures as a theme.

Allingham also kept a diary for forty years and this was published at the end of his life because it contained such vivid descriptions of his famous contemporaries.

Much of his work was illustrated by very well-known artists, including Rossetti, Millar and Kate Greenaway.

The Greeks

by John and Louise James

Rural Life

Attica 455BC

Life in the country was very hard. Away from the river plains, the land was rocky and the soil of poor quality, so few crops could be grown there. In the mountains, terraced fields had to be dug out of the hillsides. The main crops were olives, grapes and, in the plains, wheat.

This scene shows countryside in Attica, the region around Athens. Workers are harvesting olives, which will provide oil for cooking, for burning in lamps and for cleaning the skin when bathing. They are shaking and beating the olives from the trees. Two men are then using a press to squeeze the oil out. The oil will be stored in jars called amphorae, and some of it will be sold in the towns and cities. Grapes were also harvested and pressed in a similar way, and the juice made into wine.

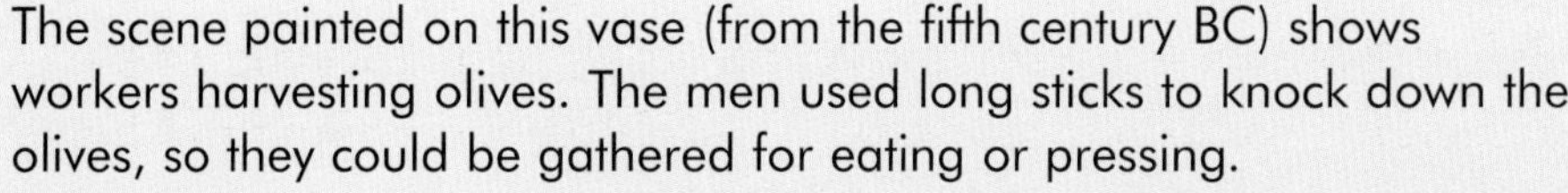

The scene painted on this vase (from the fifth century BC) shows workers harvesting olives. The men used long sticks to knock down the olives, so they could be gathered for eating or pressing.

Olive oil was one of Attica's main exports. Once collected, the olives were pulped by hand. Then the juice was squeezed from them in large presses. The same device could be used for pressing grapes.

In mountainous regions, farmers had to keep hardy, sure-footed goats and sheep rather than cattle. Farmers kept goats mainly for their milk and sheep for their wool. Meat was eaten only at festivals and when animals were sacrificed.

Other important industries were forestry, fishing and weaving. The demand for wood for furniture, ships and buildings was so heavy that many areas suffered soil erosion. In the fourth century BC, the Athenian philosopher Plato described the damage:

> "...what now remains... is like the bony body of a sick man, with all the rich and fertile earth fallen away and only the scraggy skeleton of the land left."

Crossing to Salamis

by Jill Paton Walsh

All the while my mother sat exhausted and dazed, leaning against the rock and saying nothing. I too was tired, for cutting thyme for beds, and bringing stones to build a hearth, was heavy work compared to spinning, but it was a lovely game. I was as pleased with Phryne as if she had made me another dolls' house, like the one she made once for Goose and Hare to walk in and out of.

I was falling asleep as I ate that night. We could see Athenian fires all over the plain to the north of us; we could hear a murmur of distant voices in the dark, and the strange dream-like incantation of the waves on the shore. And it was only when I crept to my bed that astonishment gripped me. I was amazed at the lack of quiet – the sounds of the night, and crackling of the prickly sweet-smelling branches beneath us, the flapping of the flimsy tent in the cool night air. I was amazed at the lack of darkness – the glow of embers on the hearth at the tent door, and the brilliant stars in a triangle of sky. I was astonished at our lack of safety – no walls, no door to shut, no bolts, only enough wool to make us a cloak apiece, and the goodwill of the gods. In the midst of my astonishment, I fell asleep.

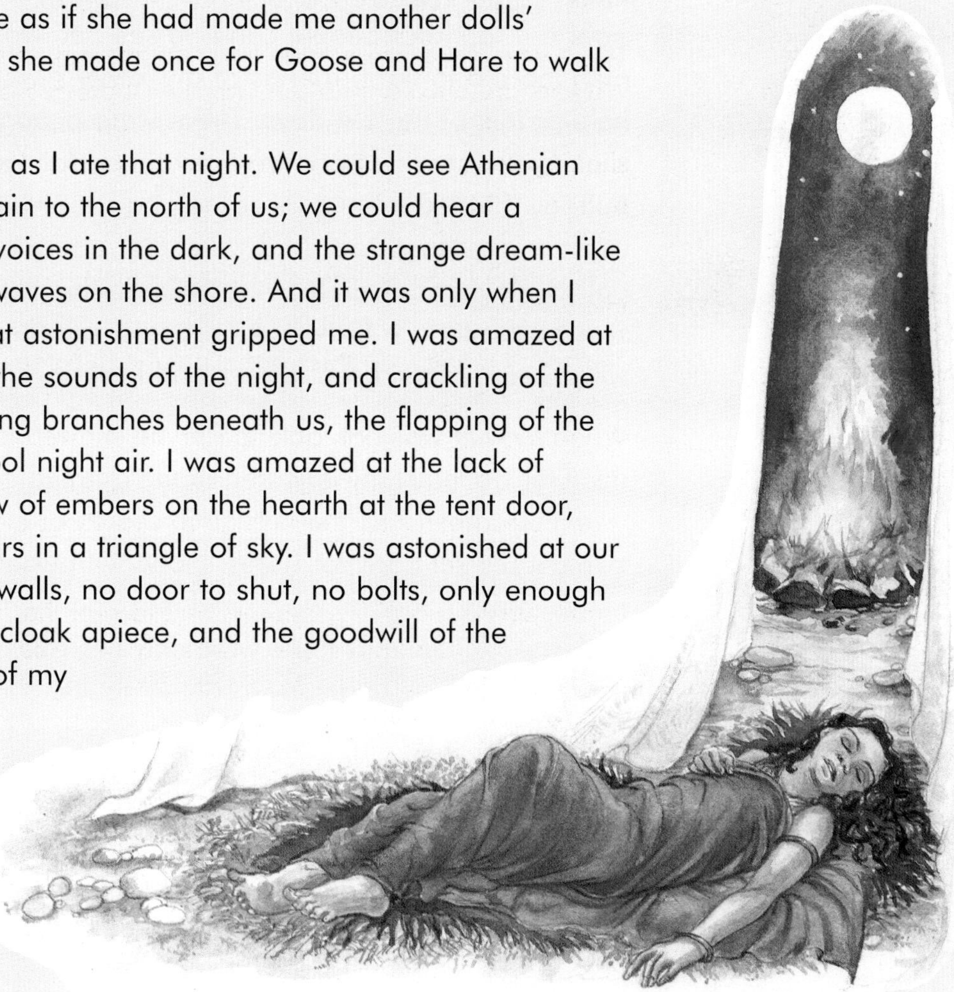

A bright dawn woke me. My astonishment continued. I had not been acquainted with the sun, until he rose high enough to shine down into our courtyard; I had not till then seen the morning glory of the sun in a wide open place, coming low and sideways, and filling the whole liquid strait of Salamis with pale molten gold. And all day long I could watch the changing shadows on the blue water, and the lilac-grey mountain side, and feel the little playful gusts of the unconfined open air.

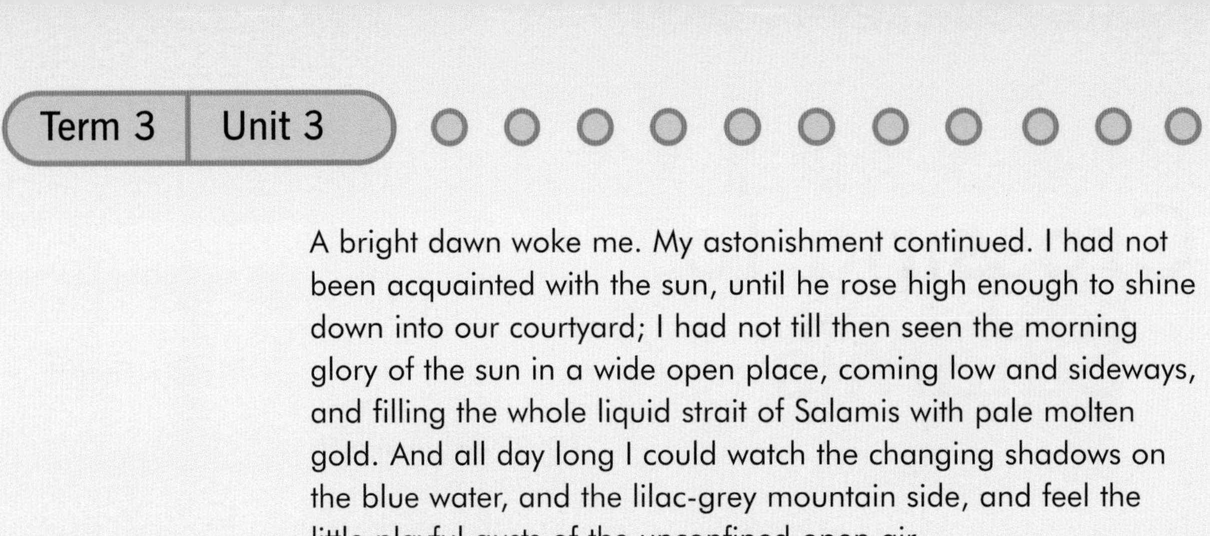

There was plenty to do on Salamis. There was coming and going among the citizens – we were not allowed to go where the men were camped in arms – people finding old friends, walking the beach in groups, talking and lamenting. My mother sat always near our tent, but people came to see her, women, and even men too old to fight, friends of my father's who came to offer help or talk of the old days. There were pedagogues on the island, and soon lessons were arranged for the boys, and nobody minded if the girls came and sat on the outside of the circle and listened too. And we could run, and skip, and throw ball all day, and even learn to swim in the clear cold water. My skin began to turn brown like a boy's; my cheeks to glow warm when I ran; I could run further and faster every day.

When Mother was not looking Phryne showed me how to gird up my tunic, to leave my legs free of the clinging cloth, and thus we went scrambling up the hillside in search of birds' eggs, and likely places to set traps for hares. Nobody frowned at Phryne now for having Spartan ways, and teaching them to me. On Salamis there were only two rules for the children – not to worry the adults, and to return to our family fires well before night.

Riddles

Riddles in Rhyme

by J. R. R. Tolkien

Crooked as a rainbow, slick as a plate,
Ten thousand horses can't pull it straight.

It cannot be seen, cannot be felt,
Cannot be heard, cannot be smelt.
It lies behind stars and under hills,
And empty holes it fills.
It comes first and follows after,
Ends life, kills laughter.

Voiceless it cries,
Wingless flutters,
Toothless bites,
Mouthless mutters.

What am I?

by Sally Angell

I'm never the same
from one minute
to the next.
In fiction writers flash
me in all directions
disrupting my flow
clocking up what
effect I have on
those who only know
part of my being.
I never stop
and am divided into
numbers and names
and sections. No one
really understands
how I tick.
Turn me round and you'll see
A widow's mite.
There is never enough of me
though I am ageless
Grandfathers speak loudly
Of my passing by.
I'm there in a way
In the song along with
Parsley, Sage, and Rosemary
The Ancient I am,
An Old father.

Two Riddles

by Eric Finney

It's what happens after
The goodbyes have been said;
Or perhaps it's a track
Through what covers your
head.

You're Emperor, Conqueror,
King,
You dead straight thing.

Riddle

by Judith Nicholls

I am
word-cruncher,
wilful, square-brain,
a mind of my own;
I am words without end,
though silent as stone.
My head is a jumble
of poems not yet done;
a mumble of stories,
of number, of song.
I'm a dream-hoarder –
snatch my words,
catch if you can!
Snatch them and mix them,
make them your own!

The Animals' Carol

by Charles Causley

Christus natus est! the cock	Christ is born
Carols on the morning dark.	
Quando? croaks the raven stiff	When?
Freezing on the broken cliff.	
Hoc Nocte, replies the crow	This night
Beating high above the snow.	
Ubi? Ubi? booms the ox	Where?
From its cavern in the rocks.	
Bethlehem, then bleats the sheep	Bethlehem
Huddled on the winter steep.	
Quomodo? the brown hare clicks,	How?
Chattering among the sticks.	
Humiliter, the careful wren	Humbly
Thrills upon the cold hedge-stone.	
Cur? Cur? sounds the coot	Why?
By the iron river-root.	
Propter homines, the thrush	For the sake of man
Sings on the sharp holly-bush.	
Cui? Cui? rings the chough	To whom?
On the strong, sea-haunted bluff.	
Mary! Mary! calls the lamb	Mary
From the quiet of the womb.	
Praeterea ex quo? cries	Who else?
The woodpecker to pallid skies.	
Joseph, breathes the heavy shire	Joseph

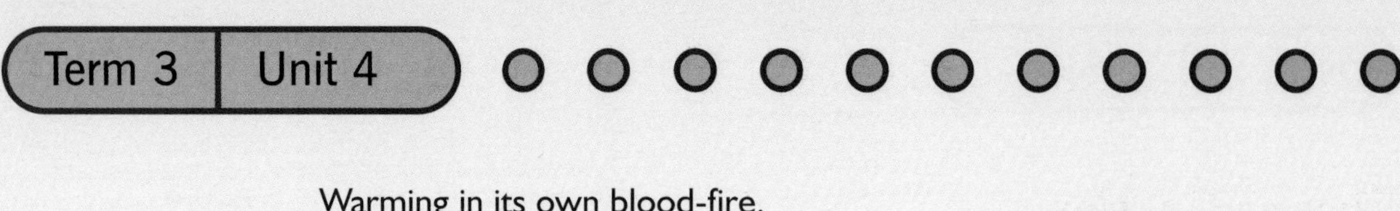

Warming in its own blood-fire.	
Ultime ex quo? the owl	Who above all?
Solemnly begins to call.	
De Deo, the little stare	Of God
Whistles on the hardening air.	
Pridem? Pridem? the jack snipe	Long ago?
From the harsh grass starts to pipe.	
Sic et non, answers the fox	Yes and no
Tiptoeing the bitter lough.	
Quomodo hoc scire potest?	How do I know this?
Boldly flutes the robin redbreast.	
Illo in eandem, squeaks	By going there
The mouse within the barley-sack.	
Quae sarcinae? asks the daw	What luggage?
Swaggering from head to claw.	
Nulla res, replies the ass,	None
Bearing on its back the Cross.	
Quantum pecuniae? shrills	How much money?
The wandering gull about the hills.	
Ne nummum quidem, the rook	Not a penny
Caws across the rigid brook.	
Nulla resne? barks the dog	Nothing at all?
By the crumbling fire-log.	
Nil nisi cor amans, the dove	Only a loving heart
Murmurs from its house of love.	
Gloria in Excelsis! Then	
Man is God, and God is Man.	

Charles Causley

Charles Causley (born 1917) is one of the best known and most highly regarded of living English poets. In other words he is a contemporary poet. He was born in Cornwall and during the war served in the Royal Navy. After the war he became a teacher and taught for several years.

All of these – Cornwall, the Navy, and his time teaching children – have greatly influenced his poetry and keep on re-appearing in it in various forms. He is particularly sympathetic to children, and has written collections of children's stories and poems for them or about them.

As a young man Causley played a piano in a dance band and many of his poems have the feeling of lively songs and music. He often writes about religion, about those who have experienced grief, deprivation and oppression and about innocence and the loss of innocence.

Much of Causley's poetry is written in such simple, clearly expressed language that it is easy to forget what a subtle, skilful and complex poet he is.

Innocent's Song

by Charles Causley

Who's that knocking on the window,
Who's that standing at the door,
What are all those presents
Lying on the Kitchen floor?

Who is the smiling stranger
With hair as white as gin,
What is he doing with the children
And who could have let him in?

Why has he rubies on his fingers,
A cold, cold crown on his head,
Why, when he caws his carol
Does the salty snow run red?

Why does he ferry my fireside
As a spider on a thread,
His fingers made of fuses
And his tongue of gingerbread?

Why does the world before him
Melt in a million suns,
Why do his yellow, yearning eyes
Burn like saffron buns?

Watch where he comes walking
Out of the Christmas flame,
Dancing, double talking:
Herod is his name.

Herod the Great (c.73–4 BC)

Herod was King of Judea. He was first appointed to be Governor of Galilee by the great Roman Emperor Julius Caesar in 47 BC and then to the even more important position of King of Judea in 40 BC by Mark Antony. When Mark Antony was defeated by Octavian, who later became the Roman Emperor known as Augustus, many people thought that his friend Herod would lose the throne. But Augustus allowed Herod to remain as King because he was so **loyal** to Rome and **ruthlessly** kept all his **subjects obedient** to the Roman Empire. He also ruled the country very **efficiently**. He made sure that the **finances** of the country were properly managed. He improved **agriculture** and **founded** a number of cities. It seems likely that he was also a cruel ruler, to judge from the iron control he **maintained** over his people and the accusations of the slaughter of innocent children made against him in the Gospels.

High in the Heaven

by Charles Causley

High in the Heaven
A gold star burns
Lighting our way
As the great world turns.

Silver the frost
It shines on the stem
As we now journey
To Bethlehem.

White is the ice
At our feet as we tread,
Pointing a path
To the manger-bed.

My Mother Saw a Dancing Bear

by Charles Causley

My mother saw a dancing bear
By the schoolyard, a day in June.
The keeper stood with chain and bar
And whistle pipe, and played a tune.

And bruin lifted up its head
And lifted up its dusty feet
And all the children laughed to see
It caper in the summer heat.

They watched as for the Queen it died.
They watched it march. They watched it halt.
They watched the keeper as he cried,
"Now, roly-poly!" "Somersault!"

And then, my mother said, there came
The keeper with a begging cup
The bear with burning coat of fur
Shaming the laughter to a stop.

They paid a penny for the dance,
But what they saw was not the show
Only, in bruin's aching eyes,
Far-distant forests, and the snow.

A Begins Another

by Julie Holder

A is for 'ungry 'orses
B is for long
C is for sailing courses
D dum D D is for song.
E eeeee for a ghostly wail
F ort to be for work
G up said the horse on a mountain trail
H lost in honour found in house and puts the sh in shirk.
I is for you and me and one
J is for bird who chatters and squawks
K for Knight is there but dumb
L leads an 'ephant by the nose and is found in the middle of walks.
M is a W on stilts or the start of drawing a crown
N is the letter for 'velope
O is the sound of surprise written down
P is found in pod or tin or finishing the soap.
Q short or long it always waits
R RRR is a cheer of sorts
S is a snake and the sound that it makes
T is for shirt for leisure or sports.
U is not for you alone
V is a spear or an arrow head
W is not your twin
X marks the spot of treasure or wrong or a kiss to be read.
Y is a question asked many times over and over and over
Z and done is this alphabet
A begins another.

Brother

by Brian Merrick

Behaves like a maniac, when grown-ups aren't watching
Rampages most when you want to be quiet
Orders you around as if you were his servant
Thinks endlessly of fresh ways to torment you
Hates above everything to hear you admired
Eats with loud noises simply to irritate
Resorts to being charming only as the last desperate bribe.

Leonardo

by Charles Causley

Leonardo, painter, taking
Morning air
On Market Street
Saw the wild birds in their
cages
Silent in
The dust, the heat

Took his purse from out his
pocket
Never questioning
The fee,
Bore the cages to the green
shade
Of a hill top
Cypress tree.

"What you lost," said
Leonardo
"I now give to you
Again,
Free as noon and night and
morning,
As the sunshine,
As the rain."

And he took them from their
prisons,
Held them to
The air, the sky;
Pointed them to the bright
heaven.
"Fly!" said Leonardo.
"Fly."

It Takes One to Know One

by Gervase Phinn

Historians take you aback;
Horologists take one's time;
Taxi drivers take you for a ride;
Kleptomaniacs take it from there.
Surgeons take it out of you;
Duellists take the point;
Washerwomen take down a peg or two;
Hurdlers take a running jump;
Pursuers take after me

The Balaclava Boys

by George Layton

Tony and Barry both had one. I reckon half the kids in our class had one. But I didn't. My mum wouldn't even listen to me.

"You're not having a balaclava! What do you want a balaclava for in the middle of summer?"

I must've told her about ten times why I wanted a balaclava.

"I want one so's I can join the Balaclava Boys..."

"Go and wash your hands for tea, and don't be so silly."

She turned away from me to lay the table, so I put the curse of the middle finger on her. This was pointing both your middle fingers at somebody when they weren't looking. Tony had started it when Miss Taylor gave him a hundred lines for flicking paper pellets at Jennifer Greenwood. He had to write out a hundred times: "I must not fire missiles because it is dangerous and liable to cause damage to someone's eye."

Tony tried to tell Miss Taylor that he hadn't fired a missile, he'd just flicked a paper pellet, but she threw a piece of chalk at him and told him to shut up.

"Don't just stand there – wash your hands."

"Eh?"

"Don't say 'eh', say 'pardon'."

"What?"

"Just hurry up, and make sure the dirt comes off in the water, and not on the towel, do you hear?"

Ooh, my mum. She didn't half go on sometimes.

"I don't know what you get up to at school. How do you get so dirty?"

I knew exactly the kind of balaclava I wanted. One just like Tony's, a sort of yellowy-brown. His dad had given it to him because of his earache. Mind you, he didn't like wearing it at

first. At school he'd given it to Barry to wear and got it back before home-time. But, all the other lads started asking if they could have a wear of it, so Tony took it back and said from then on nobody but him could wear it, not even Barry. Barry told him he wasn't bothered because he was going to get a balaclava of his own, and so did some of the other lads. And that's how it started – the Balaclava Boys.

It wasn't a gang really. I mean they didn't have meetings or anything like that. They just went around together wearing their balaclavas, and if you didn't have one you couldn't go around with them. Tony and Barry were my best friends, but because I didn't have a balaclava, they wouldn't let me go round with them. I tried.

"Aw, go on, Barry, let us walk round with you."

"No, you can't. You're not a Balaclava Boy."

"Aw, go on."

"No."

"Please."

I don't know why I wanted to walk round with them anyway. All they did was wander up and down the playground dressed in their rotten balaclavas. It was daft.

"Go on, Barry, be a sport."

"I've told you. You're not a Balaclava Boy. You've got to have a balaclava. If you get one, you can join."

"But I can't, Barry. My mum won't let me have one."

"Hard luck."

"You're rotten."

Then he went off with the others. I wasn't half fed up. All my friends were in the Balaclava Boys. All the lads in my class except me. Wasn't fair. The bell went for the next lesson – ooh heck, handicraft with the Miseryguts Garnett – then it was home-time. All the Balaclava Boys were going in and I followed them.

"Hey, Tony, do you want to go down the woods after school?"

"No, I'm going round with the Balaclava Boys."

"Oh."

Blooming Balaclava Boys. Why wouldn't *my mum* buy *me* a *balaclava*? Didn't she realise that I was losing all my friends, and just because she wouldn't buy me one?

"Eh, Tony, we can go goose-gogging – you know, by those great gooseberry bushes at the other end of the woods."

"I've told you, I can't."

"Yes, I know, but I thought you might want to go goose-gogging."

"Well, I would, but I can't."

I wondered if Barry would be going as well.

"Is Barry going round with the Balaclava Boys an' all?"

"Course he is."

"Oh."

Blooming balaclavas. I wish they'd never been invented.

"Why won't your mum get you one?"

"I don't know. She says it's daft wearing a balaclava in the middle of summer. She won't let me have one."

"I found mine at home up in our attic."

Tony unwrapped some chewing-gum and asked me if I wanted a piece.

"No thanks." I'd've only had to wrap it in my handkerchief once we got in the classroom. You couldn't get away with anything with Mr Garnett.

"Hey, maybe you could find one in your attic."

For a minute I wasn't sure what he was talking about.

"Find what?"

"A balaclava."

"No, we haven't even got an attic."

I didn't half find handicrafts class boring. All that mucking about with compasses and rulers. Or else it was weaving, and you got all tangled up with balls of wool. I was just no good at handicraft and Mr Garnett agreed with me. Today was worse than ever. We were painting pictures and we had to call it "My favourite story". Tony was painting Noddy in Toyland. I told him he'd get into trouble.

"Garnett'll do you."

"Why? It's my favourite story."

"Yes, but I don't think he'll believe you."

Tony looked ever so hurt.

"But honest. It's my favourite story. Anyway what are you doing?"

He leaned over to have a look at my favourite story.

"Have you read it, Tony?"

"I don't know. What is it?"

"It's Robinson Crusoe, what do you think it is?"

He just looked at my painting.

"Oh, I see it now. Oh yes, I get it now. I couldn't make it out for a minute. Oh yes, there's Man Friday behind him."

"Get your finger off, it's still wet. And that isn't Man Friday, it's a coconut tree. And you've smudged it."

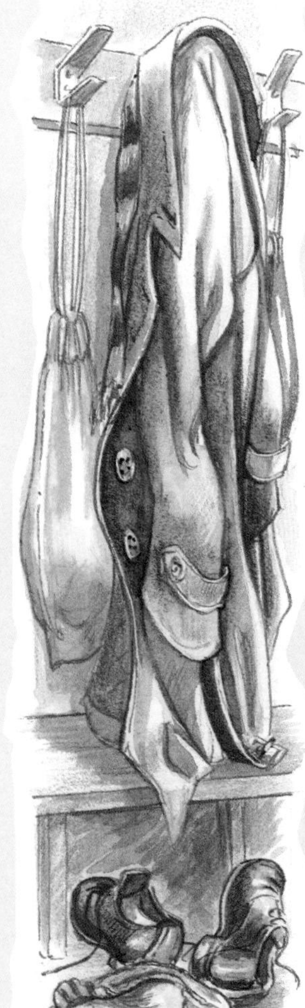

We were using some stuff called poster paint, and I got covered in it. I was getting it everywhere, so I asked Mr Garnett if I could go for a wash. He gets annoyed when you ask to be excused, but he could see I'd got it all over my hands, so he said I could go, but told me to be quick.

The washbasins were in the boys' cloakroom just outside the main hall. I got most of the paint off and as I was drying my hands, that's when it happened. I don't know what came over me. As soon as I saw the balaclava lying there on the floor, I decided to pinch it. I couldn't help it. I just knew that this was my only chance. I've never pinched anything before – I don't think I have – but I didn't think of this as... well... I don't even like saying it, but... well stealing. I just did it.

I picked it up, went to my coat, and put it in the pocket. At least I tried to put it in the pocket but it bulged out, so I pushed it down the inside of the sleeve. My head was throbbing, and even though I'd just dried my hands, they were all wet from sweating. If only I'd thought a bit first. But it all happened so quickly. I went back to the classroom, and as I was going in I began to realise what I'd done. I'd *stolen* a balaclava. I didn't even know whose it was, but as I stood in the doorway I couldn't believe I'd done it. If only I could go back. In fact I thought I would but then Mr Garnett told me to hurry up and sit down. As I was going back to my desk I felt as if all the lads knew what I'd done. How *could* they? Maybe somebody had seen me. No! Yes! How *could* they? They could. Of course they couldn't. No, course not. What if they did though? Oh heck.

I thought home-time would never come but when the bell did ring I got out as quick as I could. I was going to put the balaclava back before anybody noticed; but as I got to the cloakroom I heard Norbert Lightowler shout out that someone had pinched his balaclava. Nobody took much notice, thank goodness, and I heard Tony say to him that he'd most likely lost it. Norbert said he hadn't but he went off to make sure it wasn't in the classroom.

I tried to be all casual and took my coat, but I didn't dare put it on in case the balaclava popped out of the sleeve. I said tarah to Tony.

"Tarah, Tony, see you tomorrow."

"Yeh, tarah."

Oh, it was good to get out in the open air. I couldn't wait to get home and get rid of that blooming balaclava. Why had I gone and done a stupid thing like that? Norbert Lightowler was sure to report it to the Headmaster, and there'd be an announcement about it at morning assembly and the culprit would be asked to own up. I was running home as fast as I could. I wanted to stop and take out the balaclava and chuck it away, but I didn't dare. The faster I ran, the faster my head was filled with thoughts. I could give it back to Norbert. You know, say I'd taken it by mistake. No, he'd never believe me. None of the lads would believe me. Everybody knew how much I wanted to be a Balaclava Boy. I'd have to get rid of the blooming thing as fast as I could.

My mum wasn't back from work when I got home, thank goodness, so as soon as I shut the front door, I put my hand down the sleeve of my coat for the balaclava. There was nothing there. That was funny, I was sure I'd put it down that sleeve. I tried down the other sleeve, and there was still nothing there. Maybe I'd got the wrong coat. No, it was my coat all right. Oh, blimey, I must've lost it while I was running home. I was glad in a way. I was going to have to get rid of it,

now it was gone. I only hoped nobody had seen it drop out, but, oh, I was glad to be rid of it. Mind you, I was dreading going to school next morning. Norbert'd've probably have reported it by now. Well, I wasn't going to own up. I didn't mind the cane, it wasn't that, but if you owned up, you had to go up on the stage in front of the whole school. Well I was going to forget about it now and nobody would ever know that I'd pinched that blooming lousy balaclava.

I started to do my homework, but I couldn't concentrate. I kept thinking about assembly next morning. What if I went all red and everybody else noticed? They'd know I'd pinched it then. I tried to think about other things, nice things. I thought about bed. I just wanted to go to sleep. To go to bed and sleep. Then I thought about my mum; what she'd say if she knew I'd been stealing. But I still couldn't forget about assembly next day. I went into the kitchen and peeled some potatoes for my mum. She was ever so pleased when she came in from work and said I must've known she'd brought me a present.

"Oh, thanks. What've you got me?"

She gave me a paper bag and when I opened it I couldn't believe my eyes – a blooming balaclava.

"There you are, now you won't be left out and you can stop making my life a misery."

"Thanks, Mum."

If only my mum knew she was making *my* life a misery. The balaclava she'd brought me was just like the one I'd pinched. I felt sick. I didn't want it. I couldn't wear it now. If I did, everybody would say it was Norbert Lightowler's. Even if they didn't, I just couldn't wear it. I wouldn't feel it was mine. I had to get rid of it. I went outside and put it down the lavatory. I had to pull the chain three times before it went away. It's a good job we've got an outside lavatory or else my mum would have wondered what was wrong with me.

I could hardly eat my tea.

"What's wrong with you? Aren't you hungry?"

"No, not much."

"What've you been eating? You've been eating sweets, haven't you?"

"No, I don't feel hungry."

"Don't you feel well?"

"I'm all right."

I wasn't, I felt terrible. I told my mum I was going upstairs to work on my model aeroplane.

"Well, it's my bingo night, so make yourself some cocoa before you go to bed."

I went upstairs to bed, and after a while I fell asleep. The last thing I remember was a big balaclava, with a smiling face, and it was the Headmaster's face.

I was scared stiff when I went to school next morning. In assembly it seemed different. All the boys were looking at me. Norbert Lightowler pushed past and didn't say anything. When prayers finished I just stood there waiting for the Headmaster to ask for the culprit to own up, but he was talking about the school fete. And then he said he had something very important to announce and I could feel myself going red. My ears were burning like anything and I was going hot and cold both at the same time. "I'm very pleased to announce that the school football team has won the inter-league cup..."

And that was the end of assembly, except that we were told to go and play in the schoolyard until we were called in, because there was a teachers' meeting. I couldn't understand why I hadn't been found out yet, but I still didn't feel any better, I'd probably be called to the Headmaster's room later on.

I went out into the yard. Everybody was happy because we were having extra playtime. I could see all the Balaclava Boys going round together. Then I saw Norbert Lightowler was one of them. I couldn't be sure it was Norbert because he had a balaclava on, so I had to go up close to him. Yes, it was Norbert. He must have bought a new balaclava that morning.

"Have you bought a new one then, Norbert?"

"Y'what?"

"You've bought a new balaclava, have you?"

"What are you talking about?"

"Your balaclava. You've got a new balaclava, haven't you?"

"No, I never lost it, at all. Some fool had shoved it down the sleeve of my raincoat."

The Name of the Game

by John Foster

Play with names
And **Pat** becomes **tap**
Karl is a **lark**
And **Pam** is a **map**
Miles is **slime**
Liam is a **mail**
Bart is a **brat**
Lina's a **nail**
Star tars
Gary turn **gray**
Norma's a **Roman**
Amy makes **may**
Trish is a **shirt**
Kay is a **yak**
But whatever you do
Jack remains Jack.

Eataweek

by John Coldwell

Bunsday
Stewsday
Henseggday
Bangerday
Pieday
Spaghettiday
Sundae

The Peacock Garden

by Anita Desai

Chapter One

That summer, in 1947, the rains were late. Each day seemed hotter than the last in the little village in Punjal. The earth was scorched and every weed on it had withered. The water in the canals that criss-crossed the fields was all gone, and the clay lay cracked into smooth, pink tiles. The sky was yellow, the sun hidden by dust.

The nights, too, were so hot that it was difficult to sleep at all. As long ago as April, the family had moved its beds out into the courtyard for some cool night air. In May, they carried them up to the flat roof of their white house, to catch the few faint breezes that rose somewhere in the mango grove by the canal and murmured over the housetops.

In July, there were a few showers. The family had to wake up in the middle of the night, roll up their bedclothes and carry them down to the house and spread them out on the floor for the rest of the night. Zuni hated these nights, for it was stifling in the room with the small windows, and she wished she were allowed to stay out on the roof and feel the cool raindrops patter down on her hot, dry, dusty body. Her skin was covered with prickly heat that was raw and red and itched terribly.

In August, the heat grew worse. Night after night, the family tossed and turned on their beds, getting up every now and then to drink from the earthen jar in a corner of the parapet that kept the water cool when the hot

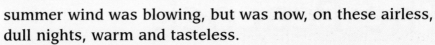

summer wind was blowing, but was now, on these airless, dull nights, warm and tasteless.

On the other rooftops, too, families were spread out on their cots. They could not sleep. Some sat in the faint starlight, playing their flutes. Some talked in low murmurs, in worried voices. Others paced the rooftops – white figures in the dark, slowly walking up and down, up and down, waiting for a breeze or a cloud – so Zuni thought. She knew they were waiting, but she did not really know what they were waiting for, nor did she know why they were so worried.

One night, when Zuni had fallen asleep very late out of sheer tiredness from tossing and turning on the burning hot bed, she was woken by a heat worse than any she had know before, and voices – low and urgent close to her, but loud and wild in the distance where the bazaar was.

"What?" she cried, sitting up, feeling the heat burning her body, and then she saw flames leaping up to the sky in the neighbour's courtyard, like a huge bonfire. That was why she was so hot that perspiration was running down from under her hair, over her face, soaking her clothes. She cried out in fear.

Her father came immediately. He was a big man, with broad shoulders and a short black beard that had red streaks in it from henna dye. When he put his arm around her, she felt at once safe. But she was curious. "What's happened, Abba?" she cried. "Has Abdulla-*mia's* house caught fire?"

"Yes," he whispered. "Speak softly, Zuni. Don't be afraid. I'll carry you away, but you must be quiet, quiet."

"Why? Why?" she cried softly, against his beard. "Why don't we go and help Abdull-*mia*?"

"No, no, he's left – he's already gone," her father said, and Zuni could not understand at all why their neighbour had run away when his house had caught fire and not stayed to put it out.

She peeped over her father's shoulder at the fire as he

carried her down the steep stairs to the courtyard, and then she was even more surprised to see her mother standing with her heavy black cloak right over her head, holding her sewing machine in her arms! What on earth was she doing with her sewing machine in the middle of the night? And behind her was Zuni's elder sister, Razia, also draped in her dark brown cloak and carrying a basket filled with pots and pan.

Zuni stretched out her arms to her mother. She cried "Amma!" She understood that they were running away, too – but why? Where to? And why in the middle of the night?

"Shh!" someone hissed, and a dark figure slipped in through the narrow doorway of the courtyard. "Come," it called to them, "follow me – but in silence."

"Who's that?" Zuni whispered, clutching her father tightly about his neck.

"It is Gopal," Abba whispered. "He is taking us to a safe place. Now Zuni, no more talking. We must be silent," and he too slipped through the doorway, followed by Amma and Razia, each walking behind the other.

Gopal was the man who watched over Abba's mango grove down by the canal and helped to look after the cattle and take them to cattle fairs to trade. Gopal was not Muslim, like Abba's family, but a Hindu. That was why he could walk out in safety. Zuni could just make out his bald head and his white clothes, dim as a moth in the darkness. He carried no light. He led the way through the fields, between the bushes, along a very narrow path on which they kept stumbling. There was a faint sound of Amma's and Razia's

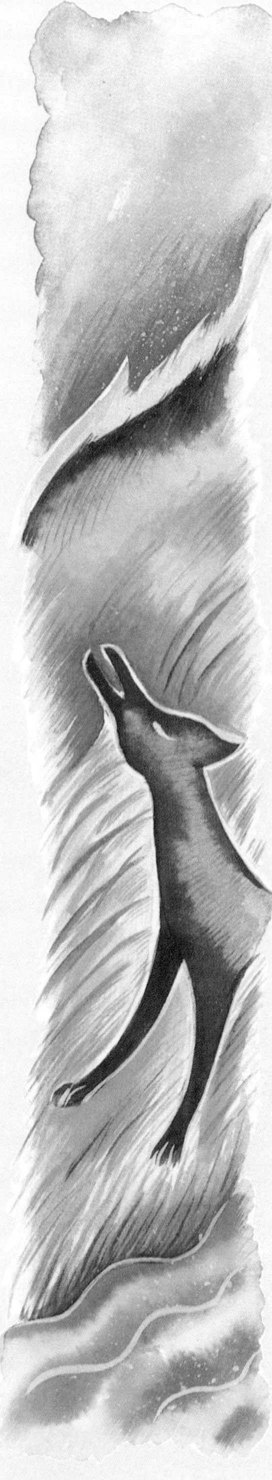

cloaks as they swished through the dry grass and bushes, and a faint tinkling of the pots and pans that Razia carried in her basket. Everyone had his head bowed, and Zuni kept hers low on her father's shoulder, but she peeped back at the village.

She saw so many bonfires there now, not just one, immense ones with hungry blue and orange and scarlet flames reaching out into the hot, parched air. It was as if the whole village was on fire. Zuni could see that it was too big a fire to put out – there was so little water in the well these days, and none at all in the canals. That must be the reason why they were running away – but why in silence? Why in hiding? And she could hear voices in the village, at the end where the bazaar was, some screaming high, thin screams like kites battling in the sky, and some hoarse yelling. The voices sounded not only frightened, but mad, wild.

Zuni hid her face in her father's beard to keep from bursting with the questions in her that she had to keep still. His arms were strong and hard around her, but his feet often slipped and stumbled on the narrow, unlit path through the fields, and he was breathing hard. She felt the perspiration roll down his cheeks, into his beard and down his neck. Every now and then she peeped to see if Gopal was still in front, leading them, and if Amma and Razia were safely following. They kept close together in the dark.

Zuni heard the stray dogs of the village howling out in the fields, wailing as if they were in tears. Somewhere down by the canal bed a jackal answered, and its voice was even more sad and frightening. Now all they could see of the fire was the glow in the sky, angry and red.

Suddenly, white walls rose above them and Gopal knocked lightly on a great wooden door. Then he put his mouth to a crack and whispered something that made the person at the other side very, very carefully open the door just a slit. Abba pressed through the narrow slit so that Zuni's legs scraped against the sides. Then Amma slipped through, struggling

and panting with the heavy sewing machine, and then Razia, and immediately the door was shut behind them and bolted.

"But Gopal!" Zuni cried out aloud. "He's been left behind."

"It is safe for him outside," Abba said in a heavy voice, and he set Zuni down on the ground and straightened his back with a groan.

It was completely dark in that courtyard enclosed on all sides by white walls. There was not a single lamp lit anywhere. Nor did the wild glow of the fire reach them there.

Then the bent white figure that had so cautiously let them in whispered, "Come, I have a room for you." He led them over the tiled floor, opened another creaking, low door and let the into a small, close room that seemed to be full of straw and stank of cattle. "You'll be safe here," he whispered and then shuffled away into the shadows.

Zuni felt her mother's hands on her head, then patting her cheeks with trembling fingers. "Lie down, Zuni," she whispered, "sleep now."

"Where, Amma?" Zuni cried. "I can't see any beds."

"In the straw, my dear," her mother replied and knelt to pat down the straw and spread her cloak on it to make a bed for her daughter.

That small, smelly, airless room was far hotter than their own room in the white house in the village. Zuni was sure it would be impossible to sleep. She lay down and the straw rose under the cloak and pricked her and scratched her in a hundred different places. She rolled over, bumped into the soft figure of her sister who lay curled up and trembling, and put her hand on Razia's arm, wishing to ask her something. But she

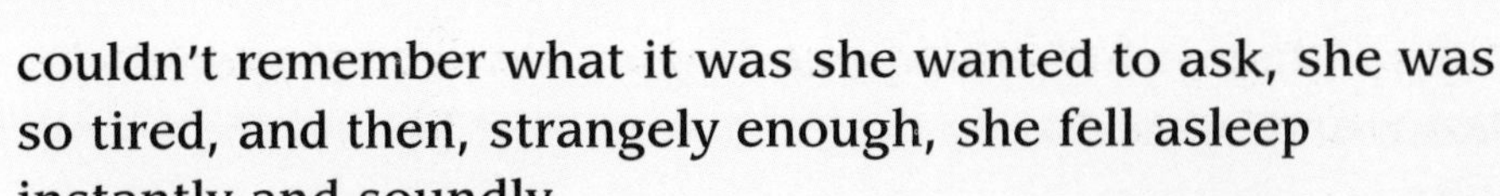

couldn't remember what it was she wanted to ask, she was so tired, and then, strangely enough, she fell asleep instantly and soundly.

Chapter Two

Zuni's family have moved, with other Muslim families, to the Mosque, where they hope to be safe. Other people, including Razia's fiancé, have fled to Pakistan. Zuni's father does not want to leave his land, so the family stays on in the mosque, but gradually more and more people leave for Pakistan.

The refugees in the courtyard of the mosque were getting worried because there was so little food left and it was not safe to go out for more. Then the trucks came at last to take them to Pakistan.

Abba and Zuni went out to watch, sleepy as they were.

"Are you all ready?" shouted the officer. "I will call out your name – step out and line up here. No big boxes allowed – only small bundles that you can carry yourselves. We haven't much space." The courtyard buzzed with life as if it were broad daylight instead of the middle of the night. The stars were covered with a blanket of dust and it was very dark. It was a wonder how fathers found their children, children their mothers, families their belongings. But in a short while they were all in a line with soldiers on either side of them to lead them out of the courtyard to the trucks that waited outside.

A few of them looked over their shoulders and called to Abba: "*Salaam Valeikum*, Habib-*mia*," and he called back in a hoarse voice, "*Valeikum Salaam!*"

Then they were all gone and the caretaker shut the heavy door and bolted it and only Abba and Zuni were left standing in the courtyard which suddenly seemed as bare and still as a graveyard. In the darkness, Zuni saw the white dome of the mosque rise above the treetops and walls, like a ghost. There was a sudden shriek that made her fly against Abba, crying, "What's that?"

It was the caretaker who answered as he shuffled off, tinkling the ring of keys tied to his side. "A peacock," he chuckled, "only a peacock." He went off towards his room in one corner of the courtyard, calling over his shoulder, "Tomorrow I'll show you your new home."

Abba lifted Zuni in his arms and called back, "We'll be ready for you in the morning." Then he hugged Zuni so that her face was pressed into his short, tickly beard and he said, "Sleep now. I'll hold you in my lap so you can sleep outdoors tonight. It's cooler here." He sat down by the doorway and was silent. He seemed to be listening for the sound of the trucks grinding up the dusty road towards Pakistan. But they could only hear the rustle of the banyan leaves and, sometimes, the sad cry of a peacock.

The Chief's Daughter: A Synopsis

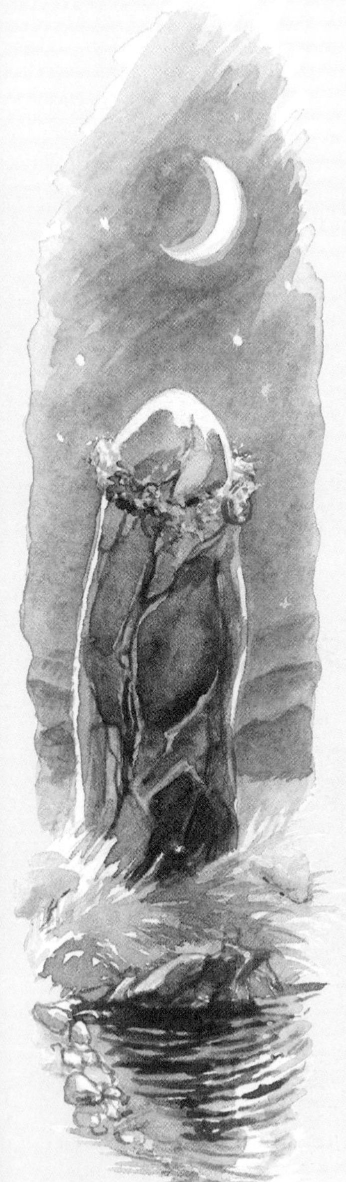

Nessan, a ten-year-old girl, is the daughter of the Chief of a Celtic tribe living in a hill village on the coast of Wales in the fifth century. Her great friend is Dara, a twelve-year-old boy who is a prisoner and a hostage, and obliged to work as a slave, having been captured from a raiding party of robbers from over the sea in Ireland.

Dara is lucky to be alive at all. According to the religious rules of the tribe he should have been sacrificed to their Goddess, the Black Mother, in thanksgiving for delivering the encampment safely from the raid. (*The Black Mother is a great stone that dominates the ridge high on the moorland above the encampment. It is the only jet black stone in a grey landscape, which persuades the superstitious tribe that is has Godlike powers.*) Dara has survived only because Nessan has pleaded desperately with her father not to allow the sacrifice to proceed and has made her own sacrifice as compensation to the Black Mother: her precious blue glass arm ring. Dara is too proud to properly acknowledge the debt he owes Nessan, but they become as close friends as it is possible for a Chief's daughter to be with a slave.

Then disaster threatens the tribe. The water pool, which has provided them over the years with a permanent supply of water, begins to dry up as the underground stream from the hills that feeds it diminishes daily to a mere trickle.

Laethrig, the old priest, convinces the Chieftain they are being punished in this way by the Black Mother for their failure to sacrifice Dara. The Chieftain reluctantly agrees that the boy must be sacrificed to ensure the preservation of the water supply.

Failing to dissuade her father from the sacrifice, Nessan releases Dara from the hut where he is imprisoned awaiting sacrifice, and sets him free to find a war band of his own people. They are both grieved to be parting. As he runs across the moor, putting as great a distance as possible between himself and the camp, Dara stumbles across the rock, the Black Mother, and at its base the spring which feeds, by means of an underground stream, the camp water pool. The spring has become choked by a dam of small branches and vegetation clustered round a spear left behind in the spring as an offering by Irish raiders. Taking the spear for his own protection (and leaving a present given him by Nessan to compensate the Black Mother) Dara hurries on his way, not realising that he has broken the artificial dam and returned the stream to its original underground route to the encampment.

The Chief's Daughter

by Rosemary Sutcliff

"Look ! This is the way you must go – they don't guard this side. And when you're away, you'll be able to find a war band of your own people."

They had scrambled down the dry runnel-bed, right to the far edge of the gap, and the cliff plunged almost from their feet to the sea creaming among the rocks far down below. Dara looked – and down – and down – and swallowed as though he felt sick.

"You've got to go that way!" Nessan whispered fiercely. "It's easy."

"If it's so easy, why don't they guard it?"

"Because the water from the spring makes it slippery, and no one could keep his footing on the wet rocks. But now it's dry. Don't you see? It's dry!"

She fished hurriedly down the front of her tunic, and held something out to him.

"Here's a barley cake. Now go quick!"

But the boy Dara hesitated an instant longer. "Nessan, why are you doing this?"

"I – don't want you to be killed."

"I don't want to be killed either. But Nessan, what will they do to you?"

"They will not do anything. No one will know that I had anything to do with it, if only you go quickly."

Dara tried to say something more, then flung an arm round her neck in a small fierce hug and next instant was creeping forward alone.

She was half crying, as he crouched and slithered away, feeling for every hand- and foothold along the grass-tufted cliff edge, and disappeared in the black moon-shadow of the turf wall. She waited shivering, ears on the stretch for any sound. Once she heard the rattle of a falling pebble, but nothing more. At last she turned back towards the Chief's Hall, and the quickening throb of the wolfskin drums.

Dara clambers along the cliff face and sets off to try to rejoin his tribe. He is keenly aware that he is alone and unarmed in an enemy country.

Presently, well into the hills, he came upon a moorland pool, where two streamlets met. It was so small and shallow that he could have waded through it in several places, and scarcely get wet to the knee. And the moon, still high in the glimmering sky, showed him an upright black stone that stood taller than a man, exactly between the two streamlets where they emptied themselves into the pool. A black stone, in a countryside where other stones were grey; and twisted about the narrowest part near the top, a withered garland of tough moorland flowers, ling and ragwort and white-plumed bog-grasses.

Dara stood staring at it with a feeling of awe. And as he did so, a little wind stirred the dry garland, and from something fastened among the brittle flowerheads, the moonlight struck out a tiny blaze of brilliant blue fire! Nessan's blue glass arm-ring! He caught his breath, realizing that this must be the Goddess herself, the Black Mother. But at the same instant, he noticed the spear which stood upright in the tail of the pool. A fine spear, its butt ending in a ball of enamelled bronze; an Irish spear!

His own people must have passed this way and come across the Goddess whose People they had been raiding, and left an offering to turn aside her anger. He noticed also that the spear, set up in what seemed to be the place where the two streams joined before the feet of the Black Mother, had caught a dead furze branch on its

way down and twigs and birch leaves and clumps of dry grass, even the carcass of some small animal, had drifted into the furze branch and clung there, building up into something like a small beaver's dam, and blocking the stream so that it had spread out into a pool. And as the pool grew high enough, it had begun to spill over a new runnel that it was cutting for itself down the hillside.

Dara was not interested in the changed course of a stream, but he needed that spear; needed it so badly that his need was greater even than his fear of taking it.

He caught a deep breath and turned to the tall garlanded stone that seemed to him now to stand like a queen in the moonlight. "Black Mother, do not be angry. I must have the spear. See, I will leave you a barley cake and my amber necklace instead. That is two gifts for one!"

And his heart racing, he stepped into the water and pulled up the spear. For a moment he expected the sky to fall on him or the hillside to open and close again over his head. But nothing happened, and he went on his way, following the faint track of the war band that he could pick up here and there by trampled grass or a thread of dark wool caught on a bramble spray, and the droppings left by driven cattle.

And behind him, now that the spear that had held it was gone, little by little the dam washed away, and the pool sank, as the water returned to its old stream bed and sang its way downhill, to disappear under a bramble bush in the place where it had always gone underground before the raider left his spear for the Black Mother.

And where it went from there, under the turf and the rocks and the hawthorn bushes on it way to the sea, was a secret that neither Dara nor the Irish raiders nor Nessan's People knew. Only the stream singing to itself in the dark, knew that secret.

Dara's escape has now been discovered by the Clan. The Chief decides that the man who had been set to guard Dara should be sacrificed in his place, if he cannot be found. The Clan all accept that this is fair and just. Nessan realises she can't let this happen.

Nessan walked forward into the torchlight, the people parting to let her through. "I helped him to escape, my Father, through the gap where the spring water goes. It is dry, not slippery, now that the water – does not run."

The Chief groaned and covered his face with his hands, and Laethrig the Priest, who had been standing by all this while, spoke for the first time. "And you are daring to come forth here and tell us of it?"

"Yes, Old Holy One." Nessan tried desperately to steady her voice.

"You are very brave, my child, or very foolish!"

Nessan drew a long, shivering breath.

"You cannot kill Istoreth. It was not his fault. I – I knew when I helped Dara away, that if the well did not fill again, I must come here instead of him."

"It is of your own choosing," said the old priest, very gently. "So be it, then; come here to me."

"No!" cried the Chief.

"Yes!" said the old priest, as gently as ever. He was holding the black pottery bowl that was used for only one thing, to hold that drink that brought the Long Sleep at the time of sacrifice.

Nessan took a step towards him, and wavered for a moment, then walked steadily forward.

Everything was very quiet, nobody moved or whispered in all the crowd; the only sound was the restless stirring of the thirsty cattle. And then into the quiet, there fell a tiny sound; a soft "plop" and then a faint trickling from the well that had been sullenly silent all night long.

"No, wait!" one of the women cried.

"Listen!"

"What to, then?"

"There it is again!"

"It is the well! The spring is coming back to life!"

That time all those near enough to the spring heard it, and a great gasp went up from them. They crowded round the well-pool; then they were parting and pushing back to make a path for the Chief and Laethrig to pass through.

Nessan did not move. She stood where she was, and shut her eyes tight; she heard another plop and a wet green trickling, and the murmur of the crowd; and then her father crying out in a great triumphant voice, "The water is rising! You see, Old Holy One? You hear?"

"I see and I hear," said the old priest. "It is in my heart that the Black Mother is no longer angry with us…"

And she knew from his voice that he had gone away small inside himself, so that if you looked into his eyes it would be like looking through the doorway of an empty hut.

Everyone waited, hearing the plop and ripple of the refilling well. And then at last Nessan heard the old man sigh, and the dry rustle of his necklaces, as he stirred and came back to himself. "The Black Mother has spoken to me. She calls for no more sacrifice in this matter; she says the willingness is enough – the willingness is enough."

Nessan opened her eyes, half dazzled for the moment by the flare of the torches, and saw the Chief her father coming towards her, and flung herself into his arms, crying partly for sorrow that Dara was gone, and partly with relief so that there was not enough room for it all inside her, and partly because she was suddenly more tired than she had ever been in all her life.

And the Chief picked her up and carried her away to her own sleeping-place in the women's hut behind the great Hall. She was asleep before he laid her down on the dappled deerskin rugs.

At the same time, far up in the hills, a broken curlew's feather, the very last that was left of the dam, shook itself clear of the bog-myrtle of the stream bank, and went eddying downstream.

Eleanor Farjeon (1881–1965)

Eleanor Farjeon was the daughter of a well-off London family. She grew up in a very privileged home and never knew anything like the kind of hardship that Mrs Malone endured. Her parents were very interested in literature and the theatre and encouraged Eleanor to read and write.

She was always very interested in children, in their world and experiences, and wrote many stories and poems both for them and about them.

Although she herself was well off, she was always aware of and concerned about disadvantaged and unfortunate people. She wrote about them with great sympathy and sensitivity.

Her poems also show great understanding of old people, and the plight of those who live their lives alone.

Eleanor Farjeon does not have a prominent reputation as a poet, like, for example, Tennyson or Wordsworth, or even Charles Causley, but her poems have a great gentleness and sympathy about them and many are lovely and memorable.

Mrs Malone

by Eleanor Farjeon

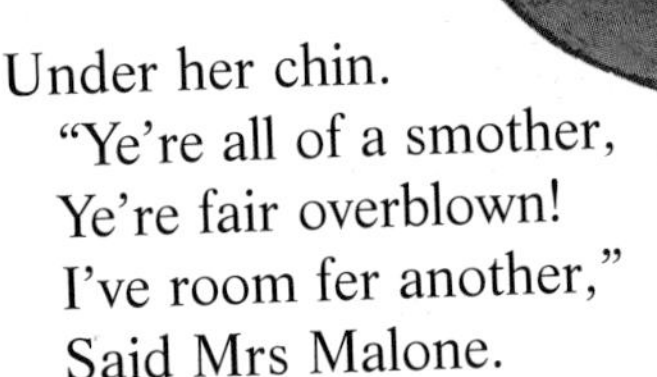

Mrs Malone
Lived hard by a wood
All on her lonesome
As nobody should.
With her crust on a plate
And her pot on the coal
And none but herself
To converse with, poor soul.
In a shawl and a hood
She got sticks out-o'-door,
On a bit of old sacking
She slept on the floor, and nobody, nobody
Asked how she fared
Or knew how she managed,
For nobody cared.
Why make a pother
About an old crone?
What for should they bother
With Mrs Malone?

One Monday in winter
With snow on the ground
So thick that a footstep
Fell without sound,
She heard a faint frostbitten
Peck on the pane
And went to the window
To listen again.
There sat a cock-sparrow
Bedraggled and weak,
With half-open eyelid
And ice on his beak.
She threw up the sash
And she took the bird in,
And mumbled and fumbled it
Under her chin.
"Ye're all of a smother,
Ye're fair overblown!
I've room fer another,"
Said Mrs Malone.

Come Tuesday while eating
Her dry morning slice
With the sparrow a-picking
("Ain't company nice!")
She heard on her doorpost
A curious scratch
And there was a cat
With its claw on the latch.
It was hungry and thirsty
And thin as a lath,
It mewed and it mowed
On the slithery path.
She threw the door open
And warmed up some pap
And huddled and cuddled it
In her old lap.
"There, there, little brother,
Ye poor skin-an'-bone,
There's room fer another,"
Said Mrs Malone.

Come Wednesday while all of them
Crouched on the mat
With a crumb for the sparrow,
A sip for the cat,

There was wailing and whining
Outside in the wood,
And there sat a vixen
With six of her brood.
She was haggard and ragged
And worn to a shred,
And her half-dozen babies
Were only half-fed,
But Mrs Malone, crying
"My! ain't they sweet!"
Happed them and lapped them
And gave them to eat.
"You warm yerself, mother,
Ye're cold as a stone!
There's room fer another,"
Said Mrs Malone.

Come Thursday a donkey
Stepped in off the road
With sores on his withers
From bearing a load.
Come Friday when icicles
Pierced the white air
Down from the mountainside
Lumbered a bear.
For each she had something,
If little, to give –
"Lord knows, the poor critters
Must all of 'em live."
She gave them her sacking,
Her hood and her shawl,
Her loaf and her teapot –
She gave them her all.
"What with one thing and t'other
Me fambily's grown,
And there's room fer another,"
Said Mrs Malone.

Come Saturday evening
When time was to sup
Mrs Malone
Had forgot to sit up.
The cat said *meeow*,
And the sparrow said *peep*,
The vixen, *she's sleeping*,
The bear, *let her sleep*.
On the back of the donkey
They bore her away,
Through trees and up mountains
Beyond night and day,
Till come Sunday morning
They brought her in state
Through the last cloudbank
As far as the Gate.
"Who is it," asked Peter,
"You have with you there?"
And donkey and sparrow,
Cat, vixen and bear

Exclaimed, "Do you tell us
Up here she's unknown?
It's our mother, God bless us!
It's Mrs Malone
Whose havings were few
And whose holding was small
And whose heart was so big
It had room for us all."
Then Mrs Malone
Of a sudden awoke,
She rubbed her two eyeballs
And anxiously spoke:
"Where am I, to goodness,
And what do I see?
My dears, let's turn back,
This ain't no place for me!"
But Peter said, "Mother
Go in to the Throne.
There's room for another
One, Mrs Malone."

In the Workhouse

by George R. Sims

It is Christmas Day in the Workhouse,
And the cold bare walls are bright
With garlands of green and holly,
And the place is a pleasant sight:
For with clean-washed hands and faces,
In a long and hungry line
The paupers sit at the tables,
For this is the hour they dine.

And the guardians and their ladies,
Although the wind is east,
Have come in their furs and wrappers,
To watch their charges feast;
To smile and be condescending,
Put pudding on pauper plates,
To be hosts at the workhouse banquet
They've paid for – with the rates.

Oh, the paupers are meek and lowly
With their "Thank'ee kindly, mum's";
So long as they fill their stomachs,
What matter is it whence it comes?
But one of the old men mutters,
And pushes his plate aside:
"Great God!" he cries; "but it chokes me!
For this is the day *she* died."

The guardians gazed in horror,
The master's face went white;
Did a pauper refuse their pudding?"
"Could their ears believe aright?"
Then the ladies clutched their husbands,
Thinking the man would die,
Struck by a bolt, or something,
By the outraged One on high.

But the pauper sat for a moment,
Then rose 'mid a silence grim,
For the others had ceased to chatter,
And trembled in every limb.
He looked at the guardians' ladies,
Then, eyeing their lords, he said,
"I eat not the food of villains
Whose hands are foul and red."

"Whose victims cry for vengeance
From their dank, unhallowed graves."
"He's drunk!" said the workhouse master.
"Or else he's mad, and raves."
"Not drunk, or mad," cried the pauper,
"But only a hunted beast,
Who, torn by the hounds and mangled,
Declines at the vulture's feast.

"I care not a curse for the guardians.
And I won't be dragged away.
Just let me have the fit out,
It's only on Christmas Day
That the black past comes to goad me,
And prey on my burning brain;
I'll tell you the rest in a whisper, –
I swear I won't shout again.

"Keep your hands off me, curse you!
Hear me right out to the end.
You come here to see how the paupers
The season of Christmas spend.
You come here to watch us feeding.
As they watch the captured beast.
Hear why a penniless pauper
Spits on your paltry feast.

"Do you think I will take your bounty,
And let you smile and think
You're doing a noble action
With the parish's meat and drink?
Where is my wife, you traitors –
The poor old wife you slew?
Yes, by the God above us,
My Nance was killed by you!

"Last winter my wife lay dying,
Starved in a filthy den;
I had never been to the parish, –
I came to the parish then.
I swallowed my pride in coming,
For, ere the ruin came,
I held up my head as a trader,
And I bore a spotless name.

"I came to the parish, craving
Bread for a starving wife,
Bread for the woman who'd loved me
Through fifty years of life;
And what do you think they told me,
Mocking my awful grief?
That 'the House' was open to us,
But they wouldn't 'give out relief'.

"I slunk to the filthy alley –
'Twas a cold, raw Christmas eve –
And the bakers' shops were open,
Tempting a man to thieve;
But I clenched my fists together,
Holding my head awry,
So I came to her empty-handed,
And mournfully told her why.

"Then I told her 'the House' was open;
She had heard of the ways of *that*,
For her bloodless cheeks went crimson,
And up in her rags she sat.
Crying, 'Bide the Christmas here, John,
We've never had one apart;
I think I can bear the hunger, –
The other would break my heart.'

"All through that eve I watched her,
Holding her hand in mine,
Praying the Lord, and weeping
Till my lips were salt as brine.
I asked her once if she hungered,
And as she answered 'No,'
The moon shone in at the window
Set in a wreath of snow.

"Then the room was bathed in glory,
And I saw in my darling's eyes
The far-away look of wonder
That comes when the spirit flies;
And her lips were parched and parted
And her reason came and went,
For she raved of our home in Devon,
Where our happiest years were spent.

"And the accents, long forgotten,
Came back to the tongue once more,
For she talked like the country lassie
I woo'd by the Devon shore.
Then she rose to her feet and trembled,
And fell on the rags and moaned,
And, 'Give me a crust – I'm famished –
For the love of God!' she groaned.

"I rushed from the room like a madman,
And flew to the workhouse gate,
Crying, 'Food for a dying woman!'
And the answer came, 'Too late.'
They drove me away with curses;
Then I fought with a dog in the street,
And tore from the mongrel's clutches
A crust he was trying to eat.

"Back, through the filthy by-lanes!
Back, through the trampled slush!
Up to the crazy garret,
Wrapped in an awful hush.
My heart sank down at the threshold,
And I paused with a sudden thrill,
For there in the silvr'y moonlight
My Nance lay, cold and still.

"Up to the blackened ceiling
The sunken eyes were cast –
I knew on those lips all bloodless
My name had been the last;
She'd called for her absent husband –
Oh God! had I but known! –
Had called in vain, and in anguish
Had died in that den – *alone*.

"Yes, there, in a land of plenty,
Lay a loving woman dead,
Cruelly starved and murdered
For a loaf of the parish bread.
At yonder gate, last Christmas,
I craved for a human life.
You, who would feast us paupers,
What of my murdered wife!

"There, get ye gone to your dinners;
Don't mind me in the least;
Think of the happy paupers
Eating your Christmas feast;
And when you recount their blessings
In your smug parochial way,
Say what you did for *me*, too,
Only last Christmas Day."

Gold Rush

Gold fever swept whole continents in the 19th century. News of a "strike", or even a rumour of one, caused an immediate stampede. Ships in the ports nearby were abandoned by their crews, while other ships set sail from countries far away, carrying thousands of passengers caught up in the same golden dream.

Many never arrived at the goldfields and many more never found any gold, but a few found wealth beyond their wildest dreams.

The most important strike of the century happened in California in 1848. A man named James Marshall found gold near a sawmill belonging to John Sutter on the American River. The pair tried to keep the news a secret among Sutter's employees, but they failed; someone brandished a bottle containing gold dust in the tiny village of San Francisco and the rush was on. Soon San Francisco was anything but tiny.

At first the rush was a local affair, as almost the entire population of the area joined in a frantic race for the hills.

(From *The Wild West* by Robin May)

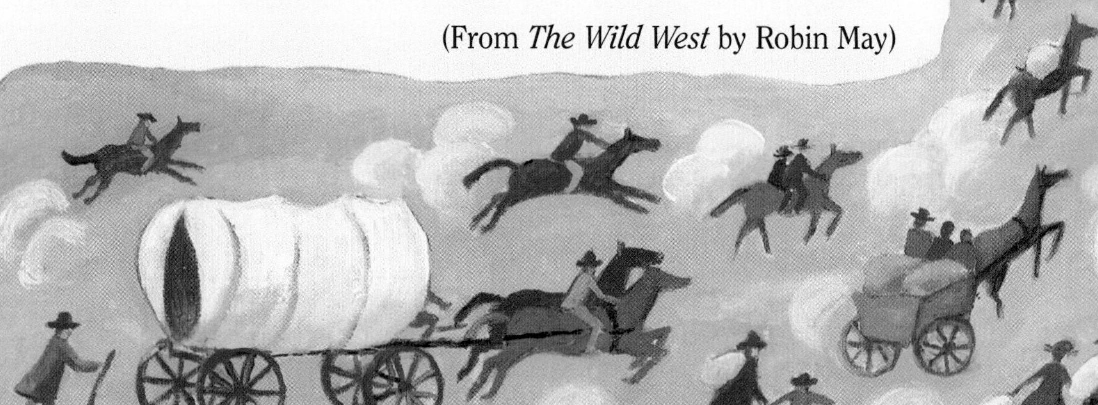

Sir Arthur Conan Doyle

In 1891 Sir Arthur Conan Doyle wrote a story about an imaginary detective, Sherlock Holmes. The story had a sensational success and Conan Doyle was persuaded to follow it up with a series of adventures about the eccentric and brilliant detective and his friend and assistant Dr Watson.

Many of the stories were published in a publication called *Strand Magazine*.

Millions of copies of the stories were sold and people wrote to Sherlock Holmes, convinced he was a real person.

But Conan Doyle, who wrote many other books and stories, including *The Lost World*, one of the first narratives about a forgotten prehistoric valley, grew tired of writing about Sherlock Holmes.

Consequently he decided to "kill him off". He did so in a fierce struggle with his great rival, the infamous Professor Moriarty, which ended in their fatal plunge over the Reichenbach Falls.

People were stunned. The story – which was entirely fictional – was reported as a real news item in the press. People wore black armbands in mourning. Over 20,000 people stopped buying the *Strand Magazine* and it almost collapsed.

Conan Doyle was besieged by people wanting him to bring Sherlock Holmes "back to life". Eventually he did, and wrote further series of his adventures, the first of which explained how Holmes had managed to avoid plunging to his death at Reichenbach.

Flying Bat

This bat flies across a room at great speed. Make it look as horrible as you can. It will look best in a fairly dark room.

You will need

a sheet of stiff black paper, or white paper and black paint

a piece of black paper, about 8cm long and 4cm wide

2 pipe cleaners

a small curtain ring

very thin nylon string or fishing line, about 8 metres long

glue, sticky tape and scissors

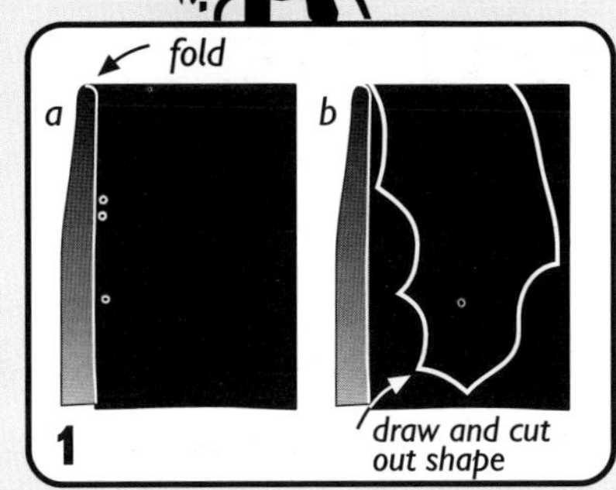

Fold the sheet of paper in half (a). Draw the shape of a bat's wing on one side (b). Cut out the shape but do not cut along the folded edge. Open out the paper.

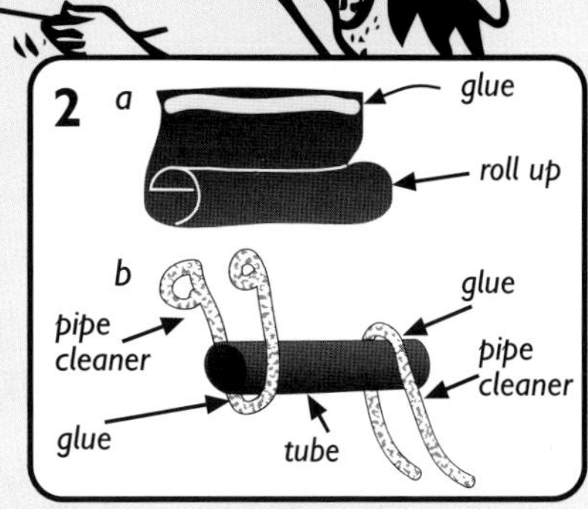

Roll up the small piece of paper to make a tube. Glue the edge (a). Bend a pipe cleaner round one end for the eyes and one round the other end for legs (b). Glue on.

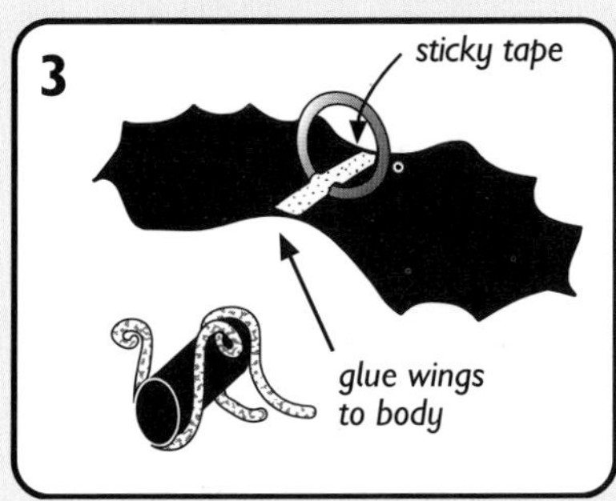

Stick the curtain ring upright to the middle of the wings with tape. Glue the wings to the body, like this. Paint the pipe cleaners black and bend them a little.

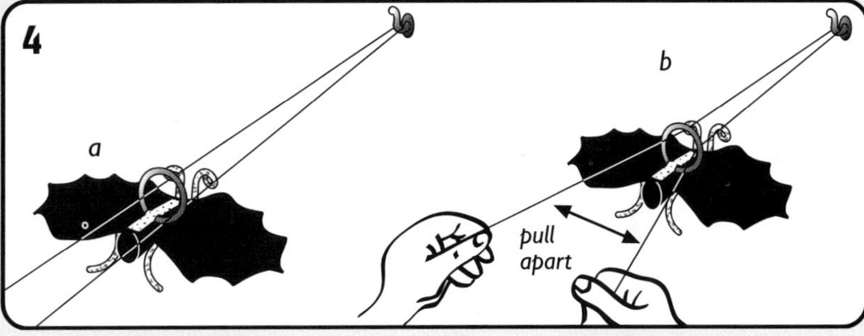

Hook the middle of the nylon string on to something high up in a room, perhaps near a door. Slide the ends of the string through the ring on the bat (a).

Hold one end of one string in each hand. Slide the bat down close to your hands. Now pull the strings apart as quickly as you can. The bat will fly along them (b).

Flies

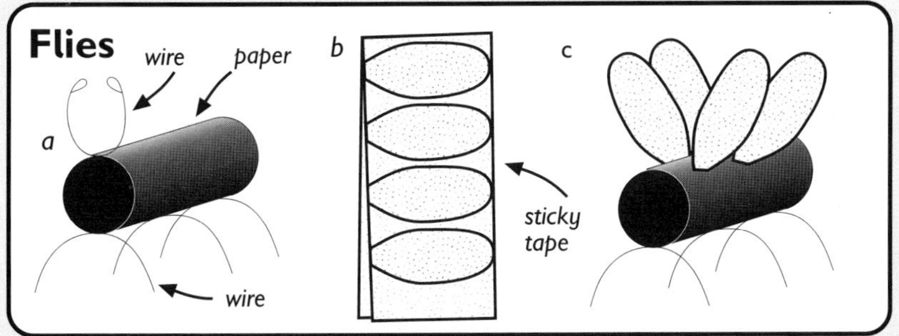

Make a little roll of paper and glue the edge. Cut some short bits of very thin wire. Glue them to make legs and antennae (a). Paint the paper black. Leave to dry.

Fold over a piece of sticky tape so the sticky sides are together. Cut out four oval shapes (b) and glue them on as the fly's wings (c). Everyone hates flies.

Wasps

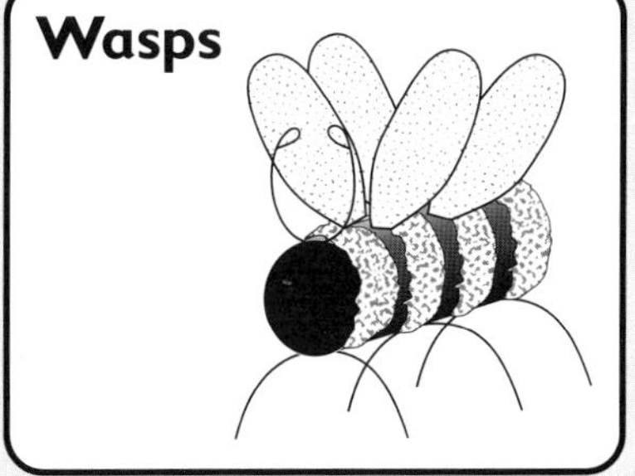

Make another fly but before you glue on the wings, wind a pipe cleaner round the body. Paint it in yellow and black stripes. Then glue on the wings.

What did one eye say to the other eye? Something has come between us that smells!

The Subtle Knife

by Philip Pullman

Chapter 1: The Cat and the Hornbeam Trees

Will tugged at his mother's hand and said, "Come *on*, come *on*..." But his mother hung back. She was still afraid. Will looked up and down the narrow street in the evening light, along the little terrace of houses, each behind its tiny garden and its box hedge, with the sun glaring off the windows of one side and leaving the other in shadow. There wasn't much time. People would be having their meal about now, and soon there would be other children around, to stare and comment and notice. It was dangerous to wait, but all he could do was persuade her, as usual.

"Mum, let's go in and see Mrs Cooper," he said. "Look, we're nearly there."

"Mrs Cooper?" she said doubtfully.

But he was already ringing the bell. He had to put down the bag to do it, because his other hand still held his mother's. It might have bothered him at twelve years of age to be seen holding his mother's hand, but he knew what would happen to her if he didn't.

The door opened, and there was the stooped elderly figure of the piano teacher, with the scent of lavender water about her as he remembered.

"Who's that? Is that William?" the old lady said. "I haven't seen you for over a year. What do you want, dear?"

"I want to come in, please, and bring my mother," he said firmly.

Mrs Cooper looked at the woman with the untidy hair and the distracted half-smile, and at the boy with the fierce unhappy stare in his eyes, the tight-set lips, the jutting jaw. And then she saw that Mrs Parry, Will's mother, had put make-up on one eye but not on the other. And she hadn't noticed. And neither had Will. Something was wrong.

"Well..." she said, and stepped aside to make room in the narrow hall.

Will looked up and down the road before closing the door, and Mrs Cooper saw how tightly Mrs Parry was clinging to her son's hand, and how tenderly he guided her into the sitting room where the piano was (of course, that was the only room he knew); and she noticed that Mrs Parry's clothes smelt slightly musty, as if they'd been too long in the washing machine before drying; and how similar the two of them looked as they sat on the sofa with the evening sun full on their faces, their broad cheekbones, their wide eyes, their straight black brows.

"What is it, William?" the old lady said. "What's the matter?"

"My mother needs somewhere to stay for a few days," he said. It's too difficult to look after her at home just now. I don't mean she's ill. She's just kind of confused and muddled and she gets a bit worried. She won't be hard to look after. She just needs someone to be kind to her and I think you could do that quite easily, probably."

The woman was looking at her son without seeming to understand, and Mrs Cooper saw a bruise on her cheek. Will hadn't taken his eyes off Mrs Cooper, and his expression was desperate.

"She won't be expensive," he went on. "I've brought some packets of food, enough to last, I should think. You could have some of it too. She won't mind sharing."

"But... I don't know if I should... Doesn't she need a doctor?"

"No! She's not ill."

"But there must be someone who can... I mean, isn't there a neighbour or someone in the family—"

"We haven't got any family. Only us. And the neighbours are too busy."

"What about the social services? I don't mean to put you off, dear, but—"

"No! No. She just needs a bit of help. I can't do it any more for a little while but I won't be long. I'm going to... I've got things to do. But I'll be back soon and I'll take her home again, I promise. You won't have to do it for long."

The mother was looking at her son with such trust, and he turned and smiled at her with such love and reassurance that Mrs Cooper couldn't say no.

"Well," she said, turning to Mrs Parry, "I'm sure it won't matter for a day or so. You can have my daughter's room, dear; she's in Australia; she won't be needing it again."

"Thank you," said Will, and stood up as if he were in a hurry to leave.

"But where are you going to be?" said Mrs Cooper.

"I'm going to be staying with a friend," he said. "I'll phone up as often as I can. I've got your number. It'll be all right."

His mother was looking at him, bewildered. He bent over and kissed her clumsily.

"Don't worry," he said. "Mrs Cooper will look after you better than me, honest. And I'll phone up and talk to you tomorrow."

They hugged tightly, and then Will kissed her again and gently unfastened her arms from his neck before going to the front door. Mrs Cooper could see he was upset, because his eyes were glistening, but he turned, remembering his manners, and held out his hand.

"Goodbye," he said, "and thank you very much."

"William," she said, "I wish you'd tell me what the matter is—"

"It's a bit complicated," he said, "but she won't be any trouble, honestly."

That wasn't what she meant, and they both knew it; but somehow Will was in charge of this business, whatever it was. The old lady thought she'd never seen a child so implacable.

He turned away, already thinking about the empty house.

The close where Will and his mother lived was a loop of road in a modern estate, with a dozen identical houses of which theirs was by far the shabbiest. The front garden was just a patch of weedy grass; his mother had planted some shrubs earlier in the year, but they'd shrivelled and died for lack of watering. As Will came round the corner, his cat Moxie rose up from her favourite spot under the still-living hydrangea and stretched before greeting him with a soft miaow and butting her head against his leg.

He picked her up and whispered, "Have they come back, Moxie? Have you seen them?"

The house was silent. In the last of the evening light the man across the road was washing his car, but he took no notice of Will, and Will didn't look at him. The less notice people took, the better.

Holding Moxie against his chest, he unlocked the door and went in quickly. Then he listened very carefully before putting

her down. There was nothing to hear; the house was empty.

He opened a tin for her and left her to eat in the kitchen. How long before the men came back? There was no way of telling, so he'd better move quickly. He went upstairs and began to search.

He was looking for a battered green leather writing-case. There are a surprising number of places to hide something that size even in any ordinary modern house; you don't need secret panels and extensive cellars in order to make something hard to find. Will searched his mother's bedroom first, ashamed to be looking through the drawers where she kept her underclothes, and then he worked systematically through the rest of the rooms upstairs, even his own. Moxie came to see what he was doing and sat and cleaned herself nearby, for company.

But he didn't find it.

By that time it was dark, and he was hungry. He made himself baked beans on toast and sat at the kitchen table wondering about the best order to look through the downstairs rooms.

As he was finishing his meal, the phone rang.

He sat absolutely still, his heart thumping. He counted: twenty-six rings, and then it stopped. He put his plate in the sink and started to search again.

Four hours later he still hadn't found the green leather case. It was half-past one, and he was exhausted. He lay on his bed fully clothed and fell asleep at once, his dreams tense and crowded, his mother's unhappy frightened face always there just out of reach.

And almost at once, it seemed (though he'd been asleep for nearly three hours) he woke up knowing two things simultaneously.

First, he knew where the case was. And second, he knew that the men were downstairs, opening the kitchen door.

He lifted Moxie out of the way and softly hushed her sleepy protest. Then he swung his legs over the side of the bed and put on his shoes, straining every nerve to hear the sounds from downstairs: very quiet sounds: a chair being lifted and replaced, a short whisper, the creak of a floorboard.

Moving more silently than they were, he left his bedroom and tiptoed to the spare room at the top of the stairs. It wasn't quite pitch dark, and in the ghostly grey pre-dawn light he could see the old treadle sewing machine. He'd been through the room thoroughly only hours before, but he'd forgotten the compartment at the side of the sewing machine, where all the patterns and bobbins were kept.

He felt for it delicately, listening all the while. The men were moving about downstairs, and Will could see a dim flicker of light at the edge of the door that might have been a torch.

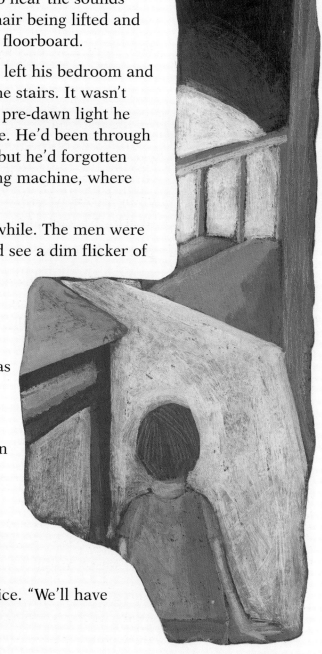

Then he found the catch of the compartment and clicked it open, and there, just as he'd known it would be, was the leather writing-case.

And now what could he do?

Nothing, for the moment. He crouched in the dimness, heart pounding, listening hard.

The two men were in the hall. He heard one of them say quietly, "Come on. I can hear the milkman down the road."

"It's not here, though," said the other voice. "We'll have to look upstairs."

"Go on, then. Don't hang about."

Will braced himself as he heard the quiet creak of the top step. The man was making no noise at all, but he couldn't help the creak if he wasn't expecting it. Then there was a pause. A very thin beam of torchlight swept along the floor outside: Will saw it through the crack.

Then the door began to move. Will waited till the man was framed in the open doorway, then exploded up out of the dark and crashed into the intruder's belly.

But neither of them saw the cat.

As the man had reached the top step, Moxie had come silently out of the bedroom and stood with raised tail just behind the man's legs, ready to rub herself against them. The man could have dealt with Will, because he was trained and fit and hard, but the cat was in the way, and as he tried to move back he tripped over her. With a sharp gasp he fell backwards down the stairs, crashing his head brutally against the hall table.

Will heard a hideous crack, and didn't stop to wonder about it: he swung himself down the banisters, leaping over the man's body that lay twitching and crumpled at the foot of the flight, seized the tattered shopping bag from the table, and was out of the front door and away before the other man could do more than come out of the living room and stare.

Even in his fear and haste Will wondered why the other man didn't shout after him, or chase him. They'd be after him soon, though, with their cars and their cellphones. The only thing to do was run.

Codes and Ciphers

Codes and ciphers are two quite different things, although most people think of them as being the same. Codes are not necessarily secret, while ciphers almost always are.

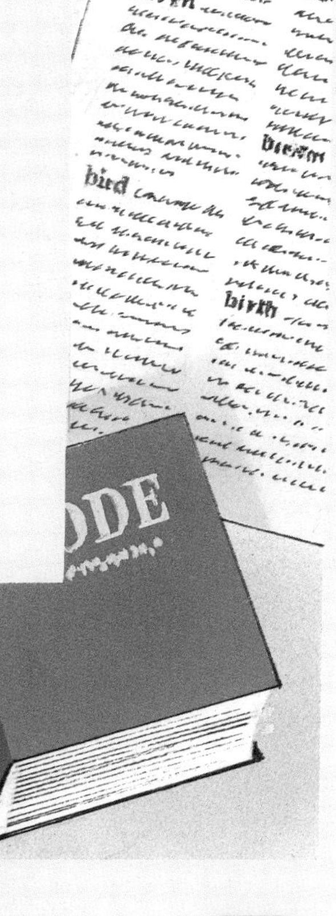

A code is simply a way of saying something by substituting different words, figures or symbols, but organising them in a particular way so they can be recognised again. Any two people can devise their own code by using two copies of an ordinary dictionary.

If, for example, you wanted to send the code word "**bird**" to your partner, your dictionary may show you the word on page 54, column 1, line 16, so "**bird**" would be encoded (i.e. written in code) as 54:1:16, giving the page, column and line.

Next, all your partner has to do is to look up page 54 in his/her dictionary, turn to column 1, line 16, and he/she will find the word "**bird**".

For this process to work it is essential for each person to use exactly the same dictionary. In fact, this is one of the weaknesses of codes generally. All codes need a kind of dictionary, or code-book, in which all the words or phrases used are listed with their meanings shown opposite. Foreign ambassadors nearly always use codes to send messages to their home countries.

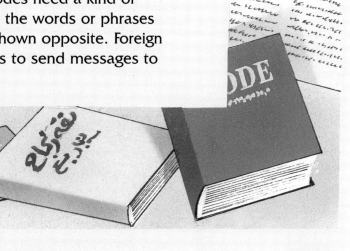

Let us suppose that the following message was received by the British Ambassador in Moscow:

SWORDFISH ARCTIC BELLFORT AFT CURRENT MIDSHIPS WALRUS BOWSPRIT DOLPHIN

It is recognised as a code message, so the Ambassador's code expert would look up the message in the latest secret code-book, which might look like this:

AFT:	P.M.	BOWSPRIT	MEET PLANE
ANCHOR:	DISPATCH NOW	CURRENT:	TOMORROW
ARCTIC:	ARRIVES BY AIR	DOLPHIN:	ARRANGE RECEPTION
BELLADONNA:	ONE	FORE:	A.M.
BELLDAME:	TWO	MERMAID:	QUEEN
BELLFORT:	THREE	MIDSHIPS:	CARRYING
BELLINGHAM:	FOUR	PACIFIC:	CANCEL INSTRUCTIONS
BELLKING:	FIVE	RIVER:	TODAY
BELLO:	ZERO	SPRAY:	LEAVING BY TRAIN
BELLPUSH:	SIX	SWORDFISH:	FOREIGN SECRETARY
BELLRING:	SEVEN	WALRUS:	SPECIAL ORDERS
BELLROCK:	EIGHT	WHALE:	PRIME MINISTER
BELLTIME:	NINE		

Such a message would quickly be decoded, and found to read:

FOREIGN SECRETARY ARRIVES BY AIR THREE P.M. TOMORROW CARRYING SPECIAL ORDERS MEET PLANE ARRANGE RECEPTION.

The code-book, therefore, is essential if the reader is to understand the message.

To cover every possible word, or group of words, such code-books have to be very large, fat volumes and must be kept in a very secret place. This can be dangerous because the books

can be stolen or copied, so the code has to be changed from time to time to make sure that secrets remain safe.

Ciphers differ from codes in a very important way that makes them more efficient for sending secret messages. The following story will help to explain the difference:

In the days before the introduction to Great Britain of the Penny Post by Rowland Hill in 1840, the charge for carrying letters was very high indeed.

A newspaper was the only article that could be sent through the post without charge. The reason was that the government had already put a heavy tax on newspapers and had decided that they could not tax such an article again. Many people tried to send letters by hiding them inside the newspapers, but the penalties for doing such a thing were severe, and the culprits were nearly always discovered. This did not stop people from trying, as a letter in those days cost about one shilling for every hundred miles, and a shilling in those days was worth a great deal.

Soon, however, people worked out a clever trick. Instead of putting a written note inside the newspaper, the sender made tiny marks or pinpricks over the tops of certain letters on the printed page. The letters, when spelled out in sequence, formed a message. This was a form of cipher, and one which was rarely discovered at the time.

This, in fact, is the big difference between a code and a cipher.

A cipher, unlike a code, needs no books to decipher or unlock it; many of the best ones could be carried by messengers in the memory. Apart from the trick of hiding a message..., there are two main types of cipher: the transposition cipher, and the substitution cipher. This article explains the **transposition cipher**.

This is not as complicated as it sounds. A transposition cipher simply means that the actual letters of the message are jumbled up in such a way that only the person who knows the secret can rearrange the letters in the correct order and so read the message.

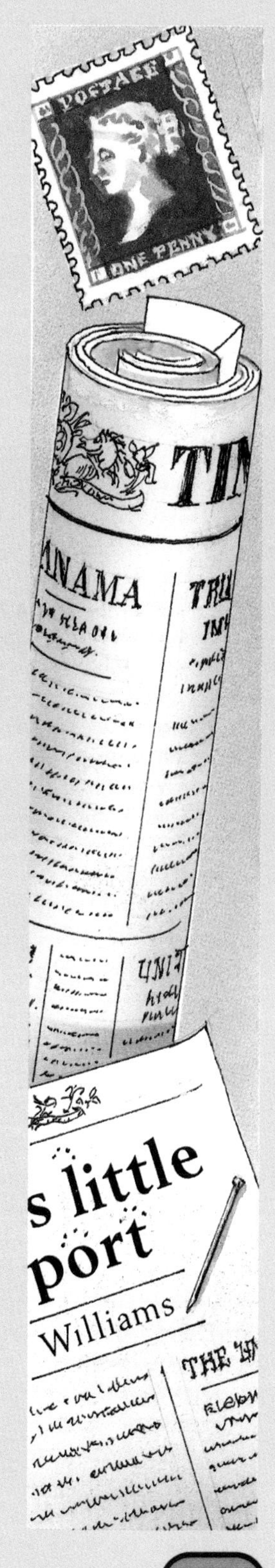

One of the surest ways to understand ciphers is to try some for yourself. However, it will help you to know some of the technical terms used about ciphers – and codes – before you begin:

Glossary

plaintext: any message written in its original sensible language.

cipher: a secret rule for changing individual letters of an ordinary plaintext message into a cryptogram or secret message.

cipher alphabet: a set of symbols, numbers or letters used to represent the 26 letters of the alphabet.

codebreaker: the common word used in ordinary speech for a cryptanalyst.

cryptanalyst: someone who tries to break or decipher cryptograms without having the key.

cryptogram: a message in which the original words are hidden according to a cipher or code.

cryptographer: someone who studies the art of secret writing and invents new codes and ciphers.

cryptography: the art of secret writing.

decipher: to turn a cryptogram or secret message back into an ordinary plaintext message.

encipher: to turn an ordinary plaintext message into a cryptogram or secret message.

transposition cipher: a cipher by means of which, all the letters of the original plaintext message are kept unchanged but are moved out of their correct order.

Book Review

The Widow's Broom is written by Chris van Allsburg, an American writer, and published by Andersen Press Ltd. It costs £8.99 in hardback, but is now more cheaply available in paperback. The author has written a number of other books, including the well-known *The Wreck of the Zephyr* and *The Polar Express*.

The Widow's Broom is presented in an unusual format. It is printed on A3 sheets and is long and slender to hold. The print is larger than usual, with a limited amount of text on each page. This makes the text very attractive to look at and gives the impression that the story is easy to read.

The powerful illustrations are all in black and white, which matches perfectly the mysterious and rather sinister theme and plot of the story.

The book is a quick and easy read. But that does not mean it is a simple story. On the contrary, it is a complex mystery with tension steadily built up so that the reader can't turn the pages quickly enough to discover the outcome and the solutions. Even then, at the end, you are still left wondering and guessing.

The outstanding features of this powerful and gripping story are:

- the original and inventive plot
- the characters, who are vividly presented in a few paragraphs through their behaviour, their relationships with each other, and their dialogue. The main "character", the broom, is a brilliant example of this. Who would have thought that a writer could make you feel so strongly and care so much about a broom?
- the wonderful language. It is easy to read, but it paints strong and memorable images and pictures: "Out of a moonlit sky a dark cloaked figure came spinning to the ground."

- the mystery at the heart of the story and the way in which it keeps the reader guessing to the end
- the tensions, suspense and the sense of terror that build up through the pages
- the conflict between good and ignorant and destructive beliefs, attitudes and values represented by the characters, which compels the reader to take sides and to hope for the triumph of the good.

The magnificent illustrations powerfully support the theme of the book.

The book is a mixture of folk tale, mystery and thriller. Apart from being a thrilling story, it contains some important messages or morals. One of these is the harm that can come from prejudice and ignorance.

The plot of the story is unusual, but easily understood – at least at the beginning.

A witch, whose magic broom has lost its power, crashes into a widow's garden. The widow, living alone in isolated countryside, takes the witch in and helps and comforts her until she is recovered and 'rescued' by her friends. She leaves the old broom behind. The broom soon recovers its magic powers and becomes a wonderful help to the widow – and very good company as well. However, the broom soon attracts the attention of the widow's ignorant and superstitious neighbours. They decide to destroy it, the widow agrees and hands the broom over to them for burning at the stake. But that is where things begin to become complicated and the reader feels icy fingers up and down the spine...!

I strongly recommend this book as a marvellous read. You will finish it in no time, but I guarantee you will go back to it again and again, it will keep popping up in your mind and you will remember it long after other more ambitious and more famous books are forgotten by you.

Different Types of Text

Holiday at Penpont Farm

We would like to draw your attention to the outstanding holidays we provide all the year around, in the beautiful county of Cornwall, at remarkably reasonable rates.

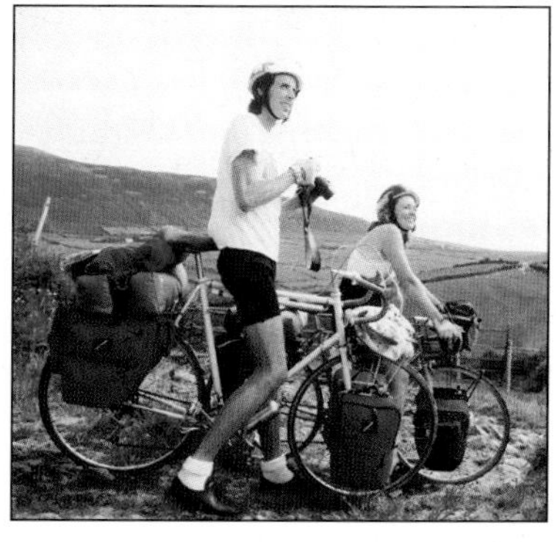

Penpont, as the farm is called, is a traditional Cornish farm, with all the activities, such as haymaking and harvesting. Guests are welcome to join in and most children find the livestock irresistible. This unspoilt part of Cornwall can provide the holiday maker with a wide range of activities at any time of year and Chapel Amble is ideally situated to take advantage of all the region has to offer.

The tiny village of Chapel Amble is just inland from the coast. It is ideally placed as a holiday centre.

The superb, safe, sandy beaches at Daymer Bay and Polzeath, for instance, offer surfing and swimming for all abilities, while Rock is a major centre for sailing, windsurfing, canoeing and waterskiing.

Try discovering the countryside on two wheels. Hire a bike and discover the Camel Trail, offering the cyclist a wonderful safe opportunity to explore the beautiful Camel River. Fishermen are also well catered for with sea fishing by boat from Padstow or Port Isaac, and salmon or trout fishing in many of the rivers, reservoirs and lakes.

An alternative to the beach, for use during dull weather, the Leisure Centre has proved to be a wonderful and most popular addition to the facilities at the Old House. Apart from the magnificent indoor heated swimming pool, with children's pool, the Leisure Centre is equipped with changing rooms, showers, toilets, a jacuzzi, sauna, solarium, full-size snooker table, lounge area with colour TV and baby's play pen.

Outside there is a patio, adventure playground, sand pit, swings and climbing frame, tennis courts and pets' corner for you to enjoy. All the facilities except for the snooker table and solarium are provided at no extra charge.

In this brochure we have tried to give an accurate impression of our Holiday Centre. Some of our guests say we have failed to do them justice, so if you have any worries or queries please give us a ring. We can really provide a "Holiday for all Seasons", so why not book now. We are sure you won't be disappointed.

Captain Cook

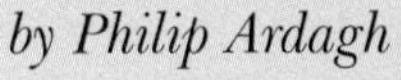

by Philip Ardagh

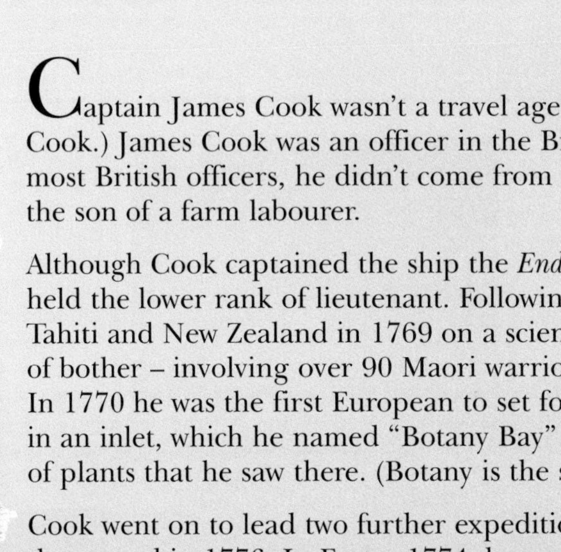

Captain James Cook wasn't a travel agent. (That was Mr Thomas Cook.) James Cook was an officer in the British Navy. But, unlike most British officers, he didn't come from the upper classes. He was the son of a farm labourer.

Although Cook captained the ship the *Endeavour* in 1768, he really held the lower rank of lieutenant. Following secret orders, he went to Tahiti and New Zealand in 1769 on a scientific mission. He had a spot of bother – involving over 90 Maori warriors in canoes – so moved on. In 1770 he was the first European to set foot in Australia. He landed in an inlet, which he named "Botany Bay" after the amazing number of plants that he saw there. (Botany is the science of studying plants.)

Cook went on to lead two further expeditions, the first in 1772 and the second in 1776. In Easter 1774, he reached an island and named it "Easter Island". There he found some incredible carved giant stone heads, some up to 12 metres tall. In 1778, he sailed to Hawaii.

To begin with, Cook and his men were treated like gods by the Hawaiians. But things took a turn for the worse. Cook set sail for home but his ship was damaged in a storm. He returned to Hawaii to carry out vital repairs, but a scuffle broke out with the locals, and Cook was stabbed and died.

Cook improved the lives of ordinary sailors. He took masses of fruit on his voyages, to help beat scurvy – the main cause of death for the sailors of the day.

He also made his men wash regularly. This may have led to a few raised eyebrows, but it resulted in far healthier crews.

The tattoo tradition

It was Cook's contact with the Maoris that led to the tradition of sailors having tattoos. Maoris loved tattoos and showed Cook's men how they were done. When the British sailors returned home, the practice spread.

Making a Mummy

by Sarah Dixon

The Ancient Egyptians believed that dead bodies had to be carefully preserved so their owners could use them in the afterlife. They used a special method called mummification. Normally, only pharaohs and wealthy people were mummified, as it was an expensive, time-consuming process.

After a person died, the body was washed; then most of its insides were removed, except for the heart and kidneys. The liver, stomach, intestines and lungs were placed in four "canopic" jars.

A type of salt called natron was heaped over the body to make it dry out. After forty days the natron was removed, and the withered body was padded out with linen and sawdust. Next, make-up was added for a life-like look.

Over the next fifteen days, the body was bandaged in linen. Much of this was recycled from old clothes. Charms called amulets were wrapped among the layers to protect the dead person in the afterlife.

Finally, a series of coffins were prepared for the mummy. There may have been as many as three or four of these, and they were normally decorated with magic spells and pictures of gods.

According to myth, the first mummy was a pharaoh called Osiris. Osiris was killed by his brother who cut his body into pieces and scattered them along the banks of the Nile for the crocodiles to eat. The pieces were found by Osiris's wife, then put back together and wrapped in bandages. Osiris came back to life and became ruler of the dead.

The Scene of the Crime

by Judith Hindley and Donald Rumbelow

Try to keep calm when you face the confusion left at the scene of a crime. A lot may depend on what you notice and what you do. Keep these rules in mind.

1. Look First – Don't Touch

Don't touch anything until the scene has been examined and dusted for fingerprints.

2. Follow a Method

Make your examination step-by-step. Look for fingerprints first. Use your kit to pick up any prints you find. Then, slowly circle the room again. Look for anything the criminal might have touched or left.

3. Use Your Notebook

Write down everything interesting you see. Don't leave out any detail that might be useful. Remember that what you notice and write down may be used as evidence.

4. Clues and Evidence

5. Take Full Statements

Ask victims and witnesses to tell you everything they can and write it down. Take the full name and address of any person mentioned.

Remember it may be a long time until your case goes to court. Your notebook must give a complete picture of what happened today.

6. Search Thoroughly

Now it doesn't matter if you disturb things. Look everywhere – even in dustbins and drain-pipes – for anything the criminal might have left. (Even the stub of a train ticket might give you an important lead.)

7. Work out a Story

From the start, try to work out what happened, to get an idea of what to look for.

A Statement

The Governors of our school are proposing a major change to the length of the school day. Lessons would start at 8 a.m.; rather than 9.45 as at present. There would be a prolonged break at 10 a.m. during which time pupils would have the opportunity for a proper cooked breakfast. The school day would finish by 1 p.m.

Pupils could bring, and eat at school, a sandwich lunch. It is intended that provision will be made by parents, voluntary bodies and some teachers for after-school activities and clubs in which all pupils can participate.

This issue has split the school **community.** The governors and some teachers and parents believe that this new system, which is common in some **continental** countries, would improve the **quality** and efficiency of education **available** to the pupils. At least as many other members of the school community seem to believe that such a large change would create hardship and **inconvenience** for many families and do nothing to improve the children's education.

Arguments in favour, together with supportive evidence:

- The new system would save money through a reduction of lunch-time services and supervisory staff. This money would be ploughed back into scarce and important school resources such as part-time teachers and books and equipment.
- The shorter day would be easier and less exhausting for young children to cope with.
- Ending the normal school day at lunch time would give pupils opportunity to take part in a wide range of clubs and activities and to learn new skills. Such activities are not possible for a considerable part of the school year because of early nightfall.

- It would make extra daylight hours free for children in winter time. The new system would remove the need for the normal lunch time, which often creates many difficulties; especially in big schools, both for the staff and for the children.
- Freedom from teaching demands in the afternoon would make it possible for teachers to do more professional training and make it easier for them to prepare lessons and mark work.

Arguments against, together with supportive evidence:

- This system would create enormous difficulties for those families where both parents are working full time. It would be necessary for them to find and pay for expensive and hard-to-secure after school care, especially for very young children. Those in favour of the scheme promise after-school activities. These could be much harder and more expensive to establish than people may think and may not be suitable for or attractive to all children.
- As a result of a system like this children could be leaving the school premises at different times during the afternoon and evening. This could clearly leave them vulnerable to various dangers; for example, in crossing busy roads unsupervised.
- So early a beginning to the school day would be very inconvenient for the parents of very young children or larger families.
- The likelihood of many children having breakfast, so necessary for the energy to enable them to work until lunchtime, would be seriously reduced by the early start.
- Even for those children who do snatch a breakfast, the wait of two or over two hours until the first refreshment break would be too long, especially for young infants.
- How likely is it that financial savings, one of the main attractions for supporters of the scheme, would be significant, since the preparation and serving of breakfasts, not to mention the ingredients, would have to be paid for?

Recommendation: a summary and conclusion or judgement.

The **proposers** and supporters of the scheme **genuinely** believe that a better and more efficient education would be provided for the children by the change. They point to the success of the scheme on the continent. I/we believe they have some strong arguments in their **favour**. For example:

- there is no doubt that considerable difficulties are created, especially for large schools, by prolonged lunch hours.
- if the scheme saved money that could be ploughed back into educational resources then the school would benefit.

However, I/we believe that the arguments against the scheme are even stronger:

- there is no guarantee that sufficient money could be saved to justify so dramatic a change.
- the difficulties and inconvenience created for many families could be intolerable.
- the arrangements could lead to hardship and strain for very young children.
- the scheme would certainly "free-up" extra hours of precious light for children in winter, but would also mean they had to turn out to go to school in dangerously dark conditions.
- there is no guarantee that a scheme that works on the continent, in very different circumstances, would work here.

In conclusion, therefore, we/I believe that the **undoubted** advantages of the scheme are seriously **outweighed** by **disadvantages** and we/I recommend that the scheme is not **adopted**.

The Earth as a Planet

by Roy Richards

For many thousands of years people believed the Earth was flat. Now we know the earth is a planet and is a **relatively** small member of a solar system, **comprised** of eight other planets, some of them gigantic by comparison. Scientists speak of the Earth as having three main layers:

The central core is about 6000 km wide and made mostly of iron. The outer core is liquid and the inner solid. It is surrounded by the **marite**, which is about 2,900 km thick and is made up of dense, very hot rocks, mostly solid but with some molten material.

The outer layer on which we live is called the **crust**. Under the oceans it is about 6 km thick, but under continents it is between 30 and 60 km thick, the thickest parts being under the mountain chains.

The crust holds the oceans, known as the hydrosphere. The crust is surrounded by the atmosphere, which extends upwards for thousands of kilometres, though most of the air is in the lower layers.

How to calculate the distance of a thunderstorm

Sound and light travel at different speeds, which is convenient in measuring roughly how far away a thunderstorm is. A lightning flash may be seen at almost the moment it occurs since its light travels at approximately 186,000 miles (300,000 km) per second. Sound travels much more slowly at about 700 mph (1223 kmph), so that by timing the difference between seeing the flash and hearing the peal of thunder we can estimate how far away the storm is. One second difference is about a fifth of a mile or 340 metres away.

(From *How to hold a Crocodile*, published by Treasure Press.)

Author Index

Acknowledgements

The editors and publishers wish to thank the following for permission to use copyright material:

A & C Black (Publishers) Ltd for an extract from *Young in the Twenties* by Eleanor Allen.

Sally Angell for 'What am I?', first published in *Crack Another Yolk*, compiled by John Foster, published by Oxford University Press, 1996.

Belitha Press for 'Captain Cook' from *History's Travellers and Explorers* by Philip Ardagh.

Sydney J Bounds for *The Ghost Train*, © Sydney J Bounds, originally published in the 4th Armada Ghost Book, edited by Mary Danby, 1972.

Town and Country Planning Act 1990 Notice of Public Inquiry by permission of Cherwell District Council.

John Coldwell for 'Life of the Nation' and 'Eataweek'.

Darton, Longman and Todd for an extract from the *Jerusalem Bible*.

'Making a Mummy' by Sara Dixon in *Ancient Egypt*, published by Design Eye Publishing.

EMI Music Publishing Ltd, London WC2H 0EA for 'The Lion and Albert' by George Marriott Edgar, © 1933 Francis, Day and Hunter Ltd, reproduced by permission of International Music Publications Ltd.

Eric Finney for 'Two Riddles', first published in *Crack Another Yolk*, compiled by John Foster, published by Oxford University Press, 1996.

John Foster for 'The Name of the Game', first published in *Crack Another Yolk*, compiled by John Foster, published by Oxford University Press, 1996.

'Codes and Ciphers' reproduced from *Codes Ciphers and Secret Writing* by George Beal by permission of Hamlyn Octopus, 2-4 Heron Quays, London E14 4JP.

HarperCollins Publishers Ltd for 'Riddles in Rhyme' from *The Hobbit* by J R R Tolkien and *The Dancing Bear* by Michael Morpurgo.

Heinemann Educational for 'The Greeks', an extract from *Digging Deeper: The Greeks* by John James and Louise James, reprinted by permission of Heinemann Educational Publishers, a division of Reed Educational & Professional Publishing Ltd.

Heinemann Young Books for the extract from *The Wreck of the Zanzibar* by Michael Morpurgo.

Crown copyright is reproduced with the permission of the Controller of Her Majesty's Stationery Office for Form SC1 Self Certificate and Sickness and Invalidity Benefit Claim Form.

David Higham Associates for *Crossing to Salamis* by Jill Paton Walsh, published by Heinemann; for 'What has Happened to Lulu?', 'Innocent's Song', 'High in the Heaven', 'My Mother Saw a Dancing Bear', 'The Animals' Carol' and 'Leonardo' by Charles Causley, from *Collected Poems* and *All Day Saturday*, published by Macmillan; for 'Mrs Malone' by Eleanor Farjeon, from *Silver Sand and Snow*, published by Michael Joseph and for an extract from *The Chief's Daughter* by Rosemary Sutcliff, published by Hamish Hamilton.

'Cat' by Rachel Myers and 'Mouth' by Anadil Hossain in *To Rhyme or Not to Rhyme* ©1994 Sandy Brownjohn, Hodder and Stoughton reprinted with permission from the publisher.

Julie Holder for 'A Begins Another', first published in *Crack Another Yolk*, compiled by John Foster, published by Oxford University Press, 1996.

J Patrick Lewis for 'A Flamingo'.

Frances Lincoln Ltd for 'The Fall of Troy' from *Black Ships Before Troy* by Rosemary Sutcliff, © 1993 reproduced by permission of Frances Lincoln Ltd, 4 Torriano Mews, Torriano Avenue, London NW5 2RZ.

Longman Education for 'The Balaclava Boys' from *A Northern Childhood* by George Layton.

Macmillan Children's Books for the extract from *Catherine Called Birdy* by Karen Cushman.

Sarah Matthews for 'Tyrannosaurus Rex' by Stanley Cook, first published in *Crack Another Yolk*, compiled by John Foster, published by Oxford University Press, 1996.

Brian Merrick for 'Brother', published in *Crack Another Yolk*, compiled by John Foster, published by Oxford University Press, 1996.

Judith Nicholls for 'Riddle', © Judith Nicholls 1996, reprinted by permission of the author.

Oxford University Press for an extract from *Moby Dick* by Herman Melville, retold by Geraldine McCaughrean, for 'Death's Murderers' by Chaucer, retold by Geraldine McCaughrean and for the extract from *Saint George and the Dragon* by Geraldine McCaughrean. Also for *A Lot of Mince Pies* by Robert Swindells from *The Oxford Book of Christmas Stories* compiled by Dennis Pepper.

'Noah's Ark' is reprinted by permission of PDF on behalf of Roger McGough.

Penguin Books Ltd for four pages from *The Stinky Cheese Man and Other Fairly Stupid Tales* by Jon Scieszka and for the extracts from *The Two-thousand-pound Goldfish* by Betsy Byars and *The Penguin Dictionary of Surnames* by Basil Cottle.

Gervase Phinn for 'It Takes One to Know One', first published in *Crack Another Yolk*, compiled by John Foster, published by Oxford University Press, 1996.

Random House Group for an extract from *King Kong* by Anthony Browne published by Julia MacRae; for an extract from *After the Goat Man* by Betsy Byars published by Bodley Head; for an extract from *The Computer Nut* by Betsy Byars, published by Red Fox; and for an extract from *Professor Branestawms's Dictionary* by Norman Hunter published by Bodley Head.

Rogers, Coleridge & White for 'Typewriting Class' by Gareth Owen, © Gareth Owen 1985 and for an extract from *The Peacock Garden* by Anita Desai, © Anita Desai 1979 reproduced by permission of the authors c/o Rogers, Coleridge & White Ltd, 20 Powis Mews, London W11 1JN;

Scholastic Ltd for an extract from *The Subtle Knife* by Philip Pullman.

The Society of Authors as the literary representative of John Masefield for the extract from 'Reynard the Fox' and L. du Garde Peach for the extract from *Napoleon Bonaparte*.

Transworld Publishers Ltd for an extract from *Truckers* by Terry Pratchett published by Doubleday, a division of Transworld Publishers. © 1989 Terry and Lyn Pratchett. All rights reserved. Also for an extract from *Clockwork, All Wound Up* by Philip Pullman, published by Doubleday, a division of Transworld Publishers Ltd and *The Firework Maker's Daughter* by Philip Pullman, published by Corgi Yearling, a division of Transworld Publishers Ltd.

'Flying Bat' reproduced from *The Know How Book of Jokes and Tricks* by Heather Amery and Ian Adair; 'The Scene of the Crime' reproduced from *The Know How Book of Detection* by Judy Hindley and Donald Rumbelow and for material from *The Usborne Book of Famous Lives* by Richard Dungworth, Philippa Wingate, Struan Reid, Felicity Everett and Patricia Fara by permission of Usborne Publishing Ltd, Usborne House, 83-85 Saffron Hill, London EC1N 8RT © Usborne Publishing Ltd.

'The Arrival of the Dinosaurs' reproduced from *Dinosaurs*, consulting editor Dr Angela Milner; and 'Gold Rush' reproduced from *The Wild West* by Robin May, published by Wayland Publishers Ltd (Macdonald Educational).

Every effort has been made to trace the copyright holders, but if any have been inadvertently overlooked the publishers will be pleased to make the necessary arrangements at the first opportunity.

Photographs ©: p65 *Bleak House*, BBC; p67 Mary Seacole, Mary Evans Picture Library; p70-71 UNEP/Angela Sands/Topham, Italy, snow scenes Topham Picturepoint; p72 Jack-knifed lorry, David Langfield, Eye Ubiquitous; p73 Ambulance, Paul Thompson, Eye Ubiquitous; p100 Arthur Kaye, "PA" News Photo Library; p102 Sidney Frank Garrett, Michael Kirby; p110 Class photo *c*.1920 Mary Evans/Bruce Castle Museum; p235 *The Toilet of Titania*, *c*.1870 (w/c on paper) by Richard Doyle (1824-83) Dreweatt Neate Fine Art Auctioneers, Newbury, Berkshire, UK/Bridgeman Art Library; p271 *Interesting Story*, 1989 (oil on canvas) by Laura Muntz Lyall (1860-1930), Art Gallery of Ontario/Bridgeman Art Library, Gift of the Government of the Province of Ontario 1972; p293 Camel Estuary, Roy Westlake/Cornwall Tourist Board, Rock, Dawn Runnals/Cornwall Tourist Board, Polzeath, David Hastilow/Cornwall Tourist Board.